THE COST OF DYING

THE VIOLENT DAYS OF
LOU PROPHET, BOUNTY HUNTER

PETER BRANDVOLD

WHEELER PUBLISHING
A part of Gale, a Cengage Company

GALE
A Cengage Company

Copyright © 2019 by Peter Brandvold.
Lou Prophet, Bounty Hunter.
Wheeler Publishing, a part of Gale, a Cengage Company.

**LIBRARY OF CONGRESS CIP DATA ON FILE.
CATALOGUING IN PUBLICATION FOR THIS BOOK
IS AVAILABLE FROM THE LIBRARY OF CONGRESS**

ISBN-13: 978-1-4328-7217-5 (hardcover alk. paper)

Published in 2020 by arrangement with Pinnacle Books, an imprint of
Kensington Publishing Corp.

Printed in Mexico
Print Number: 01   Print Year: 2020

For Alice Duncan

CHAPTER 1

"Wake up, Lou! Big trouble! Oh, Lou — plee-ease wake up! Loo-oooo!"

The voice had entered bounty hunter Lou Prophet's sleep from a long ways away, but it had quickly grown louder until it was accompanied by the tapping of running feet.

Bare running feet, judging by the *slap-slap-slap*s.

The voice was a pleasant female voice, lightly Spanish accented. It would have been a whole lot pleasanter if Prophet had heard it later — over breakfast, say, or, even better, over afternoon shots of tarantula juice. He didn't want to hear *any* voice when he was dreaming of running buck naked through spring woods near some idyllic mountain stream, trying to catch a pretty Apache princess who, just like himself, was bedecked in only her birthday suit and coaxing him on with her lusty laughter.

Run as the big bounty hunter might, he

7

couldn't catch up to the girl though he kept catching brief, enticing glimpses of her copper body through the forest's interwoven branches.

A hand grabbed Prophet's arm and shook him. Now the formerly pleasant voice was downright *un*pleasant, originating as it did just off Prophet's left ear.

"Lou!" The girl shook him again, with both hands now. *"Por favor.* Wake up! I need your help, *muy pronto"*!

The Apache princess in Prophet's dream had just stopped to let him catch up to her when the dream dissolved and Prophet was pulled up out of his fanciful slumber to blink his eyes and smack his lips, watching a small, shabby room take shape around him.

"Wha— *huh?"* The tendrils of sleep were slow to disentangle themselves from Prophet's brain while the girl on his left continued to jerk him so that the entire bed was bucking and pitching like an unbroke bronco stallion on the run from a wildfire. "Oh, Jesus . . . leave me . . . leave me alone . . . I'm . . . I'm sleepin', honey! Ole Lou's sleep-time now!"

The girl kept shaking him. *Oh, why couldn't she stop?!* "Lou, you have to help Dora!"

"Wh-who's Dora?" he asked, hoping that

8

the question might get the girl to stop her consarned shaking if only for a few blissful seconds.

"A close friend of mine! I am afraid that her life is in danger! Oh, Lou — please wake up!"

Prophet had rested his head back against his pillow. His eyelids, which weighed ten pounds apiece, had dropped shut of their own accord. But now two fingers peeled the left one open, and Prophet found himself staring up into a pair of dark brown eyes set above a fine, pale nose and ruby red lips. Curly, dark brown hair, mussed from sleep and love, framed the girl's young, pretty face that bore a heart-shaped birthmark just under her left eye.

Jasmin. That was her name, pronounced "Yas-meen." The handle floated into the bounty hunter's unconsciousness though how it made it through the gallon or so of rotgut tequila he'd soaked his brain in last night while he and Jasmin had run up one side of town and down the other, dancing to several different bands in a handful of saloons and cantinas before repairing to the *puta*'s humble crib was beyond him.

He'd met her only a few hours ago, depending on what time it was now . . .

"What the hell time is it, anyway?" he rasped.

"I don't know," the girl said. "Who cares?" She was tugging on his arm again, making the wild stallion of the bed resume running from imminent danger. "Dora is in big trouble, Lou! Only you can save her! *¡Rápido! Por favor,* Lou — there is no time to waste. *¡Rápido!*"

Prophet cursed and, merely to get the girl to stop tugging on his arm and making his hungover head pound all the harder, he sat up and dropped his bare feet to the floor. He felt as though he were speaking around a mouthful of jawbreakers. "Where is . . . where is this Dora . . . an' what trouble's she in, darlin'?"

A pistol cracked. That cleared a few more of Prophet's cobwebs, as a pistol crack tended to do for a man like Prophet, who had spent most of his life either hurling or dodging bullets and who never knew from where the next bullets would come but always knowing that there would, indeed, be more bullets on the way . . .

"What was that all about?"

"That was Dora!" Jasmin was running around the small, crudely furnished crib gathering up Prophet's longhandles, socks, and boots from where she'd tossed them on

10

the floor after she'd helped him undress —
a task which, in Prophet's condition, had
required four hands. "Well, not Dora herself . . . but the man who is going to kill
her! I just know he is going to kill her this
time for sure! He is very drunk and *very*
angry!"

She spat out several lines of unadulterated
Spanish only a few words of which Prophet,
who had only a crude working knowledge
of the border lingo, could decipher.

"Who is this rannie?" Prophet asked, running a big hand down his face as Jasmin
tossed the big loose ball of his clothes onto
the bed beside him.

"Roscoe Rodane!"

"Who in the hell is Roscoe Rodane?"
Another pistol crack issued from the open
window in the wall before Lou.

"He is the gringo *necio* who is going to
kill Dora! He is in love with her, or so he
claims! He is in the Buzzard Gulch Inn
across the street. Oh, Lou — get dressed
and hurry! Dora is like a sister to me!"

Yet another pistol report issued from out
there in the night somewhere. A cool dark
night, judging from the view from the
window and the breath of chill desert air
wafting through the ragged calico curtain
buffeting inward, rife with the smell of trash

11

heaps, woodsmoke, horses, men, and sage-brush. Typical western frontier fare.

Somewhere a dog was barking as though in response to the pistol fire. Beneath the dog's barking and between pistol shots, Prophet thought he heard a girl scream.

Jasmin sucked an anxious breath while she helped Prophet pull on his longhandles. "*Mierda.* It might be too late." The pretty *puta* sobbed, her upper lip trembling. "I might have just lost my best friend!"

"All right, all right." The girl's obvious terror sobered Prophet somewhat. At least, it got his heart going. He heaved himself up off the bed and took over his own dressing, going only as far as the longhandles, boots, and his hat. That's all he needed.

He intended to be out of bed only long enough to quiet the infernal commotion over there across the street at the Buzzard Gulch Inn, so he could return to bed in peace and catch a few more hours of shut-eye before the hot Arizona sun reared its rosy head and cast its summer rays and debilitating heat through the window, rendering further slumber impossible.

When he'd cinched his Colt Peacemaker and cartridge belt around his waist, Lou grabbed his twelve-gauge Richards coach gun, slinging its wide leather lanyard over his head and shoulder, positioning the savage double-bore gut-shredder against his back. Making his way none too steadily to the door, which Jasmin held open for him, regarding him anxiously, Prophet stepped out into the dingy hall, hearing the girl mutter a prayer in hushed, quick Spanish behind him.

She added in English for his benefit, calling cheerfully behind him, "Thank you, Lou! I will make it up to you — I promise!"

He heard her blow him a kiss.

Grumbling moodily, Prophet made his way downstairs and across the small, earthen-floored saloon called Cantina Perro de Tres Patas, or the Three-Legged Dog, taking the name from the proprietor's three-legged cur that wandered the premises all day, performing tricks for chugs of cheap ale and nibbles of beef and ham from Jimmy Rodriquez's free-lunch counter.

Prophet stumbled across the saloon occupied now by only two Mexicans, one of whom was conscious, and the three-legged cur now snoring peacefully on a straw mat beneath the pine-plank bar. Only a couple of candles burned in wall brackets, so the saloon was in more shadow than light, and Prophet rapped his knee painfully against a chair before he finally made it through the

13

batwings.

Cursing roundly and limping, he crossed the street at a slant, making his way toward the Buzzard Gulch Inn, which was a slightly tonier place than the Cantina Perro de Tres Patas, which sat on the south side of Buzzard Gulch's main street, known as the Mexican side, while the north side of the street was known as the gringo side. Prophet preferred the south side for the simple reason that the Mexicans tended to have more fun.

"I'm gonna ask y'all one more time," a man bellowed inside the Buzzard Gulch Inn, his voice badly slurred from drink. He punctuated the statement with another pistol shot. "I'm gonna ask you *one-more-time,*" he bellowed, louder, "who's been makin' time with ole Roscoe's girl when I been away?"

A girl's voice rose shrilly: "Roscoe, I told you, I am not your girl!"

She'd barely gotten that out before she screamed.

The scream was followed by another pistol report.

"Liar!" Roscoe bellowed.

Another pistol crack rocketed around inside the saloon.

"Christalmighty — ain't there any law in

14

this jerkwater?" Prophet asked himself, glancing both ways up and down the short main street and seeing no one.

Not that he could have seen anyone if anyone were out there. The night was as black as the inside of a glove save for a sky dusted with twinkling stars. Somehow, the light from the stars didn't seem to make it down to Buzzard Gulch. It was dark, all right. The only place showing any life at all was the Buzzard Gulch Inn, and the inn was showing *too* much life.

Way too much life for a fella to get a decent night's rest anywhere nearby.

Prophet hurried up the inn's three porch steps then, not wanting to waste any time, bulled quickly through the batwings, and stepped to the right, extending the Richards coach gun straight out in front of him, ready to silence Roscoe Rodane with a fist-sized wad of double-ought buck.

Lou blinked into the heavy shadows of the room before him. The Buzzard Gulch's main drinking hall was only a little better lit than the Three-Legged Dog had been, with a couple of bracket lamps and candles.

The bar ran down the wall to Prophet's left. To his right were tables and chairs. Three or four gents were crouched down behind one overturned table and a couple

15

of chairs. An old man and a blond young woman in a red and black corset and bustier, and with feathers in her hair, were crouched behind the piano abutting the wall to Prophet's right.

Prophet could see several other men pressed up against the saloon's rear wall, raising their eyes to gaze up toward the man standing slumped on the second-story balcony directly above them. The man up there was leaning forward over the rail.

He had three pistols resting atop the rail, and he was fumbling fresh shells into one of them. As he leaned forward, his longish, sandy hair hung in his eyes, so Prophet couldn't see his face. But the bounty hunter could hear the man sobbing and quietly mewling like a gut-shot coyote taking his last few breaths.

Everybody on the saloon's main floor was being quiet as a church mouse with the reverend on a tear until a man raised his head above the bar to Prophet's left and said, "Roscoe, won't you please leave those damn guns alone and listen to reason?"

The speaker was a craggy-faced gent with wavy, dark, pomaded hair and a thick dark mustache.

"I *been* listenin' to reason," Roscoe said up where he was reloading his pistols on

16

the second-floor balcony. "An' reason, she been tellin' me my purty girl, Miss Dora May, has been two-timin' ole Roscoe with a coupla the boys from the Triple-Six-Connected. An' now, lessen I don't hear which ones she been makin' time with right quick, I'm gonna kill 'em *all* right here an' now — *tonight!*"

Prophet hardened his jaws as he pushed away from the wall behind him and said, "You ain't gonna kill anybody here tonight, Rodane! Now put them pistols down an' stop this nonsense!"

Prophet glanced quickly at the man poking his craggy head above the bar. "Ain't there a lawman in town?" he asked.

The barman opened his mouth to speak but stopped when Roscoe Rodane lifted his head abruptly, tossed his long, sandy hair back from his eyes, and cast Prophet a mean-eyed stare. "Who in the hell are you and where did you come from?"

"I'm Lou Prophet, bounty hunter. Now put them pistols down and go sleep it off, amigo. The town's done tired of hearin' your caterwaulin' foolishness not to mention your infernal pistols. Don't you realize what time it is?"

"You butt out of this!" Rodane bellowed, closing the loading gate of the Colt he'd just reloaded and raising the gun to his shoulder, barrel-up. "This ain't none of your business, Mr. Bounty Hunter!"

He started to aim the pistol toward Prophet.

"Oh, Roscoe, please!" the blonde begged where she crouched with the old man behind the piano, snugged up taut against the wall. "I'm sorry if I made you think that I was your girl. I am not any one man's girl, Roscoe. I'm a *whore*!"

One of the two men crouching behind the overturned table just ahead of Prophet and to his right snorted an ironic laugh.

"You think it's funny, Norm?" Rodane yelled, shuttling his enraged gaze toward the man behind the table. "You think it's *funny*?"

He triggered a shot over the rail. The bullet plunked into the table and nearly blasted through to the other side. Prophet saw the crack it made, showing its snub nose through the crack and making both men crouching there jerk with horrified starts.

"Christ, Roscoe!" shouted the man behind the table — the one who hadn't snorted. "This is insane. It's just insane, I tell you! And it's all because you started drinkin' again, an' you know you can't hold your lightnin'!"

"Was it you, Rod?" Roscoe aimed his pistol over the rail again, narrowing one eye as he aimed down the barrel.

"Hold on!" Prophet bellowed. "Put that gun down or I'm gonna paint the wall with you, you drunken tinhorn!"

CHAPTER 2

Prophet started walking across the saloon, weaving between tables and chairs, kicking a few chairs out of his way, keeping the Richards aimed at the gun-wielding drunk on the balcony.

"Look out, mister," one of the men warned him. "He's crazy when he drinks, an' he don't care who he shoots!"

Prophet just then saw that the man wasn't exaggerating. He stopped and looked to his right. A man lay on the floor, in a pool of his own blood. He'd taken a bullet through his forehead. He was tall and lean, with long, washed-out blond hair, and his vaguely startled blue eyes stared up at Prophet.

He was dressed in crude, weathered range gear, like most of the other men in the place.

Prophet muttered a curse then looked up at the man on the balcony, who was grinning down at him, aiming his pistol at Prophet's head. He, too, had blue eyes.

Cobalt blue. The light of madness glinted in them. A two- or three-day growth of beard stubble bristled on his round, puffy face with thin yellow lips. His eyes were deep set and his nose was long and broad and splotched red and blue from burst blood vessels, a testament to too much drink.

"Drop the Greener, mister," Roscoe said through his devious grin. "Or I'll drop you right where you stand."

"Roscoe!" screamed the girl who'd been crouching behind the piano. "Stop this! Stop this right now! You know I'm not your girl! I'm not anyone's girl lessen they got the jingle for an hour's tussle!"

She came out from behind the piano and holding her hands up, palms out, placatingly, she began moving down the room toward the balcony, tripping occasionally on chair legs. "I'm sorry if you got the wrong idea about me . . . *us* . . . but that's how it is!"

"No, it ain't how it is!" Roscoe bellowed at her, angling his pistol away from Prophet now. He aimed at the girl and the fire of rage burned in his cheeks and eyes. "I told you you was mine, Dora May! When I was in Tucson you was supposed to stay true. I told you I'd marry you . . . make an honest woman out of you . . . soon as I built up a

21

grubstake! You told me you'd stay true, Dora! Damnit, you did, an' then I find out from Blue Nelson you was gigglin' an' carryin' on with a pair of fellas from the Triple-Six-Connected! Both at the same time! *Upstairs!*"

He aimed his pistol at the dead man on the floor to Prophet's right and yelled, "And Lonnie Hanks was one of 'em!"

He triggered another shot into the dead man. The dad man jerked with the impact.

Dora screamed and stopped, burying her face in her hands. "I'm a whore, Roscoe! A *whore*!"

"You're a *dead* whore — you two-timin', four-flushin' bitch!" Roscoe tightened his index finger around the Colt's trigger, his iron-hard jaws dimpling with rage as he aimed at the girl.

Prophet didn't see that he had any choice. It was either the girl or Roscoe Rodane.

He tripped both of the Richards's triggers and Rodane was picked straight up and thrown back against the wall behind him but not before he triggered a bullet into the table near Dora. The girl screamed, leaped to one side, tripped over a chair, and fell to the floor.

The blast from Prophet's shotgun echoed around the room.

Silence fell in behind it, thick and intimate with the funereal weight of death.

"There." Prophet lowered the smoking barn-blaster and swung around, muttering oaths under his breath as he retraced his path to the door. "Now, maybe the whole town can get some decent shut-eye . . . includin' me."

"He, uh . . . he dead?" asked one of the ranch hands, rising from behind the overturned table. He looked up and down the big man before him clad in only longhandles so badly faded they were a washed-out pink, boots, cartridge belt, and hat.

"Oh yeah," Prophet grumbled, chuckling his satisfaction. "The only place he'll be caterwaulin' from here on in is in the devil's own hell. I just hope Ole Scratch can shut him up before I arrive . . ." he added with a wry curl of his nose.

He glanced at the men and the girl, including the man behind the bar, slowly gaining their feet around him. They were all looking at him as though he were a two-headed panther. "You folks really oughta get some decent law in this town. No lawdog worth a good pair of socks would let a man raise that kinda hob at this time o' night."

"Mister?"

Prophet had turned back to the batwings, putting his left hand atop the left door, about to push it open, but now he turned back to the craggy-faced gent standing behind the bar, regarding the big bounty hunter in hang-jawed, brow-furled dismay.

"What is it?" Prophet asked grumpily.

The barman looked at Prophet, nervously fingering a button on his wool waistcoat, then turned away to uncertainly regard the others. "Nothin'," he said weakly.

Prophet gave a satisfied chuff then pushed through the batwings and walked out into the now-silent street. The dog wasn't barking anymore. The night, finally, was silent. Just as a night should be.

The big bounty hunter clomped back through the Three-Legged Dog, under the bar of which the dog, who was not only three-legged but apparently deaf, as well, was still sleeping on its straw mat beneath the bar. Now both remaining customers were sound asleep on their folded arms. Prophet could hear the proprietor, Jimmy Rodriguez, sawing logs in his bedroom partition behind the bar.

"You're welcome, fellas," Prophet said with another wry chuff, congratulating himself once more at rendering the night fit for slumber.

24

He climbed the creaky stairs and returned to Jasmin's crib. A candle burned, showing the girl piled beneath the sheet and thin quilt, in the room's dense shadows. She was a long lump capped with a spray of thick, chocolate hair concealing her pillow. The pretty *puta* lay curled on her side, apparently sound asleep.

Prophet skinned out of his duds, wrapped his cartridge belt and .45 around a front bedpost, within easy reach as was his custom, then crawled beneath the covers. The *puta* stirred, rolled toward him, blinking her eyes.

In a sleep-raspy voice, she said, "Did you take care of Dora's problem, Lou?"

"I took care of Dora's problem, all right." Prophet kissed the girl's bare shoulder then gazed down at her, incredulous. "You been sleepin'?"

She smiled serenely, closed her eyes. "Mhmm. I knew you would take care of the problem, Lou. A big, capable man like yourself." She wrapped her arms around him, kissed his lips. She opened her eyes, smiled into his. "Now, about that reward I promised you."

Giggling, she pulled her head down beneath the covers.

"Oh, you don't have to go to any

25

troub . . ." Prophet's resolve waned. "You don't have to . . . well . . . what the hell?" he added with a heavy sigh and a dry laugh.

Prophet had no idea how long he'd been asleep again when, *again,* he was pulled out of a deep sleep by Jasmin's urgent voice. Again, the girl shook him and said, "Lou, wake up! Wake up, Lou! *¡Mierda!* You have to *wake up!*"

"Ah, Jesus — now what?" Prophet opened his eyes and saw that the sky out the window behind the pretty *puta* was awash in the gray light of dawn. "Ah hell," he added. "It's mornin', I reckon, ain't it?" He raked a big paw down his sleep-worn face. "That had to be the shortest night's sleep —"

"Lou!"

"What is it, darlin'?"

Jasmin's wide-eyed face was only inches from his, where she knelt there on the floor beside the bed. "You didn't tell me you *killed* Roscoe Rodane, you crazy gringo!"

"Didn't I? Well, you asked me if I took care of Dora's problem, and, yeah" — Prophet chuckled and scrubbed his hand down his face once more — "I took care of her problem, all right. I reckon I just assumed —"

"Lou!"

26

"What?"

"Don't you know who Roscoe Rodane is? *Was?*"

"A caterwauling fool is what he *was.* And I reckon if I didn't blow some daylight through him, Dora would be snugglin' with the diamondbacks and you'd be out one best friend!"

"Oh, Lou — you sweet stupid gringo *cabrón!*" Jasmin rose from her knees and again began scrambling around the room, gathering Prophet's clothes. *"Out!* You must go! You must go now, or you will not live to see another sunrise. Sunrise? Hah!" She spread her arms and threw a caustic laugh at the ceiling. "You won't live to see high noon of this very day!"

"Wha— *huh?*" Prophet said, scowling at her from the bed.

The pretty *puta* threw his longhandles and socks at him. She stopped off the near corner of the bed and, clad in only a thin cream nightgown and spruce green wrap, bent forward at the waist and thrust an arm out to indicate the Buzzard Gulch Inn. "The man you killed last night . . . when I only wanted you to slap him around a little or punch his lights out and send him to bed . . . was the *law* here in town! He was a deputy sheriff — none other than the son of

27

the sheriff of Pima County. *The very prized and precious son of Sheriff Dan Rodane, Lou, you big crazy gringo!*"

The name cut through the last fog of sleep slithering around behind Prophet's eyes. He stiffened. "Dan Rodane . . ."

"Dan Rodane!"

"Damn, I knew that name rang a bell." Prophet tossed the covers aside and dropped his feet to the floor. "I reckon I was too drunk last night to ponder on it overmuch . . . or even to recognize it. But, yeah, now I recognize it, all right."

He looked at Jasmin still glaring down at him urgently, bent forward at the waist, every muscle in her lithe, buxom body drawn taut as freshly stretched Glidden wire. "Are you sure ole Roscoe is the son of Dan Rodane?" Prophet asked her.

The pretty *puta* swallowed tolerantly and spoke with strained patience. "Lou, there is no question. When I found out you had killed Roscoe last night, you fool, I also learned that one of Rodane's cronies rode to Tucson to alert the sheriff. You can bet that if Sheriff Rodane is not already in town ransacking Buzzard Gulch for the man who killed his precious son, he will be here soon!"

She scooped one of his boots off the floor

28

and threw it at him. "Go!" She grabbed his other boot and threw that one at him, too. "Go, you big galoot! He will hang you from the nearest cottonwood in Buzzard Gulch!"

Prophet heaved himself to his feet and scratched the back of his head. "Yeah, yeah, I reckon he will, all right."

Jasmin threw his pants at him. As his boots had done, they bounced off his broad, hairy chest to land on the floor at his feet. "Hurry, Lou! There is no time to lose! You are too good a man . . . and too much fun . . . to get your neck stretched for killing such a scalawag as Roscoe Rodane. Now, I sent a boy for your horse. He is to meet you in the back alley."

"Ah, you shouldn't have done that," Prophet said, stumbling around now, pulling on his longhandles.

"Why not?" the girl fairly screamed at him.

"Mean an' Ugly was aptly named, Jasmin. He's liable to tear that poor boy's arm off or, leastways, rip a seam or two out of his shirt. I hope he has at least one ear left after Mean's done with him!"

Holding his buckskin tunic, Jasmin frowned at him. "That big ugly cayuse of yours doesn't cotton to strangers?"

"That big ugly broomtail of mine don't cotton to *me*!"

Prophet gave a wry chuckle then leaned forward as Jasmin wrestled the tunic over his head, having to rise up on the toes of her bare feet to do so, for the pretty *puta* stood a whole two heads shorter than Prophet's six feet four.

Prophet was glad his hangover had all but dissipated overnight. His head ached dully, and his mouth was dry, but a few breaths of fresh air and a canteen of water would set him back right again. So, scrambling around the room, getting back into his clothes, and buckling his cartridge belt around his waist, went far smoother than it would have otherwise.

Jasmin met Prophet at the door and rose up on her toes again to smooth his short, sandy brown hair and to set his battered, bullet-torn, bleached-out, funnel-brimmed Stetson on his head. She pinched his nose and kissed his lips. "Go with God, Lou! Ride to the border and keep riding and don't come back for a good long time!"

"Mexico, huh? Yeah, well, I reckon another winter's comin' on up north, so I reckon it's a good time to go. Just wish it was under better circumstances, though. I like crossin' the border when I *want* to, not when I *have* to!"

"When are your circumstances ever good, Lou?"

Prophet winced. "You got a point." He grabbed the girl, drew her to him, and kissed her passionately. "Take care of yourself, Jasmin."

Quickly, she drew the door open and waved him through it. "Go, Lou! *¡Rápido!*"

"I'm goin', I'm goin'."

Crouching beneath the weight of his saddlebags, ancient gray Confederate war bag, Winchester '73, and Richards twelve-gauge, his Colt Peacemaker thonged on his right thigh, his bone-handled bowie knife sheathed on his left hip, Prophet hurried down the stairs. He paused when the *puta* called from her room's open door, "Lou?"

"What is it, honey?"

"Thanks for killing that drunken *bastardo!*" she rasped out from the side of the hand she held over her mouth. She winked and gave a throaty laugh.

"Anytime," Prophet said with a snort. He hurried downstairs and out through the rear door.

Just as Jasmin had said he would be, Prophet's mulish but loyal line-back dun stood in the rear alley, reins drooping to the trash-littered ground. Prophet looked around for the boy who'd fetched him. That

31

must be him, running down the alley to Prophet's right, rope-soled sandals slapping his feet. The boy, a young Mexican, cast a wary glance behind him then disappeared around the side of one of the main street buildings.

Prophet looked at Mean and Ugly, who regarded his rider with a sheepish cast to his eyes.

"You devil — I hope you didn't hurt that kid!"

As Prophet tossed his saddlebags over the mount's back, behind the saddle, Mean pawed the ground and gave a self-satisfied whicker.

Quickly, Prophet slid his Winchester into the scabbard strapped to the saddle. He hooked his war bag over the saddle horn then swung up into the leather.

He froze, looked around, frowning.

A low thunder was building. At first it seemed to be coming from his right, then his left — the rataplan of many galloping horses. The din grew quickly, injecting ice into the bounty hunter's veins. The growing din seemed to be coming from all around him until a horse and rider bounded out from around a building fifty yards away to the north, on Prophet's right.

The rider was a big man in a calico shirt

and suspenders and a big Boss of the Plains hat. He wore a thick, gray mustache on his Indian-dark face, and a shiny silver star on his shirt.

"There!" he barked, jerking his chin toward Prophet.

Several other riders bounded around from behind the same building, and they all galloped toward Prophet behind the badge-toter, Dan Rodane himself.

Prophet jerked Mean to the right. Instantly, he drew back on the reins as more riders exploded out from behind another building to the south, about thirty yards away.

"Holy crap in the nun's privy!" Prophet wailed at his horse. "We're surrounded, Mean!"

He jerked the reins hard right again and put the spurs to the hammerhead's flanks. Mean and Ugly gave a shrill whinny and exploded off his rear hooves, leaping into an instant gallop straight west, first cleaving a break between a cow pen and a board-and-batten tinker's shanty then weaving around a few scattered mud-brick cabins on Buzzard Gulch's ragged perimeter.

The horse leaped a dry wash, bulled through a stand of dusty mesquites turning silver now as the dawn grew, and then the dun and Prophet were damn near literally flying through the prickly chaparral of the open desert, hearing the nettling thunder of a good dozen or so riders nipping at their heels, whooping and hollering like the devil's slavering hounds.

Pistols crackled.

Rifles belched.

Bullets buzzed around Prophet's head, snapping creosote branches and spanging off rocks.

"I'll be damned," he said to his horse, casting a quick, anxious glance over his shoulder, "if them boys don't mean it, Mean!"

CHAPTER 3

Thunder rumbled but no storm was approaching. The Arizona skies were as clear as polished blue glass in a corner of which the sun hung like a vast bell of molten gold.

Colter Farrow slowed his horse and looked around, frowning.

As the rumble grew around him, as though an army were descending on him, a wet snake slithered in his belly. He could feel his coyote dun stallion tense his muscles beneath the saddle. The mount's name, Northwest, stemmed from the direction the prized mount always used to point his head while grazing back home in the mountain pastures of the Lunatic Range.

The horse lifted its head, sniffing the air, the cinnamon mane buffeting softly in the hot, dry Arizona breeze. It whickered edgily deep in its chest.

Colter leaned forward to pat the right withers reassuringly. "Easy, Northwest.

Easy, now — might only be cowpunchers hazing beeves to fresh pastures . . ."

The redheaded gunslinger's own belly knew it wasn't true. Colter had been on the dodge too long for his instincts not to have grown as sharp as a freshly edged Green River knife.

The rumbling grew louder and louder until Colter could feel the ground vibrating beneath Northwest's shod hooves. Colter looked around wildly. When he saw a churning cloud of tan dust rise from the incline to his left, from below the long, sage-and-cactus-spiked bench he'd been traversing for most of the past two hours, that snake in his belly coiled again quickly.

"Go, boy!" he yelled, nudging the stallion's loins with his spurs. "*He-yahhh,* boy. *He-yahhhh!* Split the wind, Northwest!"

He'd just spied a whole army of riders exploding up onto the bench on his left, a good dozen men spread out side by side and silhouetted by the brassy sun, as he swung the coyote dun hard right.

"There!" one of his pursuers shouted. "There! There! *There!*"

Leaning low over the coyote dun's buffeting mane, Colter said, "Well, so much for my original theory. They're not cowpunchers after all!" He glanced over his shoulder as the swarm of silhouetted riders, the sunlight glinting off their sidearms and rifles, bounded after him, within a hundred yards and closing.

The redheaded pistoleer didn't have time to count his shadowers, but he was sure there were a dozen or more men in hot pursuit. A couple snapped shots at him but they were still too far away and moving too hard for accuracy though there was always a chance of a lucky shot.

Colter kept his head down and gave his own mount free rein, and together they stormed across the barrel of the bench, heading for the low country. Colter might have been outnumbered, but he had a good horse, one of the best mounts that had ever been raised in the Loonies, as the Lunatics were locally called.

His pursuers had obviously been galloping after Colter for quite a distance, climbing up from the lower desert at a hard run. That meant that not only was Colter likely riding the best horse on the bench at the moment, but his mount had a fully stoked firebox, as all morning Colter had been holding the frisky beast to nothing faster than a trot, saving it for just such a situation as this.

Colter tossed another glance behind him.

Sure enough, he and Northwest were pulling ahead.

"Good boy, Northwest," Colter said, keeping his head low, his voice quavering as the horse's scissoring hooves sawed away at the ground. "You're beatin' them scalawags. What we'll do is drop into the lowlands yonder then climb that next bench to the north. That's a steep climb over there, and I'll bet silver dollars to horse fritters that that will be the end of our shadowers. They'll likely get a bad case of homesickness after that climb, and we'll be on our way to Mexico while they're back wherever they came from, pinchin' the parlor girls an' throwing back shots of Taos lightnin'!"

That last word had just made its way out of his mouth before Colter's lower jaw dropped nearly to the wash-worn red bandanna twisted into a knot around his neck. Either a cloud had just pushed over the bench before him, or yet another group of riders was storming toward him, up the north side of the bench and cutting off his escape route.

Colter blinked.

His heart thudded.

It was the latter, all right. The silhouettes of individual pursuers took shape in Colter's field of vision. Like the first group, this

38

bunch was also riding stirrup to stirrup, dusters buffeting out around them like the wings of giant birds, their dusty hat brims bending in the wind of their ground-hammering passage.

They were straight out ahead of the redhead and his galloping coyote dun, maybe seventy yards away and closing fast.

"Whoahhhhh!" Colter yelled, drawing back sharply on Northwest's reins.

Ahead, riders stormed toward him.

Behind, riders stormed toward him.

Quickly, Colter looked around. He had two directions in which to ride — to the east or the west. He couldn't ride east because of a deep cut in the bench in that direction. There was only west, straight on up the gradually rising bench.

Reining the coyote dun sharply left, Colter poked the horse again with his spurs and whipped his rein ends against the mount's left hip, though he hadn't needed to do any coaxing. This wasn't the dun's first rodeo.

He and the horse's rider had had plenty of bounty hunters and lawmen after them, after Colter had killed Bill Rondo, the rogue sheriff of Sapinero in the Colorado Territory. Rondo had killed Colter's foster father, Trace Cassidy, and then, when Colter had ridden to Sapinero to investigate, Rondo had used his legendary branding iron to burn a large, ugly *S* into Colter's left cheek. The "Mark of Sapinero" some called it, indicating the bearer of the brand was no longer wanted back in Rondo's territory.

In Colter's case, most deemed it the "Mark of Satan."

Others, especially those who'd seen the young, left-handed, redheaded, scar-faced firebrand at work with his guns, had dubbed Colter a redheaded devil, one with a good working knowledge of the old Remington .44 in the holster positioned for the cross-draw on the left-hander's right hip, and the old-model Henry Tyler .44 rifle in the scabbard jutting up from under his left thigh.

Colter's criminal reputation had grown when Bill Rondo had framed him for the murder of two deputy U.S. marshals. Now, here he was, two years later, on the run once more with a whole horde of bounty hunters or lawmen — possibly both — galloping so close behind him now that one of their bullets curled the air just off his right ear before shrieking off a rock dead ahead of him.

That caused him to flinch and for his heart to race even faster.

He glanced behind.

Again, he'd opened up a gap between himself and his pursuers. He'd been right.

He had the best horse of the lot. Still, the horde's foremost riders were only sixty or so yards behind him, and judging by how low they sat in their saddles, avoiding the wind, and by how they were spurring their mounts and whipping the horses with their reins, they were damned determined.

Still, Colter's heart was buoyed by the fact that with every long stretch of Northwest's slender but muscular legs, he and the coyote dun were widening the distance between him and the gun wolves.

But, then . . .

"Oh no," Colter heard himself say beneath the wind roaring in his ears.

He stared straight ahead over Northwest's laidback ears.

There was a problem. A big one. Not in the form of more riders, though that couldn't have been much worse.

It appeared that Colter and Northwest, storming up the gentle incline of open ground, were fast approaching the end of the bench. A shadowy line shone across the ground ahead, and as Colter and Northwest continued to gallop toward it, that shadowy line grew wider.

They were fast approaching a slender chasm.

It appeared as though, maybe several eons

41

back, something had pried both ends of the bench apart and left it with a long, jagged crack down its back, extending from Colter's left to his right. Beyond the gap, the bench continued.

Still, there was the gap. The end of the road. Not just the end of the road, but the end of Colter's life.

Should he stop and fight despite the futility of going up against thirty armed men with federal bounty money dancing in their eyes, or deprive them of their quarry by riding right on over the cliff and into eternity? Or . . .

He saw now as he closed on it quickly that the gap was no more than thirty, possibly thirty-five, feet across.

Could Northwest clear it?

Suddenly, Colter had no choice but to let the horse try. He was now too near the chasm to stop.

Colter leaned even lower, squeezing his knees taut against the horse's barrel, and shouted, "Go, boy — *gooo*!"

His blood raced like frigid snowmelt in his veins. The sweat pasting his hickory shirt to his back suddenly turned to ice.

Northwest shook his head and lunged off the bench and into thin air. Time slowed as horse and rider arced up and over the chasm.

Colter looked down.

His gut leaped into his throat as he saw that the knife slash across the bench had to be at least two hundred feet deep — a devil's red maw of churned gravel, fluted sandstone, sloping rocky shelves, and tonguelike projections of raw earth with a few tufts of wiry brown grass and desert shrubs growing amongst the debris of the planet's bowels, down there in the sun-dappled shadows of an earthen sarcophagus.

Northwest had kicked several rocks from the cliff's lip as the horse had made its leap. Colter saw those rocks tumbling down, down, down into the chasm's open jaws, one or two bouncing off the sheer wall behind Colter now as he and Northwest gained the far side of the bench.

They made it!

But as Northwest's front hooves gained the ground on the opposite side, Colter looked down and slightly behind him to see that the dun's rear hooves just barely cleared the chasm. They landed not two inches on this side of it, grinding into the black gravel and coarse brown grass, kicking the gravel out behind them and into the canyon as the horse's momentum drove horse and rider

43

forward, away from certain death.

Or maybe not . . .

Colter had just turned his head forward when the horse shifted violently. It lurched to its right. Right away, Colter knew why. He heard the grinding rasp of gravel as the horse's right hoof slid inward.

Northwest whinnied.

Instinctively, Colter pulled his feet free of his stirrups. He'd gentled horses back in his home range of the Lunatics, back before all his worldly troubles, before Bill Rondo had killed Trace, and Colter had drifted down the vengeance trail, and he knew that the first thing a horseman did when sensing trouble was to pull his boots free of his stirrups lest he wanted to get his bones pounded to chalk.

As Northwest pulled to the left, sagging beneath him, Colter flew to the right, the ground coming up fast in a gray-brown blur. It hammered Colter about the head and shoulders. It pounded a shrill *"Ohh!"* out of him and then he went rolling, rolling like a rag doll, feeling his hat flying away from him.

He felt the slashing, grinding assault of a million small rocks and some not so small before he came to a stop on his belly, his lips pressed against more dirt and gravel.

Instantly, before he even knew if he was all in one piece, he heaved himself to his feet and swung toward his horse, more worried at the moment about Northwest than he was about himself.

One, he was a horseman, born and bred. His horse was as much a part of him as his own arms and legs, his own soul.

Two, without a horse, he was dead out here even if he had shed the posse, which remained to be seen . . .

CHAPTER 4

Colter looked around him, dazed, shaking away the cobwebs.

To his left, Northwest also appeared to be shaking away the fog of the violent tumble as he regained his feet in a shroud of wafting dust. The dun clawed his front legs forward and hoisted his rear end while breaking at the hocks of his rear legs and lifting up and forward.

Colter's saddle hung down the horse's near side, along with Colter's rifle and scabbard. His saddlebags were on the ground.

Colter was relieved to see that the horse appeared all right. At least, Colter hadn't heard the horrific clatter of broken bones.

The redhead whipped his head back in the direction from which he'd come. He was roughly a hundred feet from the gap. His pursuers milled around on their horses roughly another hundred feet beyond the gap, talking amongst themselves. They were obviously discussing the gap between them and their prey. One of the riders threw lead at Colter, but there was a slight slope between Colter and the gap, and the shooter's bullet skimmed the brow of the slope before ricocheting off a rock to Colter's right.

Colter lurched to his feet. His bones felt creaky. His hips were sore and his neck was stiff. Still, he didn't think anything was broken. He quickly grabbed Northwest's reins and led the horse down into a rocky depression, out of the line of fire from Colter's pursuers trapped on the other side of the gap.

Colter shucked his Tyler Henry rifle from the scabbard then walked back up onto the relatively level ground of the gap. He dropped behind a rock and racked a cartridge into the rifle's action. He gazed across the gap at the thirty or so riders gathered there — a small army of heavily armed men speaking in hushed, angrily conferring tones.

One man — a black-bearded man in a black duster and tan Stetson sitting a fine dapple-gray stallion — spat to one side, then, pointing angrily toward the gap, yelled, "He did it — we can, too! He *ain't* gettin' away! Not again!"

Shucking his rifle from the scabbard on the right side of his saddle, the bearded man cocked it one-handed, rested the barrel across his saddle bows, then ground his spurs into his horse's flanks. He threw his head back to give a caterwauling wail as the dapple-gray lunged off its rear hooves and bolted forward, pinning its ears back against its head.

The others followed suit behind the lead rider, whooping and hollering and grinding their spurs into their mounts' flanks. The mass of men and horses, forming a triangle behind the point rider, whose duster flew out around him like giant black wings, rushed toward the gap, and Colter hunkered down behind his covering rock, grinning like a bobcat eyeing a cottontail.

Hooves rumbled. Colter could hear the squawk of leather tack and the jangle of bridle chains.

The lead rider chewed up the ground between himself and the gap. Horse and rider grew larger and larger in Colter's field of vision, the others flanking him also closing quickly on the chasm.

The lead rider's bearded face trembled with the violent jostling of his galloping mount. Colter saw fear in the man's dark

48

eyes, beneath the wide brim of his tan Stetson.

The dapple-gray lunged off its rear hooves and vaulted out over the narrow canyon, reaching desperately forward with its front hooves. At the apex of his arc over the earth's deadly grin, the bearded rider glanced down and his jaw hung in shock.

A second later, when the dapple-gray cleared the gap, landing on its front hooves, its rear hooves also just barely clearing the chasm, the rider's face stretched into a victorious grin.

Light glinted in the man's dark eyes. He started to raise his rifle. Colter's Henry spoke first. Fear returned to the man's eyes as the bullet punched through the middle of his chest and sent him howling and flying backward off the dapple-gray's hindquarters. He turned a single somersault in the air before he hit the ground, bounced, losing his hat and rifle, and rolled backward. He disappeared into the canyon.

It was as though the grinning earth had sucked him into its mouth.

Colter ejected the spent cartridge, lined up his sights on a rider just then halfway across the gap on a lunging pinto, and blew the rider out of his saddle and into the gorge.

Colter racked another round and aimed at the man to the right of the one he'd just killed. He held fire as this man's horse landed short of the ledge and plummeted into the chasm, horse and rider screaming fiercely.

Colter unseated another rider, another, and another, throwing those three men and, unfortunately, their horses into the earth's jaws. He shot another man as that man's horse gained Colter's side of the chasm. That rider didn't fall into the canyon. Instead, he rolled down the side of his horse and got a boot caught in his left stirrup.

The horse went galloping past Colter, the man screaming as the horse pulled him along beside it, the man bouncing violently. The ground ripped his duster off his shoulders and cast it into the wind, like a lover's hastily cast-off cloak.

Colter ejected the last spent round, sent it smoking over his left shoulder, and seated a fresh pill in the breech.

Several riders, having seen what had happened to the first wave, were pulling their horses sharply back from the ledge on the chasm's far side. At the same time, another horse and rider made the leap. The horse cleared the ledge but lost its nerve. Wide-eyed, it plummeted onto its knees and flipped over its left withers, throwing its rider into the air.

For a second, horse and rider were indistinguishable in the dust they kicked up, but in the next second, Colter saw the rider separate from the horse, rolling out away from it. Colter turned his attention back to the chasm as one more horse and rider disappeared into the earth's mouth while another gained Colter's side of the cleft.

Seeing Colter bearing down on him, the man leaned back in his saddle and raised his arm as though to shield himself from the bullet, shouting, *"Nooo!"*

Too late.

Colter's .44 caliber chunk of death was already on its way. It drilled the man through his right eyebrow. Colter saw the blood spray out the back of his head as he tumbled down his galloping horse's right hip and rolled off into the brush, limbs pinwheeling like those of a scarecrow torn out of a cornfield by a cyclone.

Rifles cracked from the chasm's far side. Bullets plumed the dirt and red gravel and the rocks around Colter, several spanging shrilly.

Colter pulled his head down behind his covering rock as another round zinged past his right ear to slam into a rock behind him.

When he edged another look around the rock to stare back across the chasm, he saw that the rest of the bounty hunters were sitting their restless mounts a good fifty yards back from the cut in the earth.

Their number had been winnowed appreciably.

The dust still sifted in the hot air before them, having been kicked up when, seeing that the odds of their making it across the chasm without becoming sacrifices to the dark gods at the earth's bowels, they'd wheeled their mounts and literally hightailed it back to relative safety.

Suddenly, they stopped shooting. They milled for a time in a tight cluster. Colter could hear them conferring now in the heavy silence following the carnage.

A sound rose straight out across the bench, in front of Colter. He peered that way to see the last man to make it across the chasm alive lift his head up from a brush clump. He grunted and wheezed, his clothes in tatters, his dust-soaked hair hanging in his eyes, as he heaved himself to his feet.

He looked in Colter's direction. His eyes found Colter swinging the Henry toward him.

"No!" the man cried, throwing up his hands.

Colter shot him. Why let him live only to come after Colter again? At one time, the young redhead would have done just that. But he was older now and, after three long years of being hunted across the frontier like a calf-killing coyote, he was wiser, too.

He hadn't killed any calves. At least, none that hadn't tried to kill him first.

His latest victim fell back in the brush, blood geysering from the hole in the center of his chest, painting the leaves and vines around him.

"Hey, Red!" a man called from the chasm's opposite side.

Colter shuttled his gaze in the direction of the voice. The group, dwindled by half — Colter himself hadn't killed them all; several had been claimed when they'd imprudently tried the leap on horses that couldn't make it — had drifted a hundred or so yards back from the chasm. Some were riding away with the air of disgruntled schoolboys. Several more were scattered across the bench, staring toward Colter, as was the man who'd yelled.

He was a lean man in a spruce duster on a blue roan. He held a Winchester on his shoulder as he stared toward Colter from beneath the brim of his high-crowned cream hat. A red bandanna buffeted around his neck in the wind.

"This ain't over, Red!" he bellowed, rising up slightly in his saddle. "This ain't over by a long shot!"

"Speaking of a long shot . . ."

Colter racked another round in his Henry's chamber. He snaked his rifle around the rock's left side and snugged his cheek up against the Henry's stock.

"You hear me, Red?" the lean man yelled. He canted his head slightly sideways, vaguely puzzled.

Colter lined up his sights on the man's chest. He slid the sights to the man's right shoulder then to his arm. "Yeah," he told himself. "Don't kill him. Just put him out of commission. Give him a long-distance whuppin'. That'll be good enough."

The redhead smiled to himself and yelled, "You hear this?"

He squeezed the trigger.

The rifle bucked against his shoulder, smoke and flames stabbing from the barrel. The lean man continued to stare toward him. A full second after the Henry had bucked, the man jerked back and sideways.

He dropped his rifle and reached for his right arm with his left hand. He must have dropped his reins, too, because just then his horse pitched and swung sharply, and then

54

man was flung off the roan's right hip.

He hit the ground and lay writhing before, possibly realizing he might still be in Colter's sights, he heaved himself to his feet and, leaving his hat and rifle on the ground, ran over to where the roan stood angrily switching its tail.

Crouched and in obvious pain, tossing quick, wary glances back toward Colter, the lean man grabbed the hanging reins and fought his way onto the roan's back. With one more look toward Colter, who could see the white line of the man's teeth between his stretched lips, the man swung the roan around and put the spurs to it.

He galloped off down the bench, several other bounty hunters booting their horses along behind him, also casting cautious glances over their shoulders.

Colter lowered the rifle, rose stiffly to his feet, and stepped out from behind the rock. He stared off across the chasm. The posse horde was just then dwindling from his view, swallowed now not by the earth but by the sun — by the frank glare of an Arizona afternoon.

They were gone. Colter was alone.

There was only the sun and the pale rocks and the red rocks and the dusty, spindly shrubs, few as there were. And, save for the ratcheting cry of a lone hawk hunting somewhere up in that brassy blue sky, silence.

No, he wasn't alone. Colter saw them now as he shaded his eyes with his hand — a dozen or so *zopilotes,* Mexican buzzards, circling high above the canyon. They were dropping lower and lower, likely slathering as they flew, keeping watch on the carrion around Colter and in the chasm, little hearts quickening at the prospect of a tasty meal.

Colter retrieved his hat. He spat to one side. It wasn't spittle that struck the rock he'd been aiming for, but blood. He hadn't realized in the frenzy of the dustup that in his tumble with Northwest, he'd bitten his tongue.

"Damnit," he groused, glancing once more toward where the bounty hunters had fled with their tails between their legs, one man bleeding from his arm. "You privy snipes made me bite my tongue!"

The notion suddenly struck him as funny. After all that, he was walking away with a sore tongue, and he was mad about it. His laughter was probably due to the braining he'd taken in the tumble, but he dropped to his knees, laughing, blood running from his mouth. He leaned forward, pressed his forehead into the gravelly ground, still

56

laughing, and rolled slowly onto his back. Slowly, the laughter left him.

He heard the slow clomps of a horse approaching. Northwest's shadow slid over him. The horse lowered its head over Colter, stared down at its addlepated rider through its coppery eyes that Colter had always thought showed more intelligence and character than the eyes of most of the other horses he'd known. And he'd known a few.

Northwest worked his rubbery, bristled lips and gave a snort, blowing his warm, horsey breath, rife with the smell of sun-cured brush, at Colter's face. His eyes were curious, probing, a little wary.

Colter sobered. "Yeah," he grunted out, brushing blood from his chin with his sleeve. "Yeah, I know . . ."

He sat up and looked around. Mountains, rocks, more mountains and more rocks. That was all he could see in all directions. He looked to the northern mountains and then to the southern mountains, misty blue with distance. Where in hell was he?

Somewhere west of Yuma. He'd given a wide berth to that notorious prison town for obvious reasons. He'd traveled through hot, dry, rocky desert mountains, sometimes not seeing a patch of green aside from cactus for days at a time. The sunsets had been miraculous, but the rocks had been black, as though sucked down, burned in hell, and then belched back up to this earthly perdition.

The redheaded gunslinger had been headed to Mexico, because he'd known bounty hunters were after him. He'd smelled them on his trail before he'd made it to Phoenix one week ago. He hadn't known how many. And he hadn't known they'd followed him southwest from Phoenix and around Yuma.

Now he knew.

Now there would be far fewer. At least, for a while there would be fewer.

But with a four-thousand-dollar bounty on his head, there would always be more where that posse came from — a posse likely made up of both lawmen and bounty men, both as corrupt as the most hard-bitten curly wolf to ever prowl the frontier.

Staring south, loneliness turned the redhead's heart as cold as a chunk of pure snowmelt. It lifted chicken flesh between his shoulder blades.

Mexico. He had to get down to Mexico if he wasn't there already.

He didn't want to. He wanted to ride north. He wanted to ride back to Colorado, back to his home in the Lunatic Mountains just north of the San Juans. An up-and-down land of snowy peaks and tamarack forests and cold streams chugging over boulders. He had family there, a girl who'd once loved him and probably didn't anymore — so much water under the bridge.

But he'd love her until he breathed his last.

Home.

Would he ever see it again? Would anything ever be like it was?

All he knew was that for now, he was headed in the opposite direction of home — toward Mexico.

Alone.

Leastways, just him and his horse. At least he had Northwest. That was all right. Like dogs, horses made better friends than most men did.

Colter Farrow checked Northwest over for injuries, reset his saddle, retrieved his hat, mounted up, and rode south toward Mexico.

CHAPTER 5

A bullet hammered a rock to Prophet's left.

The crashing blow sounded like a sledge-hammer smashed against a cracked bell, kicking up a clamorous ringing in Prophet's ears. He felt a burn across the outside of his left arm.

The bounty hunter sucked a sharp breath through his teeth. "Ow, damnit!"

He glanced down to see the tear in the sleeve of his sweaty, dusty buckskin tunic. Blood shone in the tear. Not much but a little. He'd cut himself worse trimming his fingernails with his bowie knife, half-drunk.

Still, it burned like the nip of a horsefly. Worse, it angered him. He cursed the shooter and, as another bullet screeched over his head to blast another rock ahead of him, he cursed that shooter, too.

"Back-shootin' sons of Satan!" he cried, turning around in the narrow arroyo he'd been following, trying to get back to where he'd left Mean and Ugly on a plateau above him, in some far-flung ruin of an ancient Mexican *pueblito,* long abandoned.

He dropped to a knee behind a pillarlike rock just as another bullet, flung from down the arroyo, smashed the face of the rock, throwing rock dust and shards in all directions. Prophet removed his battered hat and dared a glance around the rock's left side.

He could see them down there amongst the rocks — shadowy men with rifles clambering toward him, weaving around the rocks and occasionally crossing the narrow, winding arroyo that cut through the side of this low mountain strewn with rocks and boulders of every size, likely hiccupped by some volcano that had been old long before some dark god had cursed the earth with wretched humanity. All around him, the cones of ancient mountains rose, barren of anything except rocks like ivory dominoes.

The pale line of the arroyo, a strip of white sand curving through the rocks, dropped down the mountains likely emptying into the Sea of Cortez somewhere to the east. *Emptying when it had anything to empty,* Prophet thought. That sure as hell wasn't now. A fella would have a hard time finding a teaspoon of water anywhere around this dry cut in the nasty mountain desert.

Another bullet slammed the face of the bounty hunter's covering rock.

Again, the ringing kicked up in Lou's ears. Two more bullets hammered the rock's face. He could feel the vibration against his shoulders.

He knew what they were doing — the men still in hot pursuit of him after three long days of a breakneck run through southwestern Arizona and into Mexico. (Leastways, he thought he was in Mexico. There weren't any signs out here, just as there were few saloons, though he could sure do with a stiff drink.) His pursuers were flinging lead at him, with surprising venom, no doubt to keep him pinned down so another one could gain ground on him and end the chase right here and now.

Poor, drunken Roscoe Rodane would be avenged at last!

Prophet had seen the man the others were laying down cover for. He'd only glimpsed him, but he'd seen him, just the same — weaving through the rocks on the arroyo's far side, crouched over the rifle in his hands. The man hadn't thought Prophet had seen him, but the bounty hunter had spotted him, all right. That was the thing about bounty hunting. It gave you a certain savvy about those shadowing your own trail . . .

Prophet leaned back against the rock, squeezing his Richards twelve-gauge in both his sweating, gloved hands, the shotgun's leather lanyard looped over his right shoulder and neck. He'd left his rifle with Mean and Ugly. He had only the gut-shredder and the Peacemaker holstered on his right thigh. And his bowie, of course. The knife, like the revolver, had become a part of him.

Through his spine he felt the reverberations of the bullets smashing the rock's face. He squatted on his haunches, which were aching, as were his calves and ankles. He gritted his teeth, waiting, listening for the telltale scrape of a boot nearby, maybe the ring of a spur if the fool hadn't thought to remove them.

He glanced to each side, on the scout for moving shadows.

A shadow moved on his right. It was followed by the faint rasp of gravel beneath a boot.

The shooting stopped. There was a momentary silence before Prophet gritted his teeth and swung around the side of the rock, aiming the Richards straight out before him and tripping the right eyelash trigger.

Boom!

The man before him, six feet away and in

the middle of the arroyo, was picked up and blown back against a boulder that had just turned dark red with blood and organ meat blown out the man's back.

There was another man to his left.

Rather, there *had been* a man to his left.

Boom!

That sorry sack of goat dip met the same fate as his partner, blown back against another large rock and piling up at its base, his blood running down the rock above him. He'd fired his rifle just before he'd been cut in two, but now the rifle, which he'd thrown high in the air, clattered to the ground several feet down the arroyo.

Another heavy silence fell over the side of the mountain. The dead men's partners were no doubt in momentary shock at what they'd just seen from where they were poking their heads out from behind their own cover.

Taking advantage of the posse's shock, Prophet wheeled and, shoving the Richards behind him, where it jostled down his back by its lanyard, broke into a dead run up the arroyo, the floor of which rose more sharply as it climbed the side of the mountain, between larger and larger chunks of granite and limestone.

A Gila monster poked its flat, orange and

black head out from a gap beneath one such boulder, testing the air with its long, forked black tongue. Seeing Prophet, it jerked its head back into its hole. A good thing it did, for a second later a bullet hammered the rock where its head had just been.

The shooter hadn't been hunting Gila monsters. He'd been gunning for Prophet himself, just as the rest of the posse had resumed doing now, as well, bullets stitching the air around him, peppering the rocks and ground to either side of the steeply rising arroyo.

As the arroyo floor rose sharply, dangerously, and Prophet's progress slowed as he climbed, a bullet sliced across the outside of his right leg.

He cursed shrilly, grinding his teeth, but continued climbing. The pain bit him deep, and while he didn't take time to look, with bullets stitching the air all around him, he could feel the oily wetness of blood running down his leg from the hole in that denim-clad thigh.

He hoisted himself up a steep incline, grunting as his brawny arms strained to hoist his burly bulk up the side of a sheer, perpendicular stretch of rock. As he climbed, another bullet burned along the left side of his neck. Cursing, he hurled

65

himself up and to his right, into a jumble of rocks that served as a nest of sorts.

Here he sought refuge from the lead storm. Momentary refuge.

He could hear the posse members running and shouting as they ran, triggering their rifles. He knew they would try to work up and around him, and when they did, his nest would no longer be a refuge but a death trap.

He wasn't sure what to do. The way farther up the mountain offered little cover. It was mostly sand and small rocks. It was also a steep climb.

A hundred yards or so above him, the top of the mountain beckoned. But that hundred yards was a long haul for a man with a wounded leg and a passel of wild gundogs hurling lead at him every step of the uncovered way.

Lou wished he had his rifle. With the long gun, he could make a stand. He'd left the Winchester on his horse because he'd wanted only to scout his back trail after gaining the top of the mountain with Mean and Ugly. He hadn't expected to run into posse riders. At least, not this close to him. He thought he'd put more distance between himself and his shadowers and hadn't thought there'd be any need for his Winchester '73.

He'd thought . . .

"That's what you get, Prophet, you cork-headed old Confederate fool," the bounty hunter maligned himself, knowing that his sometime partner would be using those exact words or even some more colorful. *How many times have you been told that thinking ain't your strong suit?*

Of course, Louisa wouldn't have said *ain't.* No, no. The Vengeance Queen used better English than that. She didn't curse much, either, except maybe by accident when the chips were down.

He chuckled now, indulging in fleeting, appreciatory thoughts of the comely, deadly blonde with the china doll's face, smoky hazel eyes, and a hair-trigger temper. *Louisa.*

He'd parted with her somewhere up north, after an argument, of all things, over his snoring.

He chuckled again then, feeling the burn in his neck, swiped his hand across the cut. Blood shone on his fingers. That one wasn't too bad. It was the leg wound that had him worried.

On the other hand, why worry? A man worried over uncertainties. Now as he edged a look out between two rocks fronting the side of the mountain and seeing the posse riders climbing after him, spread out across the slope on both sides of the arroyo, making their way toward him, about to surround him, he was no longer uncertain of anything.

Least of all that he'd come to his own bloody end.

"Well, I'm gonna take some of these wolves with me, anyways," Prophet spat out through gritted teeth, releasing the keeper thong from over his bone-handled Peacemaker's hammer. "I can do that much, anyways. I'm gonna need all the help I can get beyond them smoking gates, shovelin' coal for Ole Scratch . . ."

He shucked the revolver, wincing as bullets hammered the rocks around him. He clicked the hammer back. Movement on his left. One of his pursuers had already worked up around him and was triggering lead as he crawled between two rocks, toward Prophet.

The bounty hunter shot the man in his left knee but only because one of the shooter's own bullets had shaved a whisker off Prophet's left cheek. The shooter dropped his rifle and grabbed his ruined knee, howling miserably.

"Stop your caterwauling, fool!" Prophet fired again, this time punching a bullet through the howler's right ear, cutting the caterwauling off midhowl.

Prophet fired at another man trying to sneak up on his other side. He couldn't tell if he hit the man or not — he just saw him jerk back behind a small snag of rocks and cactus.

"Here they come," Prophet told himself, snaking his Colt around another rock and snapping off a shot down the slope.

He missed his target, who'd just then dived down behind another rock about fifty yards away from him. More men were climbing the mountain on both sides of him, moving around him. Prophet emptied the Colt without hitting any more targets. They were moving too fast and swerving behind cover.

Quickly, Prophet flicked the revolver's loading gate open and began fumbling fresh shells from his cartridge belt.

"He's empty — rush him before he can reload!" Prophet recognized the voice of Dan Rodane.

Lou continued punching pills into the Colt's wheel. He was breathing hard and fast, his heart racing. He was sweating. "Here it comes," he told no one in particular. "I'm about to pay the price for all my tomfoolery all these years since the war, as per our agreement. Scratch, get the shovel ready — fresh blood is on the way!"

As he punched the last pill home he saw that he was too late. Another man had moved up on his left. It was Rodane himself, aiming down a cocked Winchester at him, the lawman's smile lifting his thick, pewter mustache.

"Any last words, Prophet?" Rodane said.

Prophet cursed and flicked the loading gate home. He jerked the revolver toward Rodane. The sheriff fired first, however. The rifle's bark froze Prophet. He jerked back with the impact of the bullet in his heart, the harsh blow slamming him back against a rock behind him.

Bells.

From somewhere came the sound of bells . . .

Bells tolling just for him.

This was the end. Lou Prophet, at long last, was a goner. Ole Scratch was calling his note due.

CHAPTER 6

Snarling at the pain in his chest, his life on the wane, Lou Prophet looked down at the hole in his brisket.

He frowned.

Wait.

There was no hole. No blood.

He clawed at his chest with both hands, certain he'd see blood shooting up out of the hole he felt over his heart, causing a hard, throbbing pain, like the punch from a three-hundred-pound sailor fresh from the sea and on a three-day drunk on the Barbary Coast.

No. Nothing.

What the . . . ?

He glanced up. Dan Rodane lay prone, nose down in the dirt. He still wore his hat but blood welled up out of the back of the crown, and his body was jerking as though invisible beasts were feasting on him. His rifle lay to his right.

Another man running up the slope jerked forward and went crashing to the ground, his own rifle clattering onto the rocks beside him. Another and another shooter went down, dancing, twisting, screaming, collapsing.

Again, Prophet looked down at his chest. Yep, no blood. He still couldn't quite believe it. Had he just dreamed, imagined the pain?

Taking a deep breath as though to confirm that he was, indeed, alive, he looked around his covering nest of rocks to gaze down the arroyo. Yet more posse riders were falling, cursing and screaming. Some tried scrambling for cover only to be cut down from somewhere above.

Prophet could hear the distant belches of a rifle but he couldn't . . .

Wait.

There.

On the ridge on his left, on the eastern ridge, smoke puffed from a nest of rocks. The shooter was maybe two hundred yards away, but he had the high ground, and he was picking off the posse like ducks on a millrace.

Prophet counted eight or nine posse members, including Rodane, lying amongst the rocks, unmoving. He saw three others running back down the arroyo, crouching,

72

casting quick, wary glances up the eastern ridge. The shooter up there triggered two more quick shots, pluming the dust just behind the three running with their tails up, as though to haze them on their way.

Prophet thought one of the shots broke off one of the runners' spur rowels. An accident?

Something told Prophet it hadn't been a lucky shot.

He looked up the ridge again as the last smoke puff dispersed on the wind.

"Now," he muttered, sleeving sweat from his forehead. "Who in the hell . . . ?"

No movement up there. The smoke was gone. In the harsh light, he wasn't sure he could even pinpoint the exact spot the shooter had fired from. Rocks and more rocks . . .

He looked down at his leg. He felt as though a mule had kicked him. The wound burned. He unknotted the sweaty, grimy bandanna from around his neck and tied it around his leg, breathing through his teeth, cursing the pain the dustup had caused him but thanking his lucky stars. Or, more specifically, thanking his as-yet-unknown benefactor.

Knotting the bandanna tightly, trying to get the bleeding stopped, Prophet cast his gaze once more up the eastern ridge. Still nothing.

Prophet holstered his Peacemaker, securing the keeper thong over the hammer, then reloaded his Richards, just in case. He heaved himself to his feet, an awkward maneuver, given the growing stiffness in his leg. He peered up the northern slope, sighed, then continued his ascent.

It was a ponderous, painful climb, but he wasn't complaining. He might be lying dead down there in that nest of rocks, the buzzards already tearing meat from his bones. By the time he reached the top, he was almost crawling. In fact he would have crawled if his dignity hadn't already taken a hit or two by the fact he'd let himself walk into an ambush without his Winchester.

No, he couldn't crawl, damnit.

So, with a hitch and side swing to accommodate the stiff leg, he ambled over to where he'd left Mean and Ugly ground-reined amongst big rocks that had some wiry brown grass growing up around their bases. Mean eyed him dubiously. The horse had heard the gunfire, all right. He knew Prophet had mucked up again and had nearly become crowbait.

The horse switched his tail sharply and

twitched his ears, whickering softly, reprovingly.

"I don't need any guff from you, you cussed hay-burner."

The bounty hunter grabbed his canteen off his saddle, popped the cork, and took a drink. He took several swallows, more than he would have taken normally out here in this godforsaken desert in which it was always wise to conserve water. But he knew he was close to the vineyard his pal Oscar Otero had run for many years and that, while Oscar had met his demise several years ago now, his vineyard remained. At least, the well he'd used to irrigate his vines remained, drying out in the summer but refilling at the end of every year with the winter rains.

At least, the vineyard had been here two years ago, when Prophet had drifted down this way to spend the winter soaking up the Mexican sunshine and the monetized love of the dusky-skinned, chocolate-eyed señoritas plying their parlor trade in a village near the Pacific. He hadn't yet seen the vineyard this trip. He'd paused here on this mountain to make sure he wasn't leading any unwashed types, including his shadowers seeking to avenge good old Roscoe Rodane, to the vineyard, where he had intended to stay the night.

That was when he'd walked into that ambush.

"Leastways, I didn't lead them toughnuts to the water," Prophet said. He took another deep drink of the brackish canteen water that was almost hot after so long in the sun. "At least I didn't do that."

He gave a wry chuff, adding under his breath, "Almost got myself beefed but . . . at least I didn't lead them to the water . . ."

He let his voice trail. After all, he was just talking to entertain himself, as he so often did when he'd found himself too long alone in the middle of nowhere. Looping the canteen over his saddle horn, he looked around again for his guardian angel — the one with the rifle instead of a halo.

All he saw was white-gray rock and gravel. And a washed-out blue sky bludgeoned by that giant molten bell of the sun.

Below lay the cactus-bristling desert, showing the erosions here and there, the knife-slash arroyos of previous winter rains. The flatland rolled away, pale pink as an unripe peach under a layer of dirty cream mist that was the dust suspended in the sunlight reflecting off the desert floor. Fifty, sixty miles beyond lay cool blue mountains that might have been clouds hovering just above the horizon but which Prophet knew from past experience to be the Sierra de la San Pedro in which "his" village lay — Sayulita.

That was where "his" señoritas were, gazing toward him even now, dark and smooth-skinned and ripe, wondering where he was, what was taking him so long, their lives had been so empty for the past two years without him . . .

That made him laugh.

"Okay, old son," Prophet said, mounted up now and heading down the southwest side of the mountain, along an ancient Spanish and Indian trading path that he knew led to Otero's vineyard. "You're layin' it on a little thick even for you."

Lou chuckled again despite the pain in his leg and his neck, the heat burning down on him. As the trail wound around the shoulder of a barren butte, the butte pulling back to his right, he saw the vineyard directly below, in a broad bowl between large razorbacks of red-and-cream-colored mountains clad in more of the same rocks that littered all of this part of Baja and made it so inhospitable to men that Prophet was relatively sure no one would have found Otero's old vineyard even now, these many years after the old man's death.

In fact, Prophet himself had discovered the old man's mummified carcass. Lou had had no idea what had killed Otero, but it had appeared he'd died in his sleep. He'd probably been dead a year or more before Lou had found him. When Prophet had discovered him, his old friend had been wearing a peaceful grin on his lips and in his half-open eyes beneath a gray-black shelf of coarse, unevenly trimmed bangs. A striped blanket of coarsely woven wool had been drawn up to his chin.

He'd died comfortably in his sleep, maybe dreaming of past loves. Every man should be so lucky. In his passing, he'd left casks and ollas of aging wine and a whole well and several wooden tanks full of water that changed out as the well dried and refilled, pumping water through Otero's small, painstakingly laid pipes that spiderwebbed out to his precious vines.

The vines were overgrown now, of course. They were green and brown tangles that rarely produced *uvas* for lack of pruning. Or the blossoms produced tiny grapes the birds would eat or that would simply wither on the neglected vines.

There was nothing down there now in that natural bowl between sierras except Otero's old, cracked jacal fronted by a dilapidated ramada and flanked by two or three acres of vines. Behind the vineyard humped up another rocky, cream and brown hogback, dwarfing the old Mexican wine ranch, as Prophet had always called the place. Lou had called his old friend an *uva vaquero,* or grape cowboy.

Prophet gigged Mean on down the mountain and into Otero's yard. The wind blew from the northwest, picking up dirt and sand and tossing it, obscuring the yard and moaning as it caught in the brush ramada and whistled through the jacal's open windows. One shutter banged loudly. When the gust died, it fell silent again.

Prophet cursed as he studied his surroundings. He and the old man, who'd been an outlaw in the southern reaches of Mexico long before Prophet's first kick in his mother womb, had had some good times here. They'd sipped Otero's delicious *vino* and sangria, swapping yarns, most of them lies, but having a good time because neither had held the other to the truth or even close. Otero's water, sparkling cold from the earth's bowels and gathering here in his well, was even better than his wine.

Otherwise, Prophet wouldn't be here. Not with the old man lying dead in the grave Lou had dug for him amongst the untended *vides.*

Truth was, Prophet was afraid of ghosts. Such superstitions had their roots in his Old Southern upbringing. He'd been raised by folks who believed spilled salt was an invitation to Old Scratch, as Prophet still did, and knew that when you saw three crows together in one tree, someone in the family would die, which Prophet also still believed. He believed the restless dead moved about at will and could put hexes on folks for past transgressions.

He did not, however, believe that Otero would be restless. The old Mexican had no reason to think Prophet had been anything but an amigo. So Lou nudged Mean on up to the stone-and-wood stable beside the adobe and lifted his tender leg over the dun's rump with an aggrieved groan and a heartfelt oath.

He tended his horse first, because he wasn't dead, and especially in the far-flung desert a man with any sense at all knew to tend to his horse first, no matter what — to see to its needs and comforts because without its four legs you might never see anything but this far-flung desert again. Besides, a horse was the best friend a man could have. Aside from Oscar Otero, that was.

Fortunately, Otero's well wasn't far from the jacal and *estable,* so Prophet was able to fetch water without doing significant further damage to his leg. He fed the horse a bait of oats from his saddlebags and turned him into the old Mexican's corral of woven ocotillo branches. Gathering mesquite wood from the side of the shack, he set about building a fire in the yard fronting the ancient adobe.

He dug his sewing kit out of his war bag, stripped down to his short summer underwear, and sterilized his needle in the fire's flames. He drank down a third of a bottle of whiskey from his saddlebags to kill the pain, then sutured the wound closed. The procedure was a very businesslike matter to Prophet, who'd performed the deed more times than he cared to think about though the endless maze of white, knotted scars all over his body — a tattoo diary of a violent life — were unassailable reminders.

When he had the wound tended to his satisfaction, complete with a flannel poultice of spiderwebs, mud, and whiskey (he'd found plenty of spiderwebs inside Otero's cabin), he returned to the cabin for wine. Oscar had several casks in a back room. There were a good many more spiders and scorpions in there, too, so that Prophet practically had to fight his way in, quickly filling a stone pitcher with the cool, dark red elixir from grapes of years past, then fought his way back out again.

He didn't care to linger in the old man's jacal, where Otero had breathed his last, so he'd arranged his gear outside around the fire. Benevolent or not, a ghost was a ghost. Lou didn't have much to eat except beans into which he tossed his remaining jerky, but the beans and jerky went down nicely with the *vino*.

After supper, he sat back against his saddle, rolled a smoke, refilled his tin cup with wine, and smoked and sipped the wine and missed Otero's presence around the fire. Every sip of the wine reminded him of old Oscar, and the stories he'd told about his old days running wild in Old Mexico.

Sipping the wine and communing uneasily with the old Mexican outlaw's friendly ghost, Prophet watched the rose of the sunset darken the mountains against it and turn the desert dust to a fine, other worldly mist before the sun was gone and the night was black despite the stars kindling across the zenith.

The fire snapped and crackled, resin popping. The fragrant gray smoke drifted upward to disappear in the darkness hovering low above the flames.

Coyotes yammered in the surrounding ridges.

Silence for a time, like that inside a sealed sarcophagus.

Mean gave a warning whinny, jerking Prophet out of his dolor, causing wine to splash over the rim of his cup.

A disembodied voice drifted quietly out of the eerie night: "Halloo, the camp!"

CHAPTER 7

Prophet reached for the Winchester leaning beside him. He loudly pumped a cartridge into the action and said, "Ride in. Slow."

Hoof thuds sounded from straight out away from the fire. They grew louder — the slow clomps of a walking horse.

The horse blew. Bridle chains rattled. Leather squawked.

A horse and rider materialized out of the darkness. Firelight shimmered in the eyes of the horse first and then, as they continued toward the fire, in the eyes of its rider, beneath a brown Stetson with a low crown and a wide, flat brim.

The light found the *S* that had been burned into the rider's left cheek, limning it in light and shadow, showing the knotted scar in stark relief against the otherwise long, smooth-skinned face framed by long, copper-red hair hanging straight down from the hat.

The rider wore a hickory shirt and suspenders under a faded denim jacket, and faded denim jeans. An old Remington rode in the cross-draw position on the kid's right hip. A southpaw. A Henry repeating rifle jutted from a leather scabbard on the coyote dun's left side.

The redhead was maybe twenty, lean as a rail. Prophet thought that, dripping wet and stuffed with supper, he might weigh as much as the bounty hunter's right leg.

The two men studied each other — Prophet from the ground, the kid from his saddle. Mean gave another whinny from the corral obscured by darkness. The kid's coyote dun turned his head toward Mean and pricked his ears, pawing lightly at the ground with one front hoof.

Prophet frowned as he studied the kid closely. He looked a little familiar, maybe. "Have we met?"

"Nope. Leastways, not official. I know who you are, though. Your reputation precedes you, Mr. Prophet."

"Well, ain't I the famous one?"

The kid almost smiled.

"That's Bill Rondo's tattoo on your mug."

The kid didn't say anything. He stared down from his saddle without expression;

the cheek behind the tattoo twitched slightly.

"I hear he's dead, Rondo," Prophet added. "Couldn't have happened to a more deservin' fella."

Prophet cracked a wry grin, nodding. He jerked his head toward the corral. "Since you saved my hide with that old Henry, I reckon I'd best invite you to a plate of beans. There might be a few left if you dig deep enough into that pot. Go ahead and corral your horse with mine. I hope that stallion will stand up for himself."

"Oh, he will."

Prophet glanced at the coyote dun casting the stink eye toward Mean and Ugly, and smiled. "I do believe he will at that."

When the kid had tended his horse and walked back to the camp, slouching beneath the burden of his saddle and the rest of his gear, Prophet was holding a sheet of paper up between his knees. He tossed it onto the ground beside the fire. He'd dug it out of his saddlebags where it had resided with a dozen more printed circulars. The kid's face stared up from the coffee-stained leaf — or at least a rough likeness of the kid's face — complete with the S brand on the cheek.

WANTED: DEAD OR ALIVE took up nearly a third of the heavy paper.

"Ain't this my lucky night?" Prophet said. "Not only did some mysterious shooter pluck my fat from the fire, but a four-thousand-dollar bounty just rode into my camp!" He picked up his wine cup. "My worm is turnin'. Purely it is. I might buy my own private parlor house in San Francisco."

"Those California girls would send you to an early grave, Mr. Prophet."

"Ah hell — since you saved my life and made me rich, you might as well call me Lou."

"Colter."

"I appreciate the help, Colter. I'd just as soon put off dyin' as long as possible. Costs too damn much."

"The deal you made with the devil?"

"Heard about that, did ya?"

"Who hasn't?"

"How's your leg?"

"I've hurt myself worse fallin' down drunk. Trouble is, that's no exaggeration." Prophet snorted then glanced at the redhead. "I just want you to know, young Farrow, I was just about to set those boys on the run with their tails on fire."

The kid had dropped his gear on the opposite side of the fire from Prophet and fished a spoon out of his war bag. "I decided to kill 'em fast so they wouldn't suffer."

"Why?"

"Why didn't I want 'em to suffer?"

"Why'd you save my rancid old Confederate hide?"

"Maybe I didn't want you to suffer, Lou." The kid smiled as he scraped beans out of the bottom of Prophet's cook pot.

"You got a soft spot for ole Lou, do you, Red?"

"Nah." Colter Farrow sank back against his saddle, the cook pot on his lap. "I was just hopin' that maybe one day you'd introduce me to the Vengeance Queen."

He cut another sly smile across the fire at Prophet, the fire reflecting off his eyes that matched the copper color of his hair.

"Kid, Louisa Bonaventure would turn you inside out, stomp your heart in the dirt, and leave you howlin'."

Colter shrugged as he kept working on the beans. "Not that I don't believe you, Lou, but I'd just as soon see for myself."

Prophet chuckled and sipped his wine.

Young Farrow spooned beans into his mouth then licked the spoon, stared at it, and said, "I figured I might need the favor returned someday."

"Huh?"

"You asked me why I plucked your fat

from the fire. That's why."

"Maybe you wouldn't get yourself in such a tinhorn situation in the first place."

Colter shrugged as he continued to spoon the beans into his mouth, grinning. "When I get as old as you, maybe. Old men get careless."

Prophet threw a chunk of wood at him. It bounced off the redhead's shoulder. Colter chuckled and continued eating the beans, scraping the charred leftovers off the bottom of the pot.

"Why were they after you, Lou?" Colter looked across the fire at him. "I mean . . . if you don't mind me askin'."

"Hell, my life's an open book. I shot a man I shouldn't have. A deputy sheriff. I shot him for a doxie. Never shoot a man for a doxie unless you know for sure who you're killin'. A doxie don't always tell you the whole story."

"That bad, huh?"

"She was a good doxie in other ways, though."

"Those are the important things."

"What are you doin' down here . . . so far from Sapinero?" Prophet asked the younker, glancing at the brand on the redhead's cheek again then looking away quickly, sheepishly. "If you don't mind me askin', of

89

course . . ."

"Similar trouble. I killed the wrong man. Er, men, supposedly."

"Rondo?"

Colter glanced down at the wanted dodger offering the four-thousand-dollar federal bounty on his head. "If I'd killed him quicker he might not have framed me for the murder of two deputy U.S. marshals."

"That'll boil Uncle Sam's oysters, for sure."

"Tell me about it." Colter set the empty pot aside and ran a sleeve across his mouth. He sighed, belched, spat, looked around, and said, "Somehow I attracted bounty hunters to my trail, so I decided to head for Mexico."

Prophet took another sip of Otero's well-aged *vino* and arched a brow at the redhead sitting across the fire from him. "I seen you behind me, trailin' me, so don't get to thinkin' I'm so old I don't know what's a shadow an' what ain't."

"You did?"

"I glassed you yesterday just after noon. I seen you before but I wasn't sure you was followin' me. When I realized you was followin' me but stayin' clear of Rodane's bunch of cutthroats also followin' me, I figured you might be an independent con-

90

tractor."

"Sort of like yourself?"

Prophet shook his head and gave a fateful chuff. "Believe me, there's none worse. Or more unpredictable." He chuckled as he swirled the wine in his cup, admiring the reflection of the fire off the blood-red liquid.

Colter crossed his arms on his narrow chest and regarded Prophet through the low, dancing flames. "I think our stars might be aligned, somehow."

"Oh?"

"This ain't the first time our trails have crossed. You probably don't remember, but there was a time or two . . ."

"I remember the brand. And the red hair. The left-handed gun." Prophet looked at the kid, looked away, then turned back to him again. "Tell me, kid . . . does it hurt? The brand, I mean. I apologize for the question, and you sure as hell don't have to . . ."

"Only when a purty girl looks at me and flinches. Or looks at me, just like you just did, and then turns back to stare." Colter gazed off grimly. "Then it hurts powerful bad. Almost as bad as when Rondo first pressed that red iron against my face."

"I'm sorry I stared, kid."

"That's all right." Colter curled another wry grin. "You're not pretty enough to make it ache."

Prophet laughed. "Kid, you remind me of someone."

"Oh? Who's that?"

"Me. A few years back."

"What were you doin' when you were my age, Lou?"

"Runnin' west after the war. Lookin' for any sort of trouble I could get into. Any sorta trouble that would keep me from remembering all the friends and cousins and even some of my uncles blown to bits or hacked to pieces by bayonets and minié balls, during the War of Northern Aggression."

"Well, that makes us different, then."

"What does?" Prophet asked.

Again, the young man stared grimly into the darkness. "You were runnin' *to* trouble. Me? I've been runnin' *from* trouble ever since I ran into it in the form of Bill Rondo's dead carcass on his kitchen floor."

"Mexico's not such a good place to avoid trouble, Red."

"I reckon it's a matter of which skillet is hotter at any given time."

"Tooshay, as I heard a French parlor girl say once."

"What's it mean?"

"Right as rain, but I'm no Frenchman."

92

"Ah." Colter nodded.

"You want some wine?"

Colter looked at him, flushing a little. "Truth be told, Lou, I haven't refined my drinking skills yet. I'm workin' on 'em."

"All the more for me, then, though ole Otero has a house full of the stuff."

"Really? Where is he?"

"Dead."

"Don't that beat all?"

"You didn't know about this place? I mean, before now?"

"Hell, no," Colter said. "I just followed you here."

Prophet regarded him curiously.

"Like I said," Colter explained, "our stars must be aligned. I just happened to spy a fella ahead of me — one with a fine bunch of cutthroats after him. I worked around the cutthroats an' must've glassed you right around when you glassed me. I couldn't see you very well from that distance, but I spotted your horse. I put the big man and the big horse together, an' . . . ."

"Yeah, we stick out, me an' Mean do," Prophet said.

"So, anyways," Colter continued, "I figured if you wouldn't mind, we could maybe throw in together. Fact is — and I'd appreciate if you didn't bandy this around

93

overmuch, as I embarrass easily — but I tend to get a little homesick out here all by my lonesome . . . from time to time. I thought it might be nice to have a kindred spirit to share the trail with. If I'm crowdin' you at all, Lou, just say so and I'll pull my picket pin at first light tomorrow."

"Ah hell, no, you ain't crowdin' me." Prophet refilled his wine cup from the stone pitcher. "Two pairs of eyes is better than one, I reckon. But I must say, I do have a way of attractin' teetotalers."

He chuckled dryly, thinking of Louisa, who never drank anything stronger than sarsaparilla.

"Well, then," Colter said, heeling the ground absently as he sat back against his saddle, "where we headin', Lou? Me — I got no destination in mind."

"I know this sweet little town up in them mountains yonder, on the other side of the desert," Prophet said. "The señoritas up there . . . well, let's just say they're . . ."

He spent the bulk of the next hour describing the attributes not to mention the talents of the soiled doves residing in the little village of Sayulita. Of course, he was doing more than talking. He was *remembering, anticipating,* taking himself out of this dry-as-dust world and leaping ahead to that more idyllic one across the desert. Forever across the desert . . .

He talked until he saw that he'd put his new partner to sleep over there on the other side of the fire. Chuckling, he drifted away from the fire to bleed off some of the whiskey and wine, then took a big long drink of Otero's sparkling cold water and rolled into his soogan.

He'd let the fire burn down to umber coals. The fewer folks who knew about his and Colter's presence here, the better. Even the wildcats that prowled these rocks and washes . . .

He soon learned that his new trail partner shared more than a penchant for teetotaling with his other, more comely, blond partner, Louisa Bonaventure. He shared her inclination for troubling dreams.

Prophet woke to hear the young man muttering the name "Marianna" over and over again on the other side of the fire's slowly dying coals — restlessly, anxiously, as though calling out to her over a long distance, rattling a sob from time to time before he rolled over and somewhere in the tortured caverns of his lonesome mind found peace at last.

"Sleep easy, Red," Lou whispered, and fell into a restless sleep again himself.

CHAPTER 8

"Lookee there — fresh meat," Prophet said as he stared up at the dead man hanging upside down and by one ankle from a giant sycamore.

Prophet and young Colter Farrow had been on the trail crossing the desert together for two whole days. This was the early afternoon of the third day, and they were finally starting to reach the Sierra de la San Pedro — as well as Rosario "One-Eye" de Acuna's cantina on the aptly named Arroyo de los Muertos.

"What do you suppose the poor hombre did to deserve such an end?" Colter asked.

Prophet stared up at the dead man. The corpse was badly bloated, so it had been hanging there for several days, but it was a far more recent expiration than the several other men whom Prophet and Colter had also seen in similar dispositions along the trail.

At least Prophet had assumed they were all men. He'd been able to tell for sure that only one was a man, for given the other cadavers' extreme states of putrefaction — two were veritable skeletons with only a few strips of leathery flesh clinging to the bones — it was impossible to gauge the sexes.

This was a male, all right. A Mexican in a short leather jacket, white shirt, and *pantalones* stuffed into high, brown, calfskin boots. The bloating had so disfigured the man that it was impossible to tell much else about him except that he'd been shot several times and also sliced up pretty well with a knife. Something had been shoved into his mouth, and Prophet didn't even want to think about what it might be, though, given his knowledge of the particularly grisly and punitive Baja form of punishment, he had a pretty good idea.

"No tellin'," Prophet said. "I know ole One-Eye's work, though. The severity usually only depends on what kinda mood he's in at any given time, though I'd say this fella mighta tried to take advantage of One-Eye's advanced age and rob him or abuse one of his *putas.*"

"One-Eye?"

"The old mestizo who runs the place. Rosario de Acuna. Claims to be descended

97

from Spanish kings, with an Aztec war chief hidden somewhere in a woodpile, but many a man claims to be a lot of things down here. He also claims to be a hundred years old, but he was claiming that when I first started cooling my heels down here nearly fifteen years ago now so that'd make him older'n Methuselah. So who knows? One thing I do know is that old One-Eye makes a helluva javelina stew. That's why I risk stopping here."

"Risk?"

Prophet gave a dry chuff. "You'll see."

The bounty hunter booted Mean and Ugly into the arroyo then up the other side. There was more growth here than only a mile back, which meant there was more water.

Agave cactus, elephant trees, the massive cardon cactus, tree yuccas, and spiked shrubs of many shapes and sizes pocked the desert around the rocky trail that showed the marks of recent travelers. Since One-Eye Acuna's cantina was the only place within a hundred square miles one could find water as well as food and busthead, and since it was on a main freight route from the Sea of Cortez to the Pacific Ocean, anyone passing through this part of the Baja peninsula usually stopped for an hour or two or even a night or two, to rest their horses before the hard climb over the mountains.

It was a remote, lawless place, and any man who stopped here was taking his life in his hands.

"You watch my back, kid," Prophet said as he rode on into the cantina's yard, "and I'll watch yours."

"You're makin' me nervous, Lou."

"It's good to be nervous at old One-Eye's."

Prophet and Colter stopped their horses in the middle of the dusty yard, near the windmill and stone stock tank ringing its base. The horses had smelled the water from a mile away and were eyeing the tank eagerly while Prophet and his trail companion took their measure of the surroundings, getting the lay of the land.

Several saddled horses stood before the big, boxlike, brush-roofed adobe sitting back from a wide ramada. A barn and corral sat to Prophet's right. Goats, pigs, and chickens foraged in the low, rocky desert hillocks to his left, around several small stone stock pens and an adobe chicken coop. As far as Prophet could tell, no trouble was afoot. He'd ridden up to One-Eye's place before when men from rival

99

bandito gangs were exchanging lead, so he knew from experience it paid to be cautious.

Besides, this was Mexico . . .

"All right," Lou said, reaching down to snap the keeper thong back over his Colt's hammer. He'd released the strap when they'd left the dead man hanging by the wash. "Quiet as a preacher's parsonage on Sunday after . . ."

He let the words die on his tongue when boots thumped and spurs chimed on the ramada. He glanced at the cantina. A man was just then walking through the batwing doors that were made from woven greasewood stems. The tall Mexican outfitted in the brightly colored trail garb of the border country stopped just outside the doors, as they slapped into place behind him.

He lifted his chin as though to take a deep breath, composing himself after too much drink, then walked forward with pronounced carefulness. He stepped out from under the ramada into the sunlit yard then stopped again.

Suddenly, he dropped straight down to his knees. He knelt there for a second then gave a little whining, strangling yell before falling on his face in the dust. The crown of the red velvet, silver-stitched sombrero hanging down his back poked straight up at the sky. Below the sombrero, the brass-framed, pearl handle of a stylish knife jutted from the man's back.

Something moved behind the cantina's batwings. A man stood there, staring out. He pushed through the doors and stopped under the ramada, staring straight out into the yard at Lou Prophet and Colter Farrow. He was dressed very much like the now-dead vaquero, only he was shorter, with a slight paunch, and he sported long drooping black mustaches.

As he sized up Prophet and Colter, the Mexican's right hand strayed toward a pistol holstered high on his right hip. Prophet smiled without guile at the gent and opened his hands to show that he was no threat.

Colter did the same.

The mustached Mex slid his eyes between the newcomers cautiously, then removed his hand from his gun and strode over to the dead man. He placed his left foot on the dead man's rump and pulled the knife free of the man's back with his right hand. The knife made a sucking, grinding sound as it slid free of the dead man's flesh.

The dead man's killer cleaned the blade on the dead man's short leather charro jacket, then stuck the fancy pig sticker into a sheath jutting up from the well of his right, silver-tipped, high-topped black boot. He crouched once more over the dead man and pulled something from the dead man's right coat sleeve.

He looked at it then, giving a Spanish curse, angrily flipped the object into the dirt. Prophet's eyes were good enough for him to make out the queen of hearts.

When the Mexican had returned to the cantina, Prophet turned to Colter and narrowed one eye in warning. "You don't want to cheat at cards here."

"No," Colter said, staring at the pasteboard lying faceup beside the dead man. "No, I don't."

He and Prophet swung down from their saddles and loosened their horses' latigo straps so they could drink freely from the stock tank. The men tossed their reins on the ground, effectively ground-reining the beasts, who wouldn't stray far from the water, anyway, then headed over to the cantina.

Prophet pushed through the batwings first, Colter flanking him. He looked around at the men playing cards at tables around him. Then he squinted his eyes into the smoke-hazy shadows at the rear of the earthen-floored room, where a raisin of a little one-eyed man held his place beside his range upon which a stewpot perpetually smoked, sizzled, and bubbled, filling the room with the peppery, tangy smell of Mexican stew.

The stew was One-Eye Acuna's specialty whose Spanish name Prophet couldn't remember. What he could remember was that it was one hell of a rib-sticking meal chock-full of goat or javelina and seasoned with chili peppers and several other spices Prophet didn't recognize and which he'd eaten only in Baja. (One-Eye had once confessed to the bounty hunter that his secret was simmering a goat's head in the *estofado* overnight then removing it the next morning. There was no seasoning in all of Mexico like boiled *cerebros de cabra,* or goat brains!)

Prophet stopped in the middle of the room, folded his thick arms across his broad chest, and grinned toward the old man whose head poked up maybe a foot above his plank board bar. "Lookee there, the old reprobate is still kickin'!" Prophet intoned. "Now, if that ain't proof ole *el diablo* walks amongst us, I don't know what is!"

The old man looked up from the age-yellowed newspaper spread out before him. It was a big paper likely left here by some pilgrim from Mexico City.

One-Eye's face was so dark he might have been mistaken for a full-blood Aztec. It was every bit as creased as a raisin. The man's longish, extremely thin hair was coal black and swept straight back over his head, tucked behind his tiny black ears. The hair was so thin that warts and black cancers showed through its thin screen, all over his head. He had more abrasions on his face. He squinted his lone, milky black eye toward Prophet, a black patch covering the other one.

A grin shaped itself slowly on his lipless mouth, showing what appeared to be a full set of badly tobacco-stained teeth. Ashes from the loosely rolled corn-husk cigarette dangling from a corner of his mouth dribbled onto the newspaper, which lay beside a five-gallon glass *tarro* filled with pickled baby rattlesnakes — another Baja delicacy.

Tears came to the ancient mestizo's lone eye. He shook his head as the tears started to dribble down his nearly black cheeks, the skin drawn so taut against the severe bones that it appeared on the verge of splitting.

Making a strangling sound that Prophet knew to be warm, delighted laughter, One-Eye walked out around his bar, small and frail and slightly bent forward at the waist and with a slight hump pushing his head

104

down but still fleet on his feet for all his years and ailments.

He walked up to Prophet, rose onto the toes of his desert moccasins, and placed his gnarled hands, the left one showing the middle finger hacked off at the middle knuckle, on Prophet's cheeks. He wagged the big bounty hunter's big head with affection, making Lou's lips pooch, and cried, *"¡Por todos los santos en el cielo, es una alegría rara verte de nuevo, mi viejo amigo!"*

("By all the saints in heaven, what a rare joy it is to see you again, my old friend!")

Prophet placed his gloved hands on the old man's shoulders; they appeared nearly as large as the man's head. "The pleasure is all mine, One-Eye. How you been, you old raptor?"

One-Eye lowered his head and looked up from beneath a thin, dark brow mantling his wizened eye socket. "Mean as a snake!" He grinned, wheezing out another laugh. "Who is your friend, Lou? The *rojo*. Your son, maybe, huh? I didn't know you had any, but I'm not surprised, the way you throw your seed around, uh?" He laughed until the laughter became a racking cough.

"I wouldn't be a bit surprised myself," Prophet said. "But the younker ain't mine. Leastways, not that I know about." He

105

winked at the redhead. "This here is my new pard, Colter Farrow."

One-Eye cast his one-eyed gaze over the batwings into the yard, frowning. "Where is the gringa? The *rubia* with . . ." He held his hands up to his chest as though hefting a couple of heavy melons, grinning lewdly. "She is the one I want to see!"

He laughed again until he hacked.

"The persnickety, teetotaling Vengeance Queen and I parted trails a ways back. I wouldn't doubt if she's holed up in a snake den in West Texas. Them sand rattlers can have her. She might stack up nice, but she's a harpy, just like all of . . ."

Prophet frowned. The old mestizo, apparently distracted, had walked up to Colter and now rose onto the toes of his moccasins again, placing his knobby, nearly black hands on the younker's face. With the index finger of his right hand he traced the *S* branded into young Farrow's left cheek.

Colter looked incredulously down at the old man. He shifted his uneasy look to Prophet then returned it to One-Eye, who sucked a sharp breath through his teeth, squeezing his lone eye closed, dropping his chin, and saying, "Pain, El Rojo." He placed his right hand on Colter's chest, over his heart. "So, so much pain, you have endured

— am I right?"

He opened his eye and looked up at Colter, probing the young man with his single, milky black eye, keeping one hand on his face, the other on his chest.

"What — you don't like it?" Colter asked.

One-Eye grinned. He cut his one-eyed gaze to Prophet. "*¡Fuerte!* They are tough when they are young — are they not, Lou?"

"Some of 'em have to be tougher than others."

"I know just what you need to take the pain away. Both of you. The pain of the long ride across the *desierto solitario . . .* if for no other reason." One-Eye winked his lone eye at Colter then turned toward the bar.

"The Brand of Sapinero is what that is," said a man's voice on Prophet and Colter's right. Louder, edgier, the man said, "Or, as some call it, the *Mark of Satan . . .*"

Prophet saw the speaker rise from a chair over there and flick the keeper thong free of a pistol hammer.

Ah hell.

CHAPTER 9

Peering into the shadows on the room's east side, Prophet saw the three men sitting at a table.

They were a ragged but well-armed trio in dusty trail garb. They were two gringos and a thick-set half-breed Apache with blue eyes. The man who'd spoken was sitting with his back against the adobe wall to which three translucent bark scorpions clung, twitching their tails, light from a dusty front window making them glow eerily against the sooty bricks.

The man who'd spoken held his gaze on Colter as he heaved himself up from his chair. He had long, lusterless blond hair and an angular, horsey face. Pistols resided in shoulder holsters beneath his long duster — top-break Smith & Wesson .38s, the barrels extending down past the open toes of their holsters.

"Yessir," he said, slurring his words

slightly, his faded, gray-blue eyes pinned to Colter, "the Brand of Sapinero. A skinny redhead. Southpaw. Wanted by the federals north of the border for the murder of Bill Rondo and two U.S. marshals."

"Two-thousand-dollar bounty." This from the stocky half-breed, who'd been sitting with his back to the room but who now rose slowly from his chair, the chair creaking, the breed turning, showing two Colt pistols holstered on his thighs clad in deerskin chaparajos, and another wedged behind his cartridge belt, over his belly. A long, obsidian-handled stiletto jutted from his left boot adorned with large silver Sonora rowels. A single, bushy black brow mantled his odd blue eyes, above a broad, crooked nose and a pencil-thin mustache.

He kicked the chair aside and put his back to the table, facing Colter and Prophet, menace brewing in his gaze.

"You got the bounty all wrong, friend," Colter said.

Prophet arched a brow at him.

"It's four thousand now." Colter grinned.

"Uh, kid . . ." Prophet choked out.

Now the third man rose from his chair on the room's east side. He was the tallest of the bunch, and he wore a full beard and a chilly smile, his hazel eyes glinting in the same light that had set the scorpions glowing. The scorpions held still now against the wall, as though sensing trouble and waiting with silent eagerness to see how it all played out.

"Kid," said a man on the opposite side of the room from the three gringos, "did you say *four thousand dollars?*" He'd spoken with a southern Sonoran accent.

Prophet glanced over his shoulder. The man who'd spoken was the hombre who'd killed the card cheat. He and his own two amigos sat against the building's west wall, cards in their hands, gold and silver coins, stone mugs, and the remains of a meal littering their table.

They were all brightly, ostentatiously dressed in the manner of the Mexican grandee, or those with aspirations of same. In fact, they were most likely stage robbers or cattle rustlers waiting for their trails to cool either north of the border or across the Sea of Cortez, in Sonora.

"You got it, amigo," Colter said, his pale sunburned cheeks dimpling with a winning grin. "Four thousand dollars."

"Dead . . . or alive?" asked the first man who'd spoken, the horse-faced blond.

"Either," Colter said.

"Kid . . ." Prophet's heart was thumping.

The redhead looked as pleased as a birthday boy.

The three Mexicans gained their feet, one shoving the table aside and knocking over a stone cup, making the coins jingle. Their chairs creaked beneath their shifting weight. Then they were all standing, facing Prophet and Colter as well as the men on the other side of the room.

The Mexican who'd killed the cheat lifted his chin to call to the three gringos, "What do you say, señores — we split the bounty six ways?"

"Let's see," said the blond, lifting his eyes to the ceiling and counting on his fingers. "That'd be . . ."

Still grinning like a groom with a comely bride, Colter said slowly, enunciating each word precisely, "Six . . . six . . . six." He lowered his chin, eyes glinting devilishly. "Six hundred and sixty-six dollars."

Prophet glanced at him skeptically and quietly asked, "Did you figure that in your head just now?"

Colter shrugged.

"What do you say, amigos?" the half-breed asked his gringo amigos.

The gringos glanced at each other quickly, shoving their coattails behind their holsters and flexing their hands over their pistol butts.

"We say it's fine as frog hair split six ways!" said the blond through gritted teeth, jerking his hands toward his Smith & Wessons.

Prophet's heart leaped in his throat. *"Hit the deck, Red!"*

He and Colter dropped to the floor at the same time that the gringos and the half-breed and the Mexicans jerked up their pistols. The six-guns blasted and blazed on opposite sides of the room. The bullets caromed through the air where the bounty hunter and the redhead had just been standing, the lead of the gringos and the half-breed smashing into the flesh of the Mexicans at nearly the same moment that the bullets flung by the Mexicans tore the flesh of the gringos and the half-breed.

Keeping his head down and gritting his teeth against the deafening din, Prophet had slid his own Colt from its holster. He saw that Colter, lying belly down three feet away from him, also had his Remington in his hand, cocked and ready to go.

It didn't look like Prophet and Colter were going to need their weapons, however. The Mexican and gringo bounty hunters were doing a fine job of killing one another

112

without Lou and Colter's help. On both sides of the room, the men screamed and jerked and danced around their tables. They howled enraged epithets, realizing they'd been tricked at the last second but so angered by the lead tearing into them that they couldn't stop shooting their killers.

Until they were all dead.

Until five were dead, anyway, lying in bloody piles on the floor around their respective tables.

The Mexican who'd killed the card cheat had fallen and rolled and now he lay writhing on his back, screaming in agony as well as rage. He rolled onto his belly, pushed himself onto his hands and knees. He spat a gob of dark red blood onto the earthen floor then lifted his big, silver-chased Colt and fired one more shot into the blond gringo who lay dead across the table on that side of the room.

The gringo jerked then slid off the table to land on the floor with a heavy thud.

The Mexican dropped his Colt. He rose onto his knees, stared toward the batwings as though they were the gates of heaven, and bellowed, *"Por el amor de la Madre María, ¡soy un hombre muerto!"* ("For the love of Mother Mary, I am a dead man!")

He dropped straight forward to hit the

floor on his face. He quivered slightly then lay still. A blood pool grew beneath him.

Prophet sat up, looking around. Colter did, too. "I'll be damned," the kid said, giving a low whistle. "That's the first time I ever killed six men without firing a single shot!"

Prophet looked at him. "Kid, you remind me of someone."

"You?"

"No. The Vengeance Queen, her cuckoo self. She taunts death the way you just did."

Colter gained his feet with far more swiftness than what remained in Prophet's weary bones, the bounty hunter being Colter's senior by a good fifteen years. Colter extended his hand, helped the big man to his feet.

Prophet reached down for his hat, brushed it off, and set it on his head. Looking around for the lone-eyed proprietor, whom he couldn't see for all the smoke, Prophet said, "Sorry about the mess there, One-Eye, but we . . ."

Then he saw the wizened little man crouching over the body of one of the Mexicans, the one sprawled nearest the bar. One-Eye was inspecting the ring on the man's left middle finger, holding it up and bending it to catch the light. It appeared

114

jade set in gold. The old mestizo raised his lone brow, impressed. He gave a grunt as he tried to pull the bobble from the man's finger, and winced.

No dice.

He picked up the cleaver lying on the floor beside him. He spread the dead man's hand out on the floor, palm down, and raised the cleaver. Grimacing, he thrust the blade down. *Thump!* He held up the bloody finger from which the ring dropped into One-Eye's open hand. The old mestizo held it up to the light and spread a satisfied grin.

He pocketed the ring and then ambled over to the next dead Mexican.

"A perk of the trade," Prophet told Colter.

He turned his attention to the batwings, for he'd heard a low rumbling that grew quickly louder.

"Ain't I gonna get to enjoy a single bowl of One-Eye's stew in peace?" Prophet plaintively asked.

He and Colter walked to the front of the room to stand staring over the batwings into the yard. Lou recognized the rumbling as horses coming fast and hard. A clattering sound accompanied the hoof thuds — the rattle of a wagon also approaching hard and fast.

Staring toward the brush delineating the

115

arroyo's curve just beyond the cantina, Prophet saw the first riders lunge up out of the brush on fine, tall, dusty horses with sharply arched necks bespeaking purebred Arabians. As the two riders galloped toward One-Eye's place, a four-horse team of horses lunged up out of the arroyo behind them. Hitched to the team was a natty-looking leather-and-wood carriage, fully enclosed, with fine brass fittings and high, red wheels.

As the sporty contraption turned along the trail, Prophet could see it was a custom-made rig, enclosed with glass. Red velveteen curtains jostling in the windows. A driver sat in the boot high atop the carriage. Another man sat beside him — a shotgun messenger. Leastways, he was carrying a shotgun though Prophet doubted he was a messenger. Just a guard for whatever precious cargo rode in the carriage.

The rig didn't look like any stagecoach Prophet had ever seen. But, then, leave it to a Mexican to fancy-up a simple Concord. Why not? Wasn't every day a celebration down here?

The bounty hunter chuckled at the notion then sobered as he studied the three other riders galloping up out of the wash behind the carriage, also on fine Arabians. Counting the man in the boot, that was seven guards total.

The guards as well as the driver were all dressed in the gaudy attire of the frontier vaquero, complete with short, fancily stitched waistcoats called *chaquetas,* bullhide chaparajos, and *pantalones* buttoned down the sides of their legs with silver conchos. The pants were stuffed into high, black boots with large, silver *espuelas,* or Spanish spurs. Their beards or handlebar mustaches or goatees were impeccably trimmed, and outlandish steeple-crowned sombreros were thonged securely beneath their chins. They each sat erect on a deep-seated saddle, the dinner-plate horns also trimmed in silver.

Nah, this wasn't no stagecoach. Even in Old Mexico where they shoot off fireworks on Easter, they don't natty up a stagecoach like this contraption here, and they don't guard it as well, neither.

"We getting a visit from Spanish royalty, Lou?" Colter said, standing to Prophet's right.

"If they'd sent word ahead, I'd have cleaned up a little."

The lead riders rode into the yard, followed by the carriage and the three drag-riding guards. Mean and Ugly and Colter's

117

coyote dun, Northwest, whinnied and ran around, excited by the commotion, their manes buffeting. The horseback riders and the carriage stopped between the cantina and the windmill and stock tank just beyond it, dragging their dust into the yard around them. It wafted so thickly that for a time Prophet could see only vague shadows inside it.

As the dust thinned, Prophet watched the guards swing down from their mounts and loosen the Arabians' latigo straps. The coach driver and the shotgun guard, both appearing older than the horseback-mounted guards, having liberal strands of gray in their thick beards, climbed stiffly down off the coach, unharnessed the team, and led it over to the stock tank for water.

The air continued to clear around the coach now sitting alone in the yard fronting the cantina, its tongue drooping forward into the dirt and sand. Prophet stared at it, wondering what was so precious inside that seven men had been given the duty of guarding it. He couldn't see through the window because of the red drapes, and not being able to see inside the contraption intensified his curiosity.

Suddenly, as though in response to his silent question, a slender, beringed, feminine hand slid the curtain aside. A round face appeared in the window, staring out. No, not really a round face. The impression of roundness was given by the way the woman's hair was pulled up into small buns around her regal head and covered with a white silk mantilla that hung down past her shoulders. The woman's dark brown hair was secured in the tightly coiled buns by small, ornamental gold pins.

The eyes staring toward the cantina were large and brown, almost chocolate.

Those eyes met Prophet's. The woman studied him passively for several unnerving seconds, her eyes holding his gaze with a frank one of her own. One of her brows arched. The young woman pulled her head back and let the curtain fall back into place over the window.

"Mercy," Prophet grunted to Colter. "Did you see . . . ?"

He let his voice trail off when the coach lurched slightly to one side, and the scrolled gold handle of the near-side door dropped. The door opened outward, and the young woman who'd been peering through the curtains a second before, stepped out, showing small, incredibly decorated velvet slippers and white knit stockings below the hem of her equally incredibly decorated gown of glittering brocade.

The voice of an old woman inside the carriage said something in Spanish behind the young one. The old woman prattled out the Spanish too quickly for Prophet to comprehend. Whatever she had said, in a protesting tone, it did not deter the younger woman from dropping both her slippered feet into the yard, stepping forward, and closing the coach's door behind her.

Her gown was breathtaking even for a middle-aged scoundrel like Prophet, who usually saw a woman's clothes only as an obstacle between him and the feminine body beneath. There seemed to be multiple layers and materials, though the main color was a deep chestnut brown richly embroidered in flower patterns over a frilly white *camisa* almost entirely concealed except on the woman's upper torso and shoulders. The upper torso was something to behold, however, given its roundness and the depth of the cleavage that showed there, the mouth of the deep valley exposed just above where the brown, gold, and green brocade of the main cloth started.

A raving beauty, this one. And Colter might very well have been right when he'd mentioned royalty, because the woman now striding gracefully toward Prophet and his branded partner owned the majestic hauteur and imperial carriage of a Spanish queen.

"I'll be damned if she ain't, Lou," Colter said.

Prophet watched, mesmerized. "Watch your language, Red."

CHAPTER 10

Prophet couldn't take his eyes off the Mexican beauty moving toward him, so bewitching were the eyes and the overall package. She seemed of another, heavenly world beyond the clouds, entirely separate from this lowly, scorpion-infested, bloody plain on which seven men had just died hard, the smoke smelling of rotten eggs still drifting around them.

She lifted the pleated skirts of her elaborate embroidered gown above her ankles, showing the soft shoes again, and the knit white stockings, and stepped onto the low stone walk running beneath the ramada. She stepped up before the batwings, so close to Prophet and his branded partner that the bounty hunter could smell the rosewater and sandalwood aroma wafting off her, tinged with the light musk of female perspiration.

It had to have been damn hot in that

closed-up carriage, but Prophet didn't think he saw a bead of sweat on her smooth almond forehead above thin, arched, dark brown brows that arched higher as the eyes probed his, vaguely incredulous.

Colter cleared his throat.

Prophet glanced at him. Colter jerked his chin slightly. Prophet had been held so rapt by the woman's charms and general exotic bewitchery that he hadn't realized until now that he was blocking the entrance through which she apparently wanted to walk.

"Ah hell." Prophet clumsily removed his hat. "I do apologize, uh, señorita . . . señora . . ." He couldn't tell how old she was. She was no Spanish sprite. Not with a bodice filled as well as hers was, or eyes as large and round and frank, but he didn't think she was all that deep into her thirties yet, either. If she was married, where was her husband? "I didn't realize . . ."

He pulled back away from the batwings, tripping over his spurs. Colter had already stepped back against the wall on the other side of the doors. He, too, was holding his hat as he crooked a wry grin at his big trail partner. Prophet scowled back at the younker then froze when he saw that the woman had stepped through the batwings, stopped just inside the cantina, and was gazing up at him.

Prophet became chillingly aware of all the dead men piled behind him. He fingered the frayed brim of his sweaty, salty Stetson, and averted his gaze, feeling as guilty as a schoolboy who'd just been caught tossing a snake into the girls' privy.

The woman kept staring up at Prophet. He wanted to flinch at the burn of her gaze but managed to maintain a bland expression as he stared at the toes of his boots. In the periphery of his vision, he saw her eyes wander slowly over him, across his chest and shoulders, down to his scuffed and worn boots and back up again. He could feel her disdain, as though she were regarding an ape that had just wandered into her own private boudoir.

He was glad when the woman finally pulled her scrutiny from his big ugly mug, his cheeks bristling with nearly a week's worth of trail stubble, to glance at Colter standing on the other side of the door.

Colter jerked his head back a little, as though he thought the pretty Mex was going to slap him. Then he flushed and smiled and cleared his throat, and said, "Ma'am . . ."

The woman turned her head forward, glanced around the room, turning her head slowly left then right then back again, scrutinizing the cadavers lying in twisted heaps and bloody pools of their own spilled blood. She glanced once more at Prophet, the skin above the bridge of her nose stitched with a subtle reproof, and pulled her mouth corners down.

"Is this your doing, amigo?" she asked in a low, husky voice that might have sounded intimate if not overflowing with her barely restrained hostility.

Prophet smiled, wagged his head. "No, ma'am, it purely is not." He was happy to be able to speak the truth, seeing no point in adding that the kerfuffle might have been caused *by* him and his friend with the Mark of Sapinero on his cheek. The dead men were certainly not his *doing,* however. He hadn't fired a single shot.

As the Mexican beauty stepped forward, Prophet realized that One-Eye had been standing with him and Colter, slightly behind them, peering out the batwings. Now the old man stood before the woman, a half a head shorter than she, backing away from her in his bandy-legged, stiff-kneed fashion, smiling unctuously up at her, his lone black eye glinting sharply.

"Señorita de la Paz . . ." the old man wheezed out through a toothy grin, as though the words he'd just spoken were some forbidden sacred rite rarely uttered by human lips. He gave a courtly bow, albeit a stiff one, wincing slightly at the pain it caused him, then beamed up at her again, adding in Spanish, "I am most grateful for the saints to have blessed me with a visit from one so beautiful. My heart breaks and my soul weeps."

He dipped his chin as though waiting to have his head anointed.

"Shut up, you one-eyed dog," the woman shot back at him in English, presumably for Prophet's and Colter's benefit. "I came in for a sip or two of that rancid tarantula excrement you call pulque. *¡Rápido!* My father's sister, Señora Aurora Navarro, waits in the carriage, and you know how that dried-up old crone disapproves of this perdition you have here."

"*¡Sí, sí, señorita! ¡Sí, sí!*"

"*¡Rápido!*"

"*¡Sí, rápido!*"

As One-Eye hustled back behind his bar, Prophet and Colter shared a dubious look. Prophet returned his gaze to the visual feast of the woman who was strolling toward the bar, her back and round behind facing Prophet as she stepped around dead men and avoided blood pools.

126

He glanced at Colter again and shook his head in appreciation. The redhead arched his brows in agreement with Prophet's assessment.

As One-Eye ladled his milky liquor from a clay olla on a shelf behind the bar, Prophet moseyed over to stand beside the woman, leaning forward across the bar planks. "I'll take one of those, too, One-Eye."

One-Eye glanced at him, flared a nostril in annoyance. The old man had his hands full pleasing the uppity Señorita de la Paz, who had apparently made him more than a little nervous. He was sweating, and his hands were shaking as he slowly poured the milky white liquor, fermented from the sap of the maguey plant, into the stone cup.

Prophet turned to the woman, shifting his weight to his right elbow. "Come here often?"

She blinked slowly as she turned her head to him. She regarded him blandly, maybe a little puzzledly, as though she hadn't heard what he'd said. Apparently, she was of no mind to answer a query proffered by one of the unwashed masses.

Prophet wiped his right hand on his pants and then extended it toward the woman. "Prophet's my handle. Call me Lou. I'm from up north."

"You don't say." She looked at his big open hand hovering a few inches from her belly but made no effort to shake it. She just stared at it as though it were something unappetizing that had crawled up off the floor.

"You're, uh . . . Señorita de la Paz . . . ?"

She lifted her eyes to his with a tolerant sigh then turned to One-Eye. "Hurry up with that foul milk of yours, old man. Your clientele is ogling me." She looked up at Prophet, her eyes snaking across his chest and shoulders once more before climbing his thick neck to his face. "This one is big and filthy, and he smells bad. Very bad. Besides," she added, wrinkling her nostrils and narrowing her lustrous brown eyes, "he is *americano*."

Prophet heard Colter give a sardonic snort.

Prophet flushed and turned his mouth corners down. He'd been handed his hat by a woman or two, but this one had given it to him only after smashing it pancake flat. A real piece of work, this haughty beauty. Why did such beauties always attract him — the haughtier the better?

This one reminded him of another particularly arrogant beauty — Louisa Bonaventure, the Vengeance Queen her own per-

128

snickety self. This was the Mexican version of Louisa, sure enough.

One-Eye set the half-filled cup atop the bar. The señorita lifted it to her lips, sniffed, wrinkled her nose again as though with disdain, then tipped the cup to her mouth, sliding her rich, red upper lip over the brim.

Prophet couldn't help staring at the woman's lip as she drank the pulque, her throat working as the sour substance, which tasted a little like sweetened grapefruit juice, flowed down inside that long, pretty neck of hers. So long and pale and smooth, fairly screaming for a man to press his lips to it . . .

She didn't lower the cup until she'd swallowed every drop. Prophet stared at her, his lower jaw hanging. Even he couldn't handle more than a couple of sips of the potent liquor at a time, and even then it lifted a flush to his cheeks. He didn't know for sure, of course, but he had a feeling the stuff was well over a hundred proof. He'd tasted moonshine that, by comparison, affected him no worse than lemonade. After a single cup, the world tended to swirl for a while . . .

He thought for sure the woman's eyes would roll back into her head, and she'd pass out. He shifted into position to catch her when she fell. But . . . she didn't fall.

Calmly, coolly, and quite steadily, Señorita

de la Paz set the cup on the bar, licked her lips, ran the back of her hand across her mouth, and stared stonily at One-Eye. "Foul stuff, but it cuts the trail dust well enough."

One-Eye's subservient smile broadened.

"Well, I'll be," Prophet said under his breath, staring wide-eyed at the woman before him. "Lady, you can throw back the scorpion venom!"

He fished some coins out of his pants, tossed a gold one onto the bar. "That one's on me. What say we grab another, have a seat, and swap big windies?"

He chuckled. The woman had gotten to him, all right. She was as intoxicating as the liquor she'd taken down without once coming up for air. Prophet loved Mexican women, but haughty Mexican women most of all. His loins were heavy and warm with the prospect of what this dusky-eyed viper might do behind closed doors . . .

He was so enchanted that he had only vaguely heard scuffling and light spur-ringing behind him. The quiet of the still-smoky, shadowy saloon was blown wide open by a fierce caterwauling, like that of an angry mountain lion — one that spoke fluent Spanish and was spewing it out faster than Prophet could follow beyond recognizing a few choice words, knowing the haranguing was stitched with more than a few nasty epithets.

He whipped his head toward the batwings.

A little bird of a woman clad all in black stood just inside the doors, flanked by three of the colorfully garbed vaquero guards in their steeple-crowned sombreros, their expressions grave, a little fearful, their gaudy duds caked with dust. The little bird of a woman, the female version of One-Eye though considerably more smartly attired, poked her beak-nosed, crowlike face out from the folds of the black rebozo hooding her head, and squinted her long eyes devilishly, raising one arm and pointing a withered, crooked finger at Señorita de la Paz.

When the tirade ended, the old woman doddered around, lifting a hand to gesture impatiently to the men behind her. All three hurried to make their exit ahead of the salty-tongued little crone. They stumbled into each other as they held open the batwings for her.

"Mierda," said Señorita de la Paz, having taken the withering dressing-down with the coolness of a silver-spooned debutante awaiting a hansom cab. "I have been informed we are leaving. Too bad."

She glanced up at Prophet, and for the first time a glint of ironic humor entered

131

her brown eyes as once again her gaze roamed across his chest, this time without quite as much disdain as before. "I was just starting to have fun. Thanks for the drink, amigo."

"Maybe see you around some time, señorita."

She'd turned toward the batwings but now she stopped and glanced back over her shoulder at him. "I am sorry, gringo, but I have a feeling we don't run in the same herd." She snorted a dry laugh then not so much walked as floated back across the saloon, passing Colter standing halfway between the bar and the front wall, and out through the batwings.

Like a hind-tit calf, Prophet followed her to the batwings then stood watching as one of the vaquero guards helped her back into the carriage. The vaquero closed and latched the door, mounted his sleek Arabian, and glanced behind him at Prophet. The man curled a nostril, one cur warning another cur to stick to his own pack.

The driver bellowed to his team, cracked a blacksnake over the horses' backs, and the procession was off, heading straight east through the yard. Beyond the yard, they moved off through the chaparral, tan dust rising behind them. They climbed the shoulder of a low, rocky butte then disappeared around the butte's far side.

"Damn," Prophet said to Colter, who'd walked up to stand beside him, staring over the batwings. "That there was a woman!"

"One who'd turn you inside out, stomp your heart in the dirt, and leave you howlin', Lou."

"It ain't that I don't believe you, Red." Prophet chuckled, shook his head. "But I'd just as soon see for myself."

Prophet turned and walked back toward the bar. One-Eye stood behind it, refilling the woman's cup while slowly shaking his head with the air of a man who had just cheated death. "Tell me about that sexy catamount, old man."

CHAPTER 11

"The less you know about Marisol de la Paz the better. Take it from me, Lou." One-Eye took a sip from the woman's cup. Pulling the cup back down, he smacked his lips, wiped a hand across his mouth, and added, "The de la Paz family are as crazy as owls in a lightning storm, and wild as wolves. *Muy peligroso.* Very dangerous. See this?"

He gestured toward the patch over his empty eye socket.

"Yeah, I see it," Prophet said, stepping up to the bar. "What about it?"

"Marisol's *padre,* Don Augustin Frederico de la Paz, is the *bastardo* who gouged out my eye. With a Spanish stiletto. While his men held me down, the don crouched over me, placed his boot on my head, and" — he flicked his wrist in the air — "plucked it out like he was impaling the yoke of a hard-boiled egg!"

Colter walked up to stand beside Lou at

the bar. "Why'd he do that, old-timer?"

One-Eye shrugged as he took another long drink from the woman's glass. When he pulled the cup down again, leaving a milky mustache on his upper lip, he said, "I had been rustling his cows for years and selling them across the border in California!" He slapped his thigh and had a good laugh at that. "He thought it was banditos from Sonora. All along it was me!" More cackling laughter. "I was younger then, you understand. This was thirty years ago or more."

The old man's wheezing cackles died quickly when the thud of more hooves sounded from the desert beyond the cantina yard. Mean and Ugly whinnied. Prophet could see his horse and Colter's coyote dun once more running circles around the windmill and stock tank.

"You're right popular," Prophet told One-Eye.

"*Sí.* I attribute it to my pulque and to my *serpiente de cascabel en escabeche.*" The barman gestured toward the pickled rattlesnakes. "Supposedly, they enhance a man's virility though I myself am a poor example," the old man added with a sigh.

Prophet and Colter returned to the batwings as eight men galloped into the yard. At first, Prophet thought they were

135

the vaqueros guarding the señorita's carriage, but no. These men had come from the same direction the carriage had. They were dressed in similar, gaudily colorful fashion.

The man in the lead stopped his cream Arabian stallion in front of the cantina and leaped out of his saddle, the conchos running up and down the legs of his buckskin *chivarras* flashing in the afternoon sunshine, silver spur rowels spinning.

He was tall and razor thin, with a pale face beneath a black and gray sombrero embroidered in gold. He wore a coal black handlebar mustache and a goatee that came to a sharp spade point just beneath his chin. His face looked especially pale set against the black facial fur.

He was all business as he leaped across the veranda. Prophet and Colter stepped back, making way for the tall Mex as he burst through the batwings and looked around quickly. He frowned slightly as he took in the dead men. The curious frown further ridged his brow as he turned to Prophet and then to Colter.

Then he saw One-Eye Acuna standing behind the bar at the rear of the room, and the dead men must have dispersed like morning fog from his mind. "Was she here, you old leper? Was that her carriage that pulled through here?"

"Leper, eh?" One-Eye leaned forward against his bar and glared at the rangy newcomer.

"Out with it, old man or I'll cut out your other eye! Was that the carriage of Marisol de la Paz?"

They were speaking Spanish, of course, but speaking it slowly enough that Prophet could follow though not without taxing his limited vocabulary.

"Sí, sí — it was her, all right," One-Eye said through a growl, flaring his nostrils at the rangy young man with the spade beard who also wore two ivory-gripped Bisley pistols high on his narrow hips. "She is looking well, too, after her time in Mexico City." He held his hand up to his chest, making a lewd gesture.

The tall Mexican called One-Eye an amorous old dog in need of gelding then asked how long ago the carriage had left.

"I don't know." One Eye glanced at Prophet, raising his brow in speculation. "Five, ten minutes," he said in English. "About the gelding, however," he told the vaquero, "it would be a waste of time."

The tall Mexican gave an ironic snort then wheeled quickly and ran back out to his horse. In seconds, he'd hurled himself back into the deep saddle with the dinner-plate horn, and all eight riders thundered off through the chaparral, following the trail the señorita's carriage had taken into the chaparral and around the butte.

Prophet turned back to One-Eye, frowning. "What was that all about?"

"Juan Carlos."

"Huh?" Prophet made his way back to the bar again, a curious scowl cutting deep lines across his forehead.

"That was Juan Carlos. Don't ask me about him. The whole matter depresses me with its danger. I shouldn't be living out here alone anymore — a crippled old man for whom not even the baby rattlesnakes can awaken his machismo." He gave a sad, ragged sigh, slopped pulque into a fresh gourd cup, and set it onto the bar. "Have a drink with me, Lou. A cup of the good stuff. Come on, El Rojo. One-Eye is buying, for I am sad now!"

Colter winced a little at the other cup the old man set on the bar, filled with the milky pulque. "I don't know . . . looks mighty strong."

One-Eye said, "Drink up. The fiery passion that Juan Carlos feels for Marisol de la Paz has awakened old memories of my own

138

romantic past — a past which has, sadly, disappeared into the fog of this old man's youth, leaving only wretched loneliness in its wake. These days I sleep alone but I dream vividly of past loves!"

He lifted his cup and polished off the liquor, running the front of his wrist across his mouth. A single tear rolled down his dirty cheek. "Someone should write a song about me. A ballad. A very sad ballad about a lonely, one-eyed old man in the desert, haunted by all that he has left behind. Tormented by his dreams!"

Prophet slid the cup toward Colter. "Go ahead. It'll put hair on your chest."

Colter pulled his shirt out and slid a look beneath it. He arched a brow then lifted the cup.

He froze when other sounds rose from the desert.

Still more riders?

Prophet frowned again as he turned his head toward the batwings. No. The sounds he was now hearing weren't hoof thuds. They were the crackle of gunfire.

They were followed by a woman's scream.

Prophet jerked with a start. He looked at Colter, who stared back at him, eyes wide. "You think that . . . you think that's . . . ?"

"Who the hell else would it be?"

"*¡Mierda!*" cursed One-Eye. "I *thought* I read bloody murder in that lobo's eyes! The de la Pazes and the Amadors have always gotten along like wolves and pumas! I was afraid it would one day come to this — especially after Marisol went off to the city!"

Prophet shot an exasperated look at the old man. *"Bloody murder?"*

He didn't wait for an answer. He glanced at Colter then burst through the batwings and sprinted over to where Mean and Ugly stood twitching his ears in the direction from which the gunfire had sounded. Colter ran out behind him. Lou grabbed Mean's reins and swung up into the leather.

He turned to Colter, who'd just then mounted his coyote dun. Gunfire continued to rattle in the east.

"Red, this has got bad news written all over it," Prophet said. "Me, I'm used to buckin' the Mexican tiger, even when I got no cur in the ring. You best hang back. Head on over to the ocean and lounge in the sand with the señoritas!"

"Ah hell, I'd get bored with the señoritas after a day or two. I'm with you, Lou. Even if it ain't none of our business, let's buck the Mexican tiger!"

Prophet laughed. "Yeah." He swung Mean around, facing east, and booted the mount

140

into a ground-eating gallop. "What the hell else we gonna do?"

He shot out of the cantina yard and into the bristling desert like a cannonball. Colter came up close behind, leaning forward over his horse's buffeting mane. With Colter and Northwest galloping just off Lou and Mean and Ugly's right hips, the riders stormed up and around the first butte beyond the cantina. They clattered on down the butte's far side, across a hundred-yard stretch of relatively flat desert and then up a low jog of chalky bluffs.

As they started down the other side, Prophet reined Mean up abruptly and pointed toward the east.

"There!"

The carriage sat on the far side of a wide wash, which appeared to be the dry bed of a now-dead river. It was paved in mottled black-and-white sand. The wash bristled with cactus and greasewood as well as rocks of all shapes and sizes, some as large as wagons, likely hurled down the wash by ancient floods.

The carriage sat low, slightly tilted to one side. Its four-horse team was fidgeting uneasily and looking around in the direction from which the bullets were being hurled toward them.

Several men lay around the carriage, unmoving, while a couple more were crouched behind rocks or cactus near the carriage, returning fire toward the men hurling lead at them from behind their own covering rocks and cactus on the near side of the wash. The shooters were maybe a hundred yards beyond Prophet and Colter, who had paused momentarily on the side of the bluff.

One of the shooters firing toward the carriage must have hit his mark. A man near the carriage gave a shrill yell as he lunged to his feet, throwing his two pistols into the air, then tumbled back into the desert caliche.

It took only a few seconds for Prophet to get the lay of the land. The stage must have gotten a wheel stuck in soft sand on the wash's far side. That gave Juan Carlos and his seven *compañeros* time to catch up to it and ambush the vaqueros guarding Marisol de la Paz and her aunt. There appeared to be only one more guard left alive, returning pistol fire from behind a rock not far from the carriage.

Colter glanced at Prophet. "What are you thinkin', Lou?"

"I'm thinkin' that ain't a fair fight even by Mexican standards. Let's go, Red!" Prophet shrugged the Richards twelve-gauge off his shoulder and swung it around in front of his chest, taking the savage popper in his right hand after switching the reins to his left. He gigged Mean and Ugly down the slope, yelling behind him, "You take the shooters on the right. I'll take the ones on the left!"

"You got it!"

When Mean and Ugly had gained the broad wash, Prophet swung him slightly left, toward where he could see four shooters triggering pistols toward the one remaining vaquero guard. The coach's ambushers hadn't seen him yet, but when Mean had taken two more lunging strides, the ambusher nearest Prophet, to the right of the other three, must have heard the thundering of the dun's hooves. The man swung around sharply, widening his eyes and then slamming his rifle to his shoulder.

Prophet triggered the Richards, blowing a pumpkin-sized hole in the man's belly and hurling him back onto the clump of spiky cactuses he'd been crouched behind. He triggered his rifle skyward before throwing it far and wide.

The three to the dead man's left jerked their surprised gazes toward the big bounty hunter galloping toward them, within twenty yards and closing fast. Before the man on the right of the three-man group could snap his own rifle to his shoulder, Prophet triggered the Richards's second tube, sending his target flying backward into the chaparral, howling.

The other two attackers fired shots at Prophet, who'd by now overrun them, Mean's hooves hammering into the dirt the man Prophet had just turned into a sieve, adding insult to injury.

Prophet swung Mean around sharply to face the other two bushwhackers. One triggered a Winchester carbine at him, the slug screeching past his right ear. Prophet had tossed the empty Richards behind him and whipped his Colt out of its holster. He extended the pistol straight out from Mean's right withers and blew a .45 caliber round through the man's right cheek.

Clicking back the hammer again quickly, he aimed at the last of the four bushwhackers and fired. That bullet merely blasted dust from the rock the man had just pulled his head behind.

Prophet slipped cleanly out of the saddle, threw himself to the ground, and rolled as the last of the four shooters lifted his head and rifle over his covering rock, and fired.

The bullet blew a spine off a buckhorn

cholla as the big bounty hunter rolled behind the plant. The shooter fired again, this time blowing two prickly spines off the cactus.

Prophet rolled onto his chest and belly, extended his Colt straight out from his right shoulder, lined up his sights on the bridge of the shooter's dark nose, beneath the brim of his black, steeple-crowned sombrero, and fired.

The .45 bucked, flames lapping from the barrel.

Prophet missed the man's nose. Instead, the bullet blew out his target's right eye before exiting his right ear in a spray of blood and bone matter.

"Cored you like an apple, you bush-whackin' dog!" Prophet bellowed, heart pumping hot blood like lightning through his veins.

The now-one-eyed man sat up straight, lower jaw hanging, his lone eye widening in the shock of his demise. The light of life became the shadow of death in that lone eye just before the man fell straight back and out of sight behind the broad, pale chunk of ancient, sun-bleached driftwood from behind which he'd been firing.

145

CHAPTER 12

Prophet looked around. All the shooters near him were dead.

Hearing more gunfire, he whipped his gaze to the south. Colter Farrow was on one knee over there, maybe sixty yards away from Prophet, punching lead into one man and then into another, spread out much as Prophet's own victims had been, slinging lead toward the carriage.

Two of Colter's targets were crouched behind the same boulder. Victims, rather. Calmly, the redhead jacked another round into his Tyler Henry and fired, shooting one of the two. The other one returned fire with a long-barreled revolver but his partner had just flopped against him, and his shot flew wide.

He didn't have time to get off another one. Calmly aiming down his Henry's barrel, Colter chunked a .44 round between the lapels of the man's stitched leather *cha-*

queta jacket. The man dropped to the ground on his back, howling.

Colter fired again and his third target slammed back against the broad stock of a barrel cactus and hung up there, impaled on its spines. He screamed, blood gushing from his chest, turning his head this way and that, struggling against the thorns, before ripping himself loose, dropping to his knees, then falling onto his side.

The second man Colter had shot lay writhing, digging his heels and elbows into the ground, lifting his back up off the sand and gravel. Colter pumped a fresh round into the Henry's action, rose from his knee, walked over to the man, and aimed the rifle casually in his right hand at the man's head.

"No!" the Mexican screamed.

Colter didn't hesitate. All business, he squeezed the Henry's trigger. The rifle bucked, roared, and stabbed smoke and flames at the man's head, slamming it back against the ground, where it and the rest of the man lay jerking in sudden death.

"Oh yeah."

Colter shook the rifle, cocking it one-handed, and glanced toward Prophet. The bounty hunter gave a weak smile. He'd be damned if the young redhead didn't, indeed, remind him of a particular pretty blond who was just as coolly efficient at killing.

"That all of 'em?" Colter called.

Prophet looked at the dead men around him and the redhead. "We're missing one."

He turned toward the carriage and started to raise his Colt once more. He stayed the action, seeing that the man moving over there was one of the señorita's guards. He'd obviously taken a bullet, maybe more, and was staggering around as though badly drunk. He held a hand to his belly, was clawing at the air ahead of him as though negotiating his way through a heavy curtain.

He stopped suddenly, wobbling on his hips. He gave a strangling cry then fell face-first in the sand and rocks, doing nothing to break his fall.

Prophet started walking toward the carriage, looking around for signs of life, his blood still racing in his veins but this time with worry about the señorita. "Bloody murder," One-Eye had said. It wasn't only the south-of-the-border folks who sometimes got love and murder mixed around in the same barrel, but they were especially adept at it, and ugly about it.

"You see the señorita?" Prophet called to Colter, who was roughly fifty yards to Prophet's right, also striding toward the carriage.

"Nope."

"What about Juan Carlos?"

Colter looked around some more. "Nope."

Prophet walked up to the carriage. The left side's two doors were open. Lou peered into the shadows within the contraption.

There was only one person inside. The señorita's aunt, Señora Aurora Navarro, sat slumped in the carriage's opposite rear corner, head canted back and a little to one side. The woman's eyes were open but she wasn't seeing anything. Angels, maybe, if she'd kept up with her rosary. The puckered hole in the dead center of her withered forehead dribbled blood down into the corner of her right eye and then on down her right cheek, along the base of her pointed nose. It glistened in a single beam of sunlight angling into the carriage over Prophet's left shoulder.

Prophet studied the ground beneath the door. He spied the moccasin-like impression of a woman's soft slipper. Stepping out away from the carriage and then walking up around it and the team, he spied more prints. They were overlaid with the deeper impressions of spurred boots with high heels.

The girl had run out away from the stage and a man had pursued her.

Prophet followed the sign around the front of the fidgeting team.

"You find something?" Colter asked, walking up behind Lou.

Prophet studied the rocky slope ahead and on the far side of the team. It was stippled with desert brush and cactus. He could see where rocks had recently been displaced and rolled down the slope and into the wash. "I think so."

Quickly, Lou reloaded his Colt from cartridges in his shell belt, dropping the empty casings on the ground at his boots. Flicking the loading gate closed, he spun the wheel and ran forward.

He climbed the steep slope, dropping to his hands and knees and sort of half crawling and half running up the incline, causing a landslide of sand and rocks behind him.

At the top, he paused a moment to catch his breath.

Picking up the sign again, he ran forward but quartering to his right, following the two sets of prints through the scrub, tall cactuses like misshapen, tendril-bearing monsters rising around him.

He lost the woman's and the man's trail in gravel sliding down from yet another sandy slope.

Colter ran up beside Prophet, breathing hard.

"Damnit," Lou said, raking his gaze desperately across the ground.

"There!" Colter pointed toward the indentation of a man's boot heel and the dimple of a large spur rowel.

Prophet broke into another run, scissoring his arms and legs. He pushed through some prickly shrubs, wincing as the thorns grabbed and tore at his shirt-sleeves, then dropped into another low area.

Ahead, a man gave an angry, screaming wail.

Prophet stopped, looked around, trying to locate the source of the shout.

Again, the man shouted. The señorita shouted back at the man, just as angry.

"This way," Prophet told Colter, who'd caught up to him again.

Prophet ran ahead, angling left. He ran for maybe a hundred more feet before he stopped again.

Straight ahead, the señorita stood atop a low shelf of jumbled rock. Desert willows flanked her, partly shading her.

Facing her at the base of the shelf was Juan Carlos. He had a silver-chased pistol in his right hand, aimed up the shelf at the woman. The señorita held a wicked-looking,

151

black-handled, silver-bladed stiletto, threatening Juan Carlos with it.

Juan Carlos was bent slightly forward at the waist, shouting in Spanish. He spoke so quickly it was hard for Prophet to follow, but it seemed to his crude ears that the man was professing both his love and hatred for the woman, who, it also seemed from Prophet's limited understanding of the señorita's rapid Spanish, was taking a wicked satisfaction in mocking and taunting him.

The señorita was calling Juan Carlos an ugly, gutless dog whom she wouldn't marry if . . . and here's where her voice rose to such a crescendo that Prophet couldn't understand another word.

"Carlos!" Prophet shouted.

The man and the woman suddenly stopped screaming and swung their heads toward where Prophet stood fifty feet away, Colter flanking him on his right side, both men sweating and breathing hard from the run.

"Put the gun down, Carlos!" Prophet ordered.

Juan Carlos kept his long-barreled, silver-chased Colt aimed at the señorita. He grinned at Prophet, spreading his lips wide.

"You come to watch this Mexicana *bruja,*

this cheap *puta,* die bloody, amigo?"

"Kill him!" the woman shouted at Prophet, bending forward at the waist. "Kill him *now*!"

That didn't faze Don Carlos a bit. Raising his voice and keeping his eyes glued to Prophet, he said, "She is a common hog-pen moaner, this woman. She is a mad dog in heat. A double-crossing puma with the perpetual springtime itch! That is what she is — no more and no less than the lowest of rabid animals!"

"Kill him!" Marisol shrieked at Prophet, her eyes glinting furiously. "Kill him now — I order you to shoot this devil and stop this insanity!"

Juan Carlos smiled again. He swung his pistol toward Prophet, his smile in place but a flat darkness spreading across his eyes. In half a second, his Colt would be aimed at Prophet's head. Again finding himself with no choice, Prophet squeezed his own Colt's trigger.

Juan Carlos jerked.

He took one uncertain step backward, triggering his own Colt wide of Prophet and Colter. An expression of deep surprise shone in his eyes. His face turned one or two shades paler even than its natural cream, and he looked down at the blood

153

bubbling up through the hole in his red silk shirt, just beneath the tail of the black silk bandanna knotted around his neck.

He placed a finger in the blood there then let that hand drop to his side. The Colt fell from his other hand to the ground.

Juan Carlos looked at Prophet, his brows furled as though with great concentration, his eyes still cast with exasperation. "This gringo killed Juan Carlos Anaya Amador," he announced flatly, unable to believe his own words.

He gave a dry chuckle, as though at a cosmic joke he'd found himself the butt of. His eyes crossing and lower jaw falling slack, he stumbled backward, raking his spurs across the ground, and collapsed on his back, one leg angled beneath the other one. He gave a long, ragged sigh and lay still.

Silence had fallen. The only sounds were those of the desert birds piping in the bushes.

Slowly, Prophet lowered his smoking Peacemaker.

Marisol stared in dumb shock at Juan Carlos, her beautiful mouth forming a perfect O of exasperation.

"Juan Carlos?" she said. She drew a deep breath, her well-filled bodice rising and falling sharply. "Juan?" she repeated. "Juan

Carlos?"

She dropped the stiletto, ran down the shelf, and dropped to a knee beside the dead man. "Juan?" she said, nudging the dead man's shoulder. She looked at the blood bibbing his fancy shirt then turned her head slowly to Prophet. Her own features had paled considerably.

"Oh my God — you *killed* him," she said in a voice hushed with awe. "You *killed Juan Carlos!*"

Prophet and Colter shared a dubious glance.

"You killed Juan Carlos," Marisol said again, in shock.

"Well, hell," Prophet said, aware that he seemed to have suddenly found himself in a situation far too similar to the one that had transpired in Buzzard Gulch, with Jasmin and Roscoe Rodane, only a short time ago. "I thought you wanted me to!"

"*Sí,* I wanted you to, but I didn't think you'd really do it, you crazy gringo!"

It was Prophet's turn to be exasperated. "It may be all right if a fella points a pistol at you, señorita, but it sure ain't all right if he points one at me!"

Marisol gained her feet. "*Sí.* He probably would have killed you. But you might be better off."

Again, Prophet shared an incredulous look with Colter.

"My . . . aunt?" Marisol asked. "Is she . . . ?"

"Dead," Prophet said.

Marisol bunched her lips and kicked the dead man with her slippered right foot. "Savage fool. Savage, love-struck *pendejo!*" She gazed down at the dead man. "He could never get me out of his head. He couldn't have if he'd lived to be a hundred!"

She sighed, raised her hands, and let them flop against her sides. "Well, we'd better get him back to the rancho. Tía Aurora Navarro, as well. *Mi padre* will know what to do about Juan Carlos. He'll want to bury his sister in the *cementerio familiar.*"

"You want us to take you *home?*" Colter asked her, skeptically.

The señorita looked at him, scowling. *"Sí."* She glanced around. "Who else is there to do it? I take it all of my men are as dead as Tía Aurora, or they'd have made an appearance by now."

She gave a haughty chuff, then, shaking her head as though she were dealing with morons — fools from America, no less — strode past Prophet and Colter on her way back to the carriage.

156

Prophet glanced at Colter again. "I warned you."

"Yeah," Colter said, raking his thumb across his chin, staring dubiously after the haughty señorita. "You did at that, Lou."

CHAPTER 13

The señorita didn't want to ride in the carriage, because her aunt was still in there, and Tía Aurora had given up the ghost. Señorita Marisol de la Paz might have been unafraid of the old crone in life, but in death the old bird was a whole lot more scary.

Sometimes Prophet thought that Mexicans were almost as superstitious as he himself was.

"Well, I reckon you're gonna have to ride with me, then," Lou said, glancing uneasily from the lovely señorita to the appropriately named Mean and Ugly then back again.

He looked at Colter Farrow, who sat in the carriage's driver's boot, the team's reins in his hands. They'd decided that the red-head would man the carriage to the Hacienda de la Paz. They'd laid out Tía Aurora in the carriage, along with Juan Carlos.

Those were the two most important victims of the brutal dustup, the two that must

158

be dealt with first, though, of course in starkly different ways, one being a close relation to the de la Paz family, the other being . . . well . . . Prophet still didn't know exactly the nature of Juan Carlos's family's relationship to the family of the señorita.

He had the uneasy feeling he would know soon enough. And that he might not like what that relationship might mean for him, the man who'd punched Juan Carlos's ticket.

He just hoped he didn't end up with another posse on his trail, or worse . . .

The other men, including the señorita's guards, would be left where they'd fallen. Marisol had said that her father would likely send men with a wagon to retrieve his own men, and that Juan Carlos's brutal *compañeros* could molder where they lay. She'd spat in distaste to emphasize her disdain for the men who'd attacked her and her aunt.

"How far to Hacienda de la Paz?" Colter asked from the carriage's quilted leather driver's seat.

The señorita pointed southeast. "It is over that second ridge there — a couple more hours. We are already on *mi padre*'s land, the old Cordova Grant, but the hacienda is in the valley beyond that ridge."

Prophet drew a breath. "All right, let's get

159

movin', then — it ain't gettin' any earlier in the day."

He looked at the señorita. She looked up at him stonily.

"Well?" she said.

"Well, uh . . ."

"Are you going to help me onto your horse, or I am to walk behind?"

"Ah no, no . . . I'm gonna help you up there."

"All right." She gave a cordial dip to her chin and held up her left hand.

Prophet wiped his gloved hands on his shirt and then gently took the woman's left hand. He hesitated, looking from her to his horse and then back at the lovely woman again, who was all trussed up in her gaudy, delicate attire. He sort of felt like he was having to transport a delicate figurine in a hay wagon, and he wasn't sure how best not to break it.

"Okay, uh . . ." he said.

"Sí, sí," said the señorita, growing impatient, shifting her feet around beside the horse.

Prophet stooped and started to wrap his arm around her waist then reconsidered. He straightened, tried another tack, abandoned that one, and then stepped back and grimaced down at her.

160

She scowled up at him, her dark eyes blazing again with her characteristic intolerance. "Señor Prophet, are you going to help me onto your horse or are you going to make me trudge along behind you, like a lowly peon?"

"It ain't gonna work."

"What 'ain't gonna work'?" she asked, mocking him.

Prophet shucked his big bowie knife and held it up before her. "You gittin' up on that hoss in that Sunday dress."

She frowned at him, worried. She started to step back but Prophet quickly crouched, pulled the dress out away from her legs, and cut it down the side from up near her hip to the hem.

She gasped and cursed roundly in Spanish — a few words that Prophet didn't think he'd ever heard before, in fact. And that was saying something. Before she was done, he'd returned his knife to its sheath, picked her up in his arms, and fairly hurled her onto his saddle.

The movement was so sudden and brusque that she gave another, shriller gasp that was almost a scream. Not so much a scream of fear but a scream of — what?

Pleasure? The female kind . . . ?

Marisol stared down at the big, thick-necked, broad-shouldered bounty hunter in openmouthed shock, her dark eyes wide and round.

"There, now," Prophet said, grinning from ear to ear, "that oughta . . ." He paused when he caught sight of her left bare leg peeking out from the vertical tear in her skirt. A fine leg it was. Long and creamy with just the right amount of supple female flesh. The skirt had appeared to be the only thing clothing it, he vaguely noted. Which meant she hadn't been wearing much, if anything, underneath it.

And that she still wasn't.

Not that he blamed her, riding in a pent-up carriage in the blazing desert heat. But, well . . . hell. That's all. Just . . . *hell.*

Marisol stared down at him, still shocked at his impertinence. Speechless, she followed his eyes to her leg. She glanced at him again and then slowly, with seeming vague reluctance, drew one of the torn flaps of the gown over the exposed appendage.

A high, red flush rose in her cheeks as she turned away to gaze straight out over Mean's ugly head.

Mean turned that ugly head to glance up at the unfamiliar woman residing on his back. He regarded the girl's leg peeking out from the tear in the gown and slid his vaguely insinuating gaze to his master, still standing there beside the horse, the proverbial cat having suddenly gotten Prophet's tongue.

Mean whickered, shook his head, and twitched his ears as though in amusement at the typically nonsensical situations Prophet was always getting himself into.

"Ah, shut up," Lou groused at the horse.

He looked up past the suddenly speechless Marisol to where Colter Farrow was grinning down at him from the driver's seat of the carriage, and said, "You, too!"

"I didn't say a thing," Colter said, still grinning, looking as though he were about to break out in hysterical laughter.

"Shut up, anyway."

"All right."

Trying to keep his eyes off that tear in the woman's skirt, Lou shoved his boot into the left stirrup then awkwardly heaved his bulk up onto Mean's back, settling himself behind Marisol, on his saddlebags and bedroll. Not the most comfortable place for riding, but he couldn't very well ask the señorita, obviously a Mexican thoroughbred from the higher rungs of Mexico's rung-ridden society, to switch places with him. And he didn't want to take the time to run down one of the dead men's horses.

Besides, he didn't even know if she could ride. Such a woman as this was probably more accustomed to being wheeled around in fancy carriages like the one beside him now and which had, due to a typically dark twist of Mexican fate, become a hearse.

A little stiffly, Prophet extended his arms around Señorita Marisol and unwrapped Mean's reins from the saddle horn only a few inches from her belly. "Um . . . excuse me here, Señorita," he said tightly, his lips only a few inches from her ear, as he found himself pressed up close against her, almost hugging the girl in his arms.

Her pale, lacy mantilla fluttered back against him in the hot breeze. With it came the smell of the sandalwood scent of the woman's hair, and the rosewater scent of her body from which he could feel the heat fairly radiating.

Heat from the sun?

Or from something else?

Oh, never mind, Prophet, you copper-riveted, cork-headed moron!

He glanced up at Colter still grinning annoyingly down at him. "You ready?"

"I've *been* ready."

Prophet grumbled then nudged Mean with his spurs. "All right, then, here we go . . ."

164

■ ■ ■

As he led Colter and the señorita's carriage southeast along the wagon trail, Prophet tried to ignore the woman on the saddle before him.

Of course, trying and doing are two separate things. It was hard to ignore such a woman even crossing a busy city street two blocks ahead of you. When she was sitting right in front of you — not only in front of you but practically in your lap! — well, that was an almost impossible situation.

Especially when you'd seen her bare leg and were aware of what she was wearing. Or not wearing, as the case may be . . .

Marisol de la Paz appeared to be doing her best to ignore Prophet, as well. She rode straight-backed before him, staring straight ahead, as Prophet held Mean to a comfortable walk for the sake of the woman as well as the horse, who was now carrying double in the harsh desert heat. Lou couldn't tell if she was mad at him for tossing her around like a sack of potatoes, or afraid of him. He could imagine how he might have looked to her, shucking that big, razor-edged bowie of his and cutting her dress in one violent thrust.

165

Must have scared the living daylights out of the poor gal. She acted tough, but it was a hell of a situation she'd just been through, having her aunt killed and all, and almost getting killed herself by a spurned lover . . .

He supposed he should say something to put her at ease or to throw some water on her anger, but one thing he was trying to learn was when to keep his big mouth shut.

Now seemed like a good time.

Prophet felt himself sweating inside his clothes. He couldn't tell if Marisol were sweating, as well. She had to be. But damnit, hadn't he told himself to stop thinking about her, for chrissakes? Didn't he already have enough trouble?

He'd have been better off ignoring the sound of the gunfire and just sitting down to a bowl of One-Eye Acuna's succulent stew and a second glass of pulque. But, no, he had to go fogging the sage and riding into a whole peck of trouble when he could have been continuing south to the dusky-skinned *putas* of Sayulita.

But if he had, Señorita Marisol would now be dead.

Stop thinking, Prophet. You know that ain't your strong suit. You get to thinkin' an' then you start talkin', you blame, thick-headed ole Confederate necio!

"Señor Prophet?"

Lou was surprised by the unexpected sound of the woman's voice.

He looked down at her. She had her head turned to the left, glancing back at him.

"Yes, señorita?"

"I uh . . . I wanted to, uh . . . thank you."

"You wanted to what?" He wasn't sure he'd heard her correctly.

"I wanted to thank you for saving my life. If you hadn't come along, Juan Carlos surely would have killed me. I apologize for acting so ungrateful before. It's just that . . . well, the death of Juan Carlos could mean big trouble not only for you but for us — for the de la Paz family."

"Well, I reckon your death would have meant big trouble, too — don't you think?" he added with a wry chuff, pleased with his logic. "For you *and* your family."

"Not so much for you. Besides, you didn't owe me anything. At One-Eye's cantina, I was . . . I was very impolite. I was *¡la cabróna!*"

"I've always been a sucker for purty women." Prophet grinned. "*La cabróna,* all the better."

Marisol laughed, her first unguarded moment. "Why is that?"

"Oh, I don't know. Maybe I wouldn't trust

167

a woman who didn't think I didn't deserve a good bit of nastiness."

They both laughed.

"Sure is nice to see you smile, señorita. You're a pretty woman. Maybe as purty as I ever seen. But you're a whole lot purtier when you smile. Laugh, even better!"

She flushed and turned her head to stare out over Mean's head. Prophet had a feeling the woman wasn't accustomed to blushing, and it made her uneasy.

To break the next ensuing silence, he said, "Tell me about Juan Carlos."

"He is the son of Emiliano Zapata Amador. The Amadors have been my family's rival landowners for over a hundred years. The de la Paz family and the Amadors have been feuding for generations. The fight started over disputes over the borders of our respective Spanish land grants. Once that was settled — with guns and blood, as every other disagreement in Mexico is settled — the feuding continued. The killing caused more bad blood, the need for revenge. Bad blood is impossible to wash away in Méjico. Revenge makes it flow all the faster."

"Sort of like in the Old South," Prophet remarked, remembering several family feuds that had continued long after everyone involved had forgotten what had instigated the hostility.

"From what I have read about your country, yes."

"You went to school, I take it?" Most young women from wealthy families in Mexico had a least some schooling. Prophet thought he detected a certain refinement in the señorita — underneath all her sultry bluster, that was. A refinement that came from reading and learning about the ways of the world that were far beyond Prophet's own experience and understanding, but which intrigued him, just the same.

"*Sí.* I went to school in Mexico City. A Catholic school for girls, of course."

"Is that where you're coming from now?" he asked, remembering that One-Eye had mentioned something about her returning from the city.

Marisol laughed. "No!" She glanced over her shoulder at Prophet, one brow arched. "Do I look that young?"

"I got no idea how old you are, señorita. I'm guessin' you're a helluva lot younger than this old gringo."

"I am twenty-eight."

"Pshaw!" he exclaimed phonily. In fact, being this close to her, she did look as old as twenty-eight. She'd lost the rawness of

169

youth and was in the full flower of woman-
hood. If she were a fruit, she'd be the ripest
of apples — one of a rare, ever so vaguely
tart variety, owning a complexity and danger
that enhanced her allure.

"Not all that much younger than you, eh?"
Marisol asked him, still peering at him from
over her shoulder.

"Not as much as I thought, anyway."
Wondering why she wasn't married by now
but not wanting to ask the question directly
and risk sparking another tantrum, since
they seemed to be getting on so well all of a
sudden, he said, "This Juan Carlos — he
was pretty well gone for you. That much
was obvious, though he sure had a strange
way of showin' it."

Marisol frowned, curious. "Gone for . . . ?"

Lou shrugged. "In love with."

"Ah." She nodded and turned her head
forward. "*Sí*. He thought he was in love
with me, at least. At one time I thought I
was in love with him."

"How did that work — him bein' an Amador, your own family's blood enemy?"

Marisol shrugged as she continued staring
straight over Mean's head, her shoulders
moving with the easy pitch and sway of the
dun's walk. "We met when we were very
young. Thirteen, fourteen years old. Not

170

formally, of course, but my family's and Juan Carlos's family's ranges abut each other to the south of the *compuesto* of my father's hacienda. The compound where our casa sits. I would go out riding, usually against *mi padre*'s orders, as banditos and the descendants of the Pericúes, a savage native tribe of Baja, were a bigger problem back then than they are now. Juan Carlos liked to ride off by himself, as well. That's how we met — one day by a small lake in the mountains between our haciendas. At that age, we had little understanding of our families' hatred for each other. For whatever reason — maybe because there was simply no one else around or because we were soul mates at the time — we fell in love. *Forbidden* love."

"Did your families know?"

"Not at first. We'd have been whipped! But later, *mi padre* ordered one of his vaqueros to follow me. He must have become suspicious of my long sojourns into the mountains. The vaquero reported back and I was promptly forbidden ever to see the boy again. Of course, I didn't listen. I was very shrewd, very sneaky. I continued to steal out at night, under cover of darkness, to visit my life's one true love — Juan Carlos Anaya Amador!"

She gave a caustic laugh that sounded a little like a hawk strangling on viscera. "What a fool I was! Juan promised himself to me, I to him. We planned to run off to America together and to be married. But, then . . . I heard from *campesinos* that were friends of both Juan's and mine, that he was riding over to the Sea of Cortez and lying with fallen women."

She stiffened her back in the saddle as she sucked an angry breath. "I wanted to gut him like a pig! In fact, I brought a stiletto to our next planned meeting and would have done just that if he hadn't found the knife in my riding dress. He cried. He fell to his knees and begged me for forgiveness. I refused him. I refuse him to this day and I would have continued to refuse him if . . . well, if . . ."

"I hadn't finished him off for you," Prophet said.

"*Sí.* You did me a favor in more ways than one. He was weak. There is nothing worse than a weak, simpering man. I hated Juan Carlos to his very fiber after I learned of his sinning with the *putas* on the seashore. He didn't love me. Not really. He only wanted what he couldn't have. Well . . . now he's dead. You have put me at ease."

She paused, then added ominously, under

her breath, "Juan's *padre,* Emiliano Zapata Amador, on the other hand . . ."

Prophet's loins tightened at the thought of a slow death in Mexico. They tightened more when Colter called from the carriage behind him, "Lou! Looks like trouble ahead!"

Ah hell.

CHAPTER 14

Prophet glanced back at Colter, who, seated atop the tall, stagelike carriage, had a better view of the terrain ahead than he did.

"Several riders," announced the redhead.

Prophet turned forward to see men on horseback galloping down two ridges, one on each side of the trail. Three galloped down the ridge on the left while four galloped down the ridge on the right, angling toward Prophet's party.

Even from this distance, Lou could see the gaudy vaquero attire complete with steeple-crowned sombreros and the arched necks of the fine Arabian horses galloping sleekly through the high yellow grass. For the past hour or so, Prophet, Señorita Marisol, and Colter had been riding in lusher country than that in which they'd left the dead men.

Around them now was still some cactus, but not nearly as much as before. Greasewood and cholla had given way to stands of willows and mesquites lining arroyos through which clear water coursed. The fuzzy yellow grass sometimes grew nearly as high as Prophet's stirrups.

This was high desert country, reminding Lou a little of the Montana Territory in his own country, with its broad, bowl-like valleys carpeted in wheat-colored grass and with small hills peppered with cedars and pines, and striped with racing cloud shadows. As here, the valleys swept upward toward far blue mountains brooding along the horizon in all directions. It was a vast landscape created by the sky as well as the land; throughout the day it was imbued with the rich colors of a painter's palette.

Pretty it was, but dangerous, too.

Prophet reached around the señorita to slide his rifle from its scabbard. She placed her hand on his. "It is all right. Those are *mi padre*'s men."

Lou frowned down at her, keeping his hand on the Winchester's stock. She patted his hand reassuringly. "We are nearly to Hacienda de la Paz. I assure you, we are safe."

Removing his hand from the rifle, Prophet sank back onto his bedroll, grumbling, "Maybe *you* are . . ."

He wasn't sure how Marisol's old man was going to take the news that he, Prophet, had killed Juan Carlos, the son of his blood enemy. The way Prophet saw it, he'd saved the woman's life. On the other hand, he might have kicked up an old blood feud. While Don de la Paz would naturally be happy to have his daughter home safe and sound, that didn't necessarily leave Prophet in the clear.

Not in Mexico, where nothing ever worked out the way you'd think it should.

Prophet glanced over his shoulder at Colter driving the carriage behind him. "Easy, Red. The señorita thinks we're all right."

"You are with me," Marisol said. "You are safe."

Prophet kept Mean moving as the riders approached, coming at a slant from ahead and along both sides of the trail. Their hoof thuds grew louder. They'd all slid rifles from their saddle scabbards and several were cocking the rifles now, the metallic rasp of cartridges being seated into breeches making the hair along the base of Prophet's neck prick.

When the vaqueros were within fifty feet and still coming, frowning beneath the brims of their sombreros, likely puzzled by the señorita riding with one of the two gringo strangers, Marisol held up her right hand, palm out. "Reynosa, Huerta — stand down," she ordered in Spanish. "We ran into trouble but I am all right. These two are friends. Ride ahead and alert *mi padre!*"

While the others slowed their horses to near stops, turning them, one man from the group on the right continued forward, scowling incredulously. He was a stocky, middle-aged Mexican with long, black sideburns liberally stitched with gray, as was his thick mustache. "Señorita Marisol — are you sure you're all right?"

He looked at Lou and Colter, no doubt appraising the carriage, as well, wondering where his own men were, then returned his skeptical gaze to the woman.

"I am all right, Miguel. Alert my father. Tía Aurora is dead. It is a sad day at Hacienda de la Paz. *¡Vamos!*"

Astonishment widened the man's eyes. He neck-reined his bay Arabian around sharply and, leaning forward, nudged the mount's loins with his large Spanish rowels. He lunged into a gallop in the direction of the hacienda headquarters now spreading out in front of Prophet, a hundred or so yards farther along the trail.

The ranch, a large one, nestled at the base

of a high tabletop mesa — a table with two legs far shorter than the other two. The mesa slanted sharply down to the south. It dwarfed the hacienda headquarters beneath it, several red tile roofs glowing in the late-afternoon sun. Prophet put Mean into a fast trot now that they were in sight of their destination.

The contrary dun gave a snort and complied. Marisol bounced back against Prophet, her mantilla billowing against his face. He drew a deep breath of the woman's scent — intoxicating, relaxing despite his natural unease with the situation before him.

He'd killed an important man. And this was Mexico, where revenge was a dish served cold.

Marisol didn't help any when she turned her head to say, "Do not be offended if *mi padre* is not on his best behavior. He is an ill man and . . . well, trouble has been afoot here at Hacienda de la Paz."

"I thought you said the tensions between you folks and the Amadors had eased."

"*Sí.* It does not involve Amador. It is something . . . some*one* else entirely. Do not worry, Lou. It is not your problem."

Prophet raked a thumb across his chin,

inwardly groaning. *Where have I heard that before?*

Mean trotted into the yard between two large stone pylons roughly fifteen feet high. Across the top of the pylons, over the trail, stretched a heavy oak beam with the words HACIENDA DE LA PAZ ornately burned into it and painted red. *Red for blood?* Prophet silently, absently mused.

He looked around the broad, hard-packed earthen yard strewn with straw as chickens of every color, squawking angrily, scattered from Mean's trotting hooves. The yard was sprinkled with large trees — mostly sycamores and nut trees, Prophet thought. There were others he couldn't identify. The trees shaded sun-bleached, age-cracked, tile-roofed adobes — living quarters for the don's men and peons as well as workshops, barns, and stock pens.

Several goats as well as pigs — one with a small litter — foraged freely in the trees and shrubs, some nibbling watermelon rinds. In fact, a goat and one large sow were just then kicking up dust over what appeared to be a cantaloupe rind, playing a tug-of-war of sorts, the pig squealing, the goat bleating.

There were several corrals to the right, and in one a vaquero in a bright red shirt and black sombrero appeared to be putting the finishing touches on the gentling of a young, mouse-colored bronc. Three other vaqueros sat on the corral's fence, idly watching, though now as the newcomers and the carriage jounced across the yard, heading for the casa, the vaqueros turned their attention to Prophet and Marisol. The Indian-dark vaqueros, some wearing serapes, stretched their lips back from their teeth, squinting and shading their eyes with their hands.

The vaqueros who'd ridden into the yard ahead of Lou's party milled under the brush ramada of a long, pale adobe bunkhouse to Prophet's left. They, too, watched the newcomers, muttering amongst themselves, no doubt darkly speculating on the trouble that had killed the don's sister, Marisol's aunt, as well as seven of their own *compañeros.*

A single Arabian stood in front of the main casa, in the shade of several fruit trees — lemons and oranges, it appeared — growing inside the adobe wall ringing the house. The branches, speckled with young lemons and oranges, angled out of the wall and into the yard, and the Arabian was tugging on a low-hanging leaf. That would be the horse of the man whom Marisol had addressed as Miguel. Miguel was no doubt

180

inside, giving the don the tragic news.

Prophet stopped Mean near the Arabian and peered up at the casa. It was a grand adobe dwelling in the old Spanish style, though it was hard to see much of it from here because of the fruit trees growing in the courtyard inside the adobe wall. Prophet was about to step down off Mean's back but stopped when voices rose from inside that junglelike patio — men's voices speaking Spanish too quickly for Prophet to follow beyond the random phrase.

The voices grew louder, and then two men pushed out through the black, wrought iron gate in the wall's arched entrance. They were flanked by Miguel, who stepped to one side and held his hat in his hands, demurely averting his gaze.

The other two men were old — in their sixties, at least. One was on crutches. He stood maybe six feet tall, but age had whittled his body to sinew. He was bald, and his shriveled face sported thin, patchy side-whiskers and a mustache and goatee that showed only a little dark brown through the gray. He was dressed in white doeskin leggings and a hand-tooled vest of calfskin over a red embroidered shirt open halfway down his pale, warty, birdlike chest.

The man beside him, clad in a *mayordo-*

181

mo's, or butler's, livery appeared just as old but not as infirm as the man he attended, who was, Prophet opined, Don Augustin Frederico de la Paz. The *mayordomo* stood near the don, turned slightly toward him as though to catch him in case he should fall. The don stood unsteadily on both feet but with the help of two crutches over which he was crouched.

The don's watery brown eyes went directly to his daughter. He frowned deeply, lips moving inside his goatee, then looked at Prophet and the carriage where Colter sat with the reins in his hands.

"Marisol . . . ?" said the don only slightly above a whisper.

"Papa," Marisol said.

"What is this I heard . . . about . . . Doña Aurora . . . ?"

Prophet swung down from Mean's back. He extended his hands to Marisol, who turned toward him, sagging into his arms, letting him lift her down from the saddle. As soon as her feet were on the ground, she hurried over to the old don and wrapped her arms around him, hugging him tightly. The don did not hug her back, for his arms were occupied with the crutches, but he lowered his withered old head to her neck.

The embrace was both a greeting and a

consolation.

Marisol spoke into the old man's ear. Prophet couldn't hear, not that he'd understand if he could hear, but he assumed she was telling her father about the dustup back along the trail.

Prophet saw the old man's forehead crease and turn red. The don lifted his head from his daughter's shoulder, pulling away from her. And now his face was a deeply creased red mask of grief and rage.

Gritting his teeth, his eyes filling with tears, he bellowed, *"Ciaran Yeats!"* A veritable volcano of barely restrained rage, he staggered a little to one side and might have fallen if the *mayordomo* hadn't grabbed him, steadied him.

"No!" Marisol shook her head. "No, Papa. Not Yeats. This time, no."

Ignoring her, the don looked beyond her to several of the men who'd come up from the bunkhouse, moving as shyly as prospective suitors at a debutante's ball, muttering softly amongst themselves, the dust puffing up from their high-topped, spurred boots. The don told them in Spanish, his voice high and raspy, that he wanted to see his *hermana,* his sister.

As Marisol turned to face the carriage, standing close to the don, one hand on his arm, several men gathered around the fancy rig. Prophet, holding Mean's reins, stood to one side of the don, Marisol, and the *mayordomo*. Prophet doffed his own hat as the vaqueros opened the carriage door and gently pulled out the old woman's lumpy body clad nearly all in black. Colter watched from the carriage's driver's seat, no doubt feeling, as Prophet did himself, like the fifth wheel on a lumber dray — awkward and out of place.

He glanced at Prophet, and then, seeing Lou holding his hat in his hands, quickly removed his own topper and hooked it over a knee.

As gingerly as possible, the four vaqueros carried the old woman's body up to the don. The sunlight glistened off Doña Aurora's open eyes and off the blood that had welled up from the hole in her forehead to dry in a long crust down her prunelike face.

The don drew a deep breath as he looked down at his sister. He scowled, jaws hard, a single tear dribbling out of his right eye to roll down his craggy cheek. He removed an arm from one of his crutches, which Marisol caught before it could fall, then reached forward and closed the old woman's eyes with his long, clawlike fingers.

He turned to look at Miguel standing

behind him, and said in Spanish, "Take her to Seville. Seville will tend her now, prepare her for burial."

"Sí, patrón," Miguel said. He glanced at the men holding the old woman gently between them, then turned and strode into the patio, heading for the casa. The four vaqueros bearing the old woman's body stepped around Marisol, the don, and the *mayordomo,* and disappeared into the courtyard.

The don turned to his daughter, drew a deep breath, and said in raspy voice taut with barely restrained fury, *"Dime, hija, ¿quién mató a mi hermana?"* ("Tell me, daughter — who killed my sister?")

Marisol didn't have to answer. Four other vaqueros were just then hauling the second body out of the carriage. They all stared in glint-eyed shock at the body of Juan Carlos Amador as they carried the body up to the don, who stared down at the dead man with his own wide-eyed exasperation.

"In the name of the saints," intoned Don de la Paz, "who in the devil's own hell killed the son of Emiliano Zapata Amador?" He was almost breathless, and he wobbled on his crutches so that both Marisol and the *mayordomo* had to grab him.

Marisol looked at Prophet then lowered

185

her eyes uncertainly to the ground.

The don followed his daughter's gaze to the big gringo standing by the ugly horse, holding his badly weathered hat in his hands.

"Uh . . ." Prophet gave a wooden grin. "*Hola,* there, Don. Uh . . . name's Prophet. Lou Prophet. I'm from up north, don't ya know . . ."

"Colter Farrow, Colter Farrow," the don

CHAPTER 15

"I'm from up north, don't ya know," the
don said, mimicking Prophet in nearly
perfect English, including the big bounty
hunter's pronounced Southern accent. It
was as though he were repeating the phrase
not only to absorb it for himself but also to
brush up on his English. "Lou Prophet."

"How-de-do, Don." Prophet stepped
forward and extended his big, gloved right
paw. "Pleased to make your acquaintance,
though, uh . . . I sure wish it was under different circumstances. Poor ole Doña Aurora."

"*Sí, sí* . . . poor ole Doña Aurora." The
don frowned, cutting his curious gaze from
Prophet to Colter Farrow sitting in the carriage and then to his daughter. "How did . . .
how did . . . ?"

"We met at One-Eye's place," Marisol
said, now speaking in English out of respect
for their gringo guests. "I stepped in for a

187

drink of water and became acquainted with Señor Prophet and his friend" — she glanced at the redhead — "Colter Farrow."

Colter smiled and dipped his chin at the don.

"Colter Farrow, Colter Farrow," the don said, again speaking in near-perfect English, with only a hint of a Spanish accent. "Where have I heard that name befo . . ." He let his voice trail off as he studied the tattoo on the redhead's cheek.

Colter flushed and glanced away.

"Anyway," the don said, shaking his head as though to clear it of unnecessary thoughts and looking at the body of Juan Carlos still being held before him by the grunting vaqueros. "I don't understand . . . what happened here . . . with Juan Carlos?"

"He must have learned somehow that I would be returning from Mexico City today," Marisol said. "He was quite passionate. Him and a half dozen of his cutthroats ran down the coach. He must have wanted to kidnap me, the fool. They killed all the men when a wheel got stuck in a sand trap. One of the bullets punched through the carriage and killed Tía Aurora. I tried to make a run for it during the shooting. I thought I would hide and wait for dark, then try to slip out of that crazy man's clutches. But he ran me down. He threatened to kill me. He said if he couldn't have me, no one would. That's when Lou appeared and shot the *pendejo loco.*"

She gazed beseechingly up at her father. "*Por favor* — you must understand. Lou had no choice but to kill Juan Carlos. It was him or me. The poor fool has obviously gone even crazier than he was before. To think that I would marry such a fool against your own forbiddance!"

The don nodded, smiling at Marisol. "*Sí, sí . . .* I know you would never do such a thing, *mi amada hija.*" ("My beloved daughter.")

Prophet had a feeling the old man didn't know the full story of Marisol's and Juan Carlos's forbidden relationship, that she'd only turned on the young man because he'd cheated on her and not because her father had forbidden her to see him. Prophet choked back a chuckle. The woman was obviously quite adept at manipulating her father, as she was any man. As beautiful and captivating as she was, it couldn't be too hard.

Don de la Paz returned his attention to Juan Carlos. He looked at Prophet and then at the dead man hanging slack in his vaqueros' arms. Miguel, who Prophet assumed was the don's *segundo,* or foreman, walked up to the old man and said in a tone hushed with foreboding, "*Patrón,* do you know what this means? This man has killed the son of your blood enemy. The *only child* of Don Amador. Up to now, the fighting has stopped . . . more or less. But when Don Amador gets wind that . . ."

Miguel stopped, frowning at the old don, who had turned his head to stare off across the yard as though collecting his thoughts. The don was turned away from Prophet, but the bounty hunter thought the old man's eyes were squeezed shut. The don's shoulders shook. He lowered his chin nearly to his chest and drew a ragged breath.

"Papa?" Marisol asked him, tentatively. She glanced with concern at Miguel, who returned her look. She looked at Lou, who gave a noncommittal shrug.

Don Amador appeared to be sobbing. Why? Surely not over the death of Juan Carlos. He must be enduring another wave of grief for his sister.

But, no. Wait.

The old man lifted his chin and turned toward Prophet. Tears were streaming down his cheeks. Not tears of sorrow, however. They were tears of laughter. He drew another, even more ragged breath and

190

pointed at Prophet and then to the dead man still being held, suspended above the ground by the four straining vaqueros.

"The gringo," he said through his breathless laughter, leaning on one crutch while raising his other arm to point at the bounty hunter, "he . . . he killed Juan Carlos! The *norteamericano . . .* ha-hah! — he comes down here . . . and . . . *hah-hah-hah!* — he shoots that no-good walking louse — *hahhh!* — of a misbegotten Amador through his black heart — the very thing I have wanted to do for the past twenty years! *Ohhhh-ha-ha-ha-hah-hah-hah!*"

He laughed almost violently, sort of wheezing and making choking sounds, leaning forward to slap his thigh. His left crutch slipped out from under his arm and Miguel quickly grabbed it, staring in shock at the old don, who was laughing so hysterically that he appeared on the verge of a stroke.

The old don's laughter was infectious. Miguel looked at him, a smile building slowly on his mustached mouth until suddenly he was leaning back and throwing loud guffaws at the heavens. He, too, pointed at Prophet and then at Juan Carlos and laughed even louder. Then his men started laughing until they were having even more trouble than before keeping the heavy, dead burden of Juan Carlos above the ground.

Prophet glanced a little uneasily, self-consciously, at Señorita Marisol and was somewhat surprised to see that even she had broken out in laughter. She covered her mouth with one hand and looked at him, tears streaming down her cheeks.

That made Prophet feel even more self-conscious and truly bewildered, not entirely sure what everyone was laughing about. He looked over his shoulder at Colter, who appeared as taken aback by the scene as he himself was. Then Colter spread a smile of his own. The redhead chuckled and then he was laughing, too, albeit not with quite as much unrestrained vigor as the Mexicans, but laughing just the same.

Suddenly, the four men holding Juan Carlos let the body slip out of their weakening hands. The cadaver dropped to the ground with a hard thud, dust puffing up around it.

That stopped the laughter cold. Everyone looked down in shock at Juan Carlos staring up at them through half-closed lids, tongue sort of lolling against one corner of his mouth. He looked like a man so drunk he'd passed out with his eyes open.

Several seconds of absolute silence passed. Even the birds seemed to stop piping in the fruit trees.

Staring down at the body, Don de la Paz gave a snort. Then another, louder snort.

He threw his head back on his shoulders, laughing wildly once more.

The others snorted, as well, and then they all were once more rocking with ribald guffaws. They were all laughing so hard, even Colter now, that Prophet himself couldn't help becoming infected. He gave a snort and then threw his own head back, bellowing laughter at the sky. Even as he laughed, he had the strange, unsettling feeling he was laughing at the prospect of his own funeral, but he went on laughing, anyway.

When they were finally all laughed out, and chuckled out, and had wiped the tears from their eyes, Miguel said to the don, a tone of wariness returning to his voice: "*Patrón,* the shit is really going to fly when Don Amador gets wind of his son's demise." That wasn't what he said exactly; it was Prophet's rough translation in terms he himself could best understand.

The don stared down at the dead man. The old *hacendado* also appeared a little rocked back on his heels again by the dark turn of events. "*Sí, sí.* Juan Carlos wasn't much, but he was the old puma's only child. Hmmm." He fingered his chin whiskers as he continued staring down at the deceased.

The don wrapped his free arm around Miguel's neck. "I tell you what we'll do. *You'll* do, rather, Miguel."

"*¿Qué?*"

"I want you to throw a blanket around Juan Carlos and lay him out in a wagon . . ."

"*¡Sí, sí, patrón!*"

"And then you and a half-dozen men of your choosing drive Juan Carlos over to Hacienda del Amador. Wrap white cloths of truce to your rifles. Politely inform Don Amador of what happened — that Juan Carlos was caught trying to ravage my older daughter and swallowed a pill he couldn't digest" — he chuckled devilishly then swiped his fist across his nose — "only, possibly not in those exact words!"

He chuckled again as he cut a glance at Prophet, who felt a dark worm of dread turn in his belly.

The don leaned close to Miguel to whisper in his *segundo*'s ear. While he talked, Miguel frowned and nodded, both men cutting several quick, meaningful glances at Prophet, who again felt that black worm writhe around in his gut.

"Okay, Miguel?" said the don, pulling his head back from the *segundo* and patting his shoulder. "Do you have all that? Everything

194

should be fine. For whatever differences we have, Don Amador and myself, we are men of honor and mutual respect. He will see how Juan Carlos's killing has been the result of a sad misunderstanding, one that has resulted in a tragic loss for each of us, and that there is no reason for further conflict."

Looking a little like he'd swallowed rat poison, Miguel handed the don's crutch back to him. The don slipped it under his arm. Miguel glanced at his men, who regarded him dubiously, warily, then sprang into action when the *segundo* ordered them to stop standing there like they were men of leisure and to pick up Juan Carlos and haul him over to the wagon barn.

"*¡Vamos!*" intoned Miguel, taking out his sudden case of biliousness on his men. "*¡Vamos!* You heard the don! *¡Vamos! ¡Vamos!*"

Just then, the vaqueros who'd carried Tía Aurora into the casa came out. The don ordered two to unload his daughter's and sister's belongings from the carriage and to take them inside. He ordered the other two to take the carriage back to the wagon barn and to unhitch the team. He told them that at first light of the next day they were to take a wagon out and pick up the dead men from Marisol's traveling party.

Colter had climbed down out of the carriage by now, and, as the don's men hurried about their business, soon leaving only himself, Marisol, Prophet, Colter, and the *mayordomo* standing just outside the wrought iron gate to the courtyard, the don turned to his guests.

"It has been a sad day," said the don. "I think we could all do with a few drinks and a hearty meal. *Por favor, amigos — ¡mi casa, tu casa!*"

"Ah, that's all right, don," Prophet said, feeling as though it might be a good idea to make himself scarce sooner rather than later. "We don't want to put you out, Colter an' me. We'll just be foggin' the sagebrush."

"Nonsense!" said the don. "I insist! You saved *mi hija*'s life." He leaned over and pressed his lips to Marisol's forehead. "The least I can do is stuff you full of good wine and food before you resume your journey. Besides . . ." The don lowered his voice conspiratorially. "I have something to discuss with you both. A most important matter, in fact."

"Oh?" Lou said, suddenly curious despite his compulsion to light a shuck.

"*Sí, sí — ¡por favor!*" The don jerked his chin to indicate the casa.

Prophet hesitated. Staying on here seemed like an even less favorable idea when he saw

Marisol regarding her father with brows furled warily, suspiciously.

"¡Por favor!" the don said again, insisting.

Prophet looked at Colter. The redhead shrugged.

"All right," Prophet said.

He and Colter followed Marisol into the courtyard, the don trudging along behind them on his crutches, like the grim reaper with a hitch in his gait.

CHAPTER 16

"Pulque?" asked the don. "I ferment it myself right here at Hacienda de la Paz. Er . . . I should say my peons ferment it, but under my close supervision, of course." Holding up a slender, brown stone jug he'd removed from the top of a heavy wooden cabinet beneath a framed, painted map of Baja, the old *patrón* smiled at his guests.

Prophet salivated. "That's one of the two things that calls me to Mexico year after year."

The don switched his gaze to Colter, raising the jug a little higher and arching a brow. Colter glanced sheepishly at Prophet, flushing.

"Red don't imbibe, Don," the bounty hunter answered for the younger man. "He's still —"

"What do you mean I don't imbibe?" Shifting uncomfortably in the big, deep leather chair he'd dropped into when the don had invited them into his personal library for presupper drinks, Colter beetled his brows at his new partner, as though he'd never heard anything so silly. He looked at the don and curled his upper lip in an ironic smile. "Lou's just sore 'cause he knows I can drink him under the table. Sure, fill 'er up, Don. I got a mouthful of trail dust beggin' to be cut."

"Kid," Prophet said under his breath and with a wooden grin. "There's no shame in —"

"No shame in what, Lou?" Colter shifted around again. "No shame in throwing back too much busthead and howling at the moon? Pshaw! I can hold my liquor." He smiled at the don. "Even the black powder variety you brew down here in Méjico."

"All right." Prophet dropped his arms to the sides of his own leather chair. "It's your head, El Rojo."

"All right, then." The don glanced at his *mayordomo* standing just inside the open door. "Raoul, three pulques, if you will."

"*Sí,*" said Raoul, a straight-backed, elegant-looking old Mexican with a carefully trimmed gray mustache. The don placed a hand on the servant's shoulder and whispered into his ear.

As he did, Colter turned to Prophet again,

199

and said under his breath with more than a little indignation, "What do you think I'm gonna do — sit here and drink goat's milk like a blame nancy boy while you two swill Mexican busthead and compare knife scars and scorpion bites? This is Mexico, Lou!"

Prophet shrugged and sat back in his chair.

While the *mayordomo,* Raoul, walked over to the liquor cabinet, the don got both his crutches under him and ambled over to a chair near where Prophet and Colter had parked themselves at angles before the small fire snapping and crackling in a deep stone hearth. The library was a testament to old Spanish wealth — opulence that had gone somewhat to seed, however. The furniture was stately and Old Mexican in the best Spanish tradition, and the full armor of a Spanish conquistador was mounted on a wooden pedestal beside the fireplace, complete with jewel-encrusted sword.

But the leather furniture was badly cracked, the seams frayed. Wooden chair arms were splintering and showing the wear of the ages. In fact, most of the wood in the room, and there was a great deal including that of heavy shelves bearing the weight of hundreds of handsome cloth- or leather-bound Spanish volumes, had long since lost its luster.

There were patches of dust here and there, in hard-to-reach places, and cobwebs hung like tangled threads in wall corners. The heavy drapes thrown back from two long, arched windows, open to the cool night air and citrus aromas wafting from the surrounding patio, owned their own patina of dirt and soot from the fireplace.

Not that Prophet put any stock in neatness and maintenance himself, but the shabbiness, which he'd spied in other parts of the grand old house as he and Colter had been led here from the front entrance, spoke to him of better days at Hacienda de la Paz. Of younger housekeepers, perhaps, a younger don better equipped to stay on top of such supervision, and no doubt an overseeing lady of the place who had long since passed on.

Seeing that the don was having trouble with his crutches, Lou rose to help, taking the crutches from the old man, easing him into a chair near himself and Colter, at the end of a low table, then leaning the crutches against the man's heavy leather armchair.

"Gracias, amigo," the don said as he sank back in his chair, a little breathless. "It is no good — getting old."

"I don't look forward to it," Prophet said.

The don looked at Colter. "You are still quite young."

"I reckon in years, Don."

"You feel older, eh?" The don fingered his left cheek. "Maybe it has something to do with the scar, eh?"

"Maybe."

"La Marca de Sapinero." Keeping his eyes on Colter, the old don gave a grim, knowing smile. "Sheriff Bill Rondo's brand."

Colter frowned at him in astonishment. "You know . . ."

"Sí, sí." On the table before the don were three short stacks of reading material — books, magazines, and dime novels with yellow pasteboard covers. He leaned forward and with his arthritic hand riffled through a couple of the stacks, knocking the books around the table. "I try to brush up on my English from time to time by reading books from America. In my old age, I have wearied of the more serious fair" — he tossed a heavy, cloth-bound volume aside — "and indulge myself with more romantic tales of derring-do on the wild 'n' woolly American frontier. Ah, here it is . . ."

He plucked a slender pasteboard volume from a now-messy stack and shoved it across the table toward Colter. The redhead stared down at it, deep lines cut across his forehead, pale where his hat had shaded it from the sun.

Leaning forward, Colter plucked it off the table and held it up so Prophet could see the cover on which a crude drawing showed a slender, long-haired young man bearing down on three obvious curly wolves with exaggeratedly savage faces. The young man wore a grisly S on his left cheek. He held a pistol in his left hand, flames stabbing from the barrel. One of the cutthroats facing him was thrown off his feet by the bullet. One man still standing wore a big silver star and held a gun in one hand, a branding iron in his other hand.

The brand on the end of the iron was a large, bright-red S.

The title in large dramatic letters read: *THE SAPINERO BRAND.*

Below, in smaller letters: *The redheaded gunslinger wore the Brand of Sapinero on his face . . . or was it the Mark of Satan? The man who branded him found out for sure — the hard way!*

"Well, I'll be damned," Prophet said. "Kid, you've ridden into dime-novel country."

Colter scraped his thumb across the edge of the book, riffling the pages. "Reckon I have at that." He didn't seem quite sure how

203

he felt about it.

"Just like Louisa," Prophet groused. The Vengeance Queen, too, had had a dime novel written about her. "Me," Prophet said, wryly, "all I get is shot at!"

"Ah, you are famous in your own right, Señor Prophet," said the don. Raoul had given the old *patrón* a stone mug of pulque, and it quivered now in the oldster's shaking hands. Raoul had set mugs of the astringent Mexican liquor on the low table near Prophet and Colter, and then after a quick nod to his *patrón,* retreated from the room. The don smiled around the mug he held up close to his spade-bearded chin. "Or, shall we say, *infamous*?"

"That'd likely be a better word — you're right on that score, Don," Prophet growled, lifting the mug and taking a small sip of the liquor.

The don sipped his own brew then smiled over the lip of the mug. "The big ex-Confederate bounty hunter who sold his soul to the devil . . ."

"I see my reputation precedes me, as well."

"I read about you in a book about the Vengeance Queen."

Prophet laughed. "Ain't it just like her to get most of the glory."

"You are her partner, are you not, Señor

Prophet?"

"She's mine. When I feel like indulging her persnickety ways, that is."

The don frowned curiously, sliding his glance between Lou and Colter. "But, now . . . you two are partners . . . ?"

"For the time bein'," Prophet told him.

"We found ourselves in similar situations, you might say," Colter explained before taking a tentative sip of the pulque. He swallowed and his cheeks instantly flushed but he tried not to grimace.

He shot a quick glance at Prophet, who hooked a half smile at him.

"I see, I see," said the don, studying each man in turn.

The man's stare made Prophet feel like a horse the man was thinking about making an offer on. Apparently, the don's scrutiny made Colter uneasy, as well, for the redhead glanced again at Prophet, this time with a question in his eyes.

After a long, uneasy silence, the don turned to Prophet. "You said, señor, that there were two things that lured you to Méjico. One was pulque. And the other . . . ?"

As if to dramatize the bounty hunter's response, there was a soft knock on the library door. Not waiting for a response, Señorita Marisol poked her head into the room to say, "Papa, Seville wanted me to ask if you would like corn or beans with the *birria.*" She must have seen the three regarding her with a bemused half smile, for she froze there, frowning curiously back at them.

Prophet's heart did a little Indian dance in his chest. Marisol looked even more beautiful now than before. She must have bathed after the long journey, for her heart-shaped face had a fresh-scrubbed look, enhancing its rich earthy tones, and her hair still showed a little dampness. She wore it down now, tucked behind her ears and spilling down her shoulders; it shone with a recent brushing. It was as rich and glossy as her eyes.

She wore a sleeveless, salmon-colored gown with a very low-cut neck and a bodice edged with gold embroidery. The gown enhanced the ripeness of her figure. A lacy, sheer, cream shawl was drawn around her shoulders.

"*¿Qué es?*" she asked, befuddled.

The don looked at Prophet then at his daughter and shaped a toothy smile. He blinked once, slowly, then said, "Tell Seville that the corn will suffice, *mi hija.*"

Marisol continue to stare at the three men, perplexed. She looked at Prophet.

There must have been something about his own expression that affected her, for a flush rose into her smooth cheeks. She averted her eyes and, muttering softly under her breath, pulled her head out of the room and drew the door closed with a soft, slow click.

The don turned to Lou, smiling. "Could that other thing be the señoritas, Señor Prophet?"

"It might just be at that, Don. I hope I'm not being impolite by saying your daughter might just be the most beautiful señorita I've ever laid eyes on." Lou smiled. "And I've seen a few."

The old *hacendado* studied him shrewdly, nodding. "You are a good judge of woman-flesh, Señor Prophet."

"Call me Lou. I mean, I am sitting in your library, drinking your liquor — which is mighty fine, if I might add."

"*Sí, sí.* And you did save my daughter's life."

"Sorry about your sister, Don," Colter said through a slight rasp after taking another small sip of the pulque. "I wish we could have saved her, too."

"Of course, I am bereaved," the don said, waving a hand in the air, at once accepting and dismissing the notion. "But *mi hermana* lived a good, long life. One of great adventure. She has been ill for years, an illness similar to the one that took my wife five years ago, but only after eating away at her slowly for the previous ten, the past six of which she was a mere ghost of her former self. This way was better. A bullet to the head. It was almost a merciful thing Juan Carlos did. I didn't want to see Aurora linger. Besides . . ." The don turned again to Prophet. "I guess Juan Carlos got his — how do you say? *Just desserts?*"

"About that," Prophet said, shifting uneasily in his seat. "Just how mad is . . ."

"Don't worry about that. You are safe here at Hacienda de la Paz, I assure you. Besides, I ordered Miguel to assure Don Amador that he got what he deserved by a stranger who did not know who he was. I told the don that his son was about to kill my daughter. That he will believe. He knows how Juan Carlos felt about Marisol, and how hot Juan Carlos's blood ran. No, no. I assure you both that while a few years ago such a happening would have resulted in all-out war between our haciendas, both Don Amador and myself are far too old and worn-out to fight. Or to send others to do our fighting."

The don paused to take a deep drink of the pulque. "Besides," he continued, thumbing some of the liquor away from the corner of his mouth, "we both have another problem that has us both badly preoccupied. At least, I'm sure Don Amador is as preoccupied with Ciaran Yeats as I am, for I am told the bloodthirsty devil has done as much damage over at Hacienda del Amador as he has here."

That was the second time Prophet had heard the name. Now he had an opportunity to voice his curiosity. "Who is Ciaran Yeats, pray tell?"

"He is the, uh, *matter* I mentioned. The reason I summoned you here for a private conversation."

"I don't understand," Colter said, cutting a quick glance at Lou.

Don de la Paz stared at the redhead. His rheumy brown eyes flickered with emotion. His hands shook, including the one holding the pulque. It shook so badly that the creamy white liquor splashed up over the brim to run down the sides of the cup.

"Easy, Don," Prophet said when forked veins bulged so severely in the old man's forehead that Lou was afraid he was about to have a stroke and die right there in his chair.

The don drew a breath as though to calm himself. It didn't work. His raspy voice quavered as he said, "He is the vile gringo jackal who has kidnapped my youngest daughter. *He is the vile son of a wild lobo bitch I am going to pay you both most dearly to kill!*"

CHAPTER 17

Again, Prophet and Colter shared a dubious glance. Scowling deeply, Prophet leaned forward in his chair, resting his elbows on his knees. "Wait a second. Your, uh . . . your youngest daughter was *kidnapped*?" He was having trouble working his mind around the information, wondering why, if such a thing had occurred, he hadn't learned about it until now.

"And . . . you want us to, uh, kill a man?" Colter asked in the same halting, incredulous manner of Lou.

"Ciaran Yeats!" The name had flown out of the don's mouth like a choking wail.

He took a calming drink of his pulque and then sank back in his chair, the forked veins in his forehead contracting somewhat, which Prophet was relieved to see. For a minute he'd honestly been worried about the old man's health. "He took my daughter, Alejandra, in a raid. Six weeks ago. That is why I summoned Marisol home from Mexico City, sending my dearly departed sister as her chaperone."

He sat there staring across the room as though he himself could not believe the words he'd just spoken. His spindly chest rose and fell heavily. Sweat glistened across his forehead. A single bead ran down the side of his face. "My dear Alejandra . . ." he muttered.

"Ciaran Yeats," Prophet said, frowning. "I've heard that name."

"He was a major in the Ninth Cavalry stationed in California," said the don in a soft, raspy voice, still staring across the room at a faded painting of a beautiful, red-haired woman on the wall — probably his dead wife, Lou assumed. "He was court-martialed for . . ."

"Leading a raid on a small Mojave village in southeastern Arizona, murdering mostly old women and children," Prophet said. "Not long after his court-martial, he was busted out of a guardhouse by a gang of his loyal supporters, including a lieutenant named . . ."

"Will-John Rhodes," the don finished for him. "They are still together, thick as thieves. Hell, they *are* thieves. Loco *americano* bandits riding wild in Baja!"

"So the old coyote is still alive, after all these years." Prophet nodded slowly in surprise, remembering the tale he'd been told late one night in a Nogales gambling den by the quartermaster from Fort Bowie. "I heard Rhodes is as crazy as Yeats."

"*Sí,*" said the don. "Maybe crazier."

"Still addicted, then . . ."

Colter furled a curious brow at Prophet. "Addicted?"

Lou set his cup on the table and laced his fingers together between his knees. "I heard the major contracted a case of rabies after being bitten by a rabid coyote he tried to chase away from his dog. A medico pre-scribed a powerful hemp extract to treat the rabies. It takes great doses of the stuff to hold it at bay, and you have to keep taking it or the rabies will come back, even years after you first contracted it. So you can either go mad from the cure or die about as painfully as any man can, from the rabies."

Colter whistled softly at the prospect of such a miserable death.

"Yeats became obsessed with his medicine, which he could only get from back East somewhere. Tilden's India Extract, I think it was called. When he became anxious about the reliability of his supplier, the major decided to grow the weed himself and extract it. I heard he had acres and acres of the stuff growing at Fort Davis. He had his men cultivating the crops and formulating a powerful liquid extract. They must have done some sampling, because, as the story goes, many of the enlisted men, noncoms, and even officers at Fort Davis became as addicted as Yeats.

"The major and his men did a lot of loco things before they ever killed those Mojaves. It's said they'd all turned outlaw and were extorting money from gold mines they'd been assigned to protect from Indian raids and banditos. They took over one mine and ran it themselves. There's also a story they got involved in a rustling ring and were even kidnapping young Mojave girls and selling them into sex slavery in Mexico. All hearsay, of course. No one was able to prove anything. When Yeats and his men killed those Mojaves they claimed were holding up stagecoaches, the army finally had the devil locked up for good. Or so they thought."

"*Sí,* or so they thought," said the don. "The major's loyal, addicted supporters wouldn't have it." The old *hacendado* was still staring at the painting of the red-haired woman who must have been his wife, depicted in her much younger years. Prophet saw where Marisol had gotten her looks. If possible, the señorita's mother was even more spectacular, unless the painter had added his own romantic touches to the image.

Prophet sipped his pulque then set the cup back on the table. "Yeats's men busted him out of the guardhouse where he was waiting to be moved to a permanent military pen, and they all ran to Mexico. A good fifty U.S. soldiers armed to the teeth. Deserters, every one. All in allegiance to a crazy son of Satan. The Mad Major, they called him."

The don turned his head slowly to Prophet. "He is crazier now than ever."

Prophet's brows furled tightly, skeptically. "Are you sure it's him, Don? I mean, Yeats was busted out of the Fort Bowie lockup damn near twenty years ago. Surely, he's not still alive. Not with the rabies, the addiction. He must have been forty, forty-five years old back then. He'd be in his sixties now. Hell, his youngest men have to be in their forties. Still running off their leashes down here in Baja?"

The don's eyes glinted wildly. "Most of his original gang is dead from illness or violence. But . . . am I sure it's him? Madre María, he was here less than a month ago, and him and his men, most of them the lowest of *bandidos mexicanos,* had the run of

215

the place! Most of my men had gone to the ocean coast to sell beef and produce and to return with supplies. Hacienda de la Paz was undermanned. Yeats and his men rode in under cover of darkness, slipped into the casa" — he pointed a finger like a pistol barrel at the floor — "as silent as ghosts in the night! I woke up to the sharp chill of a knife held to my throat, to the horrible aroma of that ungodly substance the old devil doesn't stop smoking!"

"You mean Yeats himself stole into your room?" Prophet asked.

"Sí, sí." The don poked a long, crooked finger to his throat. "He held a big *cuchillo* to my neck! He pulled my bedcovers away and said, 'Come downstairs, Don de la Paz. It is time to negotiate for your life and the life of Hacienda de la Paz.'

"He continued his siege throughout the next day and the next night. It was like a celebration for him and his men. They kept my men in their bunkhouses but forced the peons' women to dance with them — I won't tell you what else they were forced to do! — while their husbands were forced to play guitars and mandolins. Yeats and that wicked Lieutenant Rhodes forced me to sit out on the patio with them, watching the festivities. They held guns and knives and machetes on us all. They butchered several pigs and a goat and roasted them over big fires, and we sat there on the veranda, drinking pulque and wine together, as though we were old amigos!"

The don placed a hand to his temple then flung that hand toward the ceiling. "*¡Mierda!* They smoked that evil weed of theirs and sipped their evil drink that has obviously pickled that old gringo devil's brains. Oh, he is quite mad!"

"What were they here for?" Colter asked. He'd been listening closely, riveted.

"Gold! And guns! And women, of course! That is what Yeats does — he travels around Baja laying siege to villages and ranchos and haciendas, plundering the hard-earned wealth of others, raping women, hoarding the fruits of his pillaging, fostering this demented idea that he is the governor of Baja and that he, in time, will take over all of Sonora and, after a few more years, all of Méjico! Oh, he is quite mad. See? Do you understand now? He is quite mad!"

He turned to Prophet and choked out, "And he took my daughter. My beautiful Alejandra!"

"So you said. Why?" Prophet turned to the painting the don had been gazing at earlier. Lou thought he knew why she'd been taken. At least, if Alejandra looked anything like her mother, he knew why Yeats had taken her.

The don followed Prophet's gaze to the picture and said nothing for nearly a minute before muttering, "*Sí, sí.* Now you understand." He raised a knotted hand slowly to his face and thumbed a tear from his cheek. "Like her mother before her, she is more beautiful than Madre María, and more saintly, more divine. Yeats told me that he was taking my daughter in exchange for my life, for the lives of everyone else at Hacienda de la Paz, and for not burning the hacienda to the ground."

The old *hacendado* gritted his teeth, stifling a sob. "Alejandra's parting words to me were: 'Do not worry, Papa, my life for yours and Hacienda de la Paz is a sacrifice I am honored to make.' Then she told me she loved me." His fingertips fluttered against his cheek as he stared dreamily at the painting. "My dear *hija,* my youngest, my most ravishing, *mi bebé* . . . she kissed my cheek most tenderly — it was like an angel's kiss — and then they took her away, all of them mounting their horses and thundering off into the mountains . . . gone forever with my last-born, my angel. My Alejandra!"

The old don propped his elbow on the

arm of his chair, rested his head in his hand, and cried like a baby for several minutes.

When he finally stopped, he looked from Prophet to Colter then back to the bounty hunter again, his eyes swimming in tears. "*Por favor.* I beg you both. Only you two can get her back for me. Only you two can kill that mad devil, Ciaran Yeats. I have treasure. They didn't take it all. I have gold. It's buried, but I will dig it up for you. It is not much, but it is all yours. There is probably enough to equal around five thousand of your American dollars out there. I was saving it for an emergency. If this is not that, I don't know what is."

He gave a heavy sigh that was part sob.

Don de la Paz treated his guests to an opulent, savory meal.

Prophet couldn't remember enjoying a meal more than he enjoyed the succulent Spanish dishes laid out by Marisol and the tall, gaunt Mexican woman — the wife of the *mayordomo,* Raoul, it turned out — whose name was Seville. No, he couldn't say he really enjoyed the meal. The food satisfied him no end, as did the wine from the don's own vines cultivated by his peons.

But it was hard to enjoy a meal under the cloud of all that had happened that day, starting with the murder of Doña Aurora and ending with the don's horrible story of Yeats's siege and the don's pleas for Prophet and Colter Farrow to find his beloved daughter and bring her back to the hacienda but only after assassinating the mad jackal who'd kidnapped her — the notoriously savage Ciaran Yeats.

The Mad Major, as he was called.

Before leaving the library, having been called to *la cena,* or supper, by Marisol, Prophet and Colter had told the don they'd sleep on his proposition and give him their response in the morning. There wasn't much talking during dinner. As could have been predicted, a funereal pall had fallen over the casa. As soon as the don had finished his plate, he wiped his mouth with a cloth napkin and excused himself for the evening. He was going to light a candle for his dearly departed *hermana* and sit with her awhile, in her bedroom upstairs, where Marisol and Seville had washed her and dressed her and laid her out on her bed for visitation.

Before he left the dining room, the crippled old don wished Prophet and Colter a good night's sleep and announced in his raspy voice that he hoped they would, in the morning, accept his offer for the job he so badly needed them to do.

Prophet and Colter thanked him for the meal. The don gave a formal bow then hobbled on out of the room, his *mayordomo* in close attendance. Prophet caught Marisol studying him closely from where she sat directly across the heavy wooden table. Her lovely, chocolate-eyed face wore a faintly skeptical expression. An oblique one, as well.

Did she know about her father's request?

If so, she didn't offer commentary. Instead, she politely excused herself, as well, announcing that she'd best sit with her father. As Prophet and Colter slid their chairs back and climbed clumsily to their feet, she moved swiftly to the dining room's broad, arched door. She stopped and glanced back at both men standing at the table, the light from the table's three candles flickering in her eyes. Light and shadows were shunted this way and that across her beautifully gowned body, the deepest shadows of all lingering in the cleavage of her low-cut bodice.

Prophet flushed when, lifting his eyes from the woman's bosom, he saw her staring at him, a very faint smile pulling at the corners of her full, wide mouth. He flushed with embarrassment. *Prophet, you goatish old*

*devil. You done been caught with your hand
in the cookie jar, old son. Leastways, your
eyes where they had no business bein'* . . .

Marisol blinked once as she kept her
frank, lustrous gaze on Prophet. "I will have
Raoul show you to your rooms, señores."

"Rooms?" Prophet hooked a self-
deprecating smile. "The closest pile of hay
is all I need."

"Me, too," Colter agreed.

"Nonsense," said the señorita. With that
she abruptly turned away and left the room,
her high-heeled, side-button shoes clacking
off down a stone-paved hall. The clacking
dwindled slowly, and Prophet found his ears
straining to keep listening, his heart reluctant to let her go . . .

Finally, she was gone. Only the light,
intriguing scent of her remained.

Prophet and Colter were now alone in the
room lit by only the three candles. They
could hear Seville moving around in the
kitchen off the dining room, but otherwise
they were quite isolated here in the deep
recesses of the sprawling, ancient casa.

Colter sat back down in his chair and
fingered the handle of his coffee cup. He
studied the cup for a time and then looked
across the table at Prophet. "What do you
think?"

Prophet sank back into his own chair, which creaked beneath his weight. "About the señorita?"

Colter chuffed a laugh and tossed a grape across the table at Lou. They'd been served grapes and coffee for desert. "I already know what you think about the señorita, Proph." He chuckled again. "That's more than obvious. I'm talkin' about the don's offer."

"Oh, that." Prophet sat back in his chair and heaved a slow sigh. "Yeah . . . that . . ."

CHAPTER 18

Prophet and Colter were each given their own separate rooms.

Nice rooms they were, too — large and well-appointed with big, canopied beds and tall glass doors that opened onto a patio that ran along the rear of the casa. There were more fruit trees here, lending their citrus aromas to the chill air of the silent night. The rooms were likely reserved for the don's most important guests. Prophet didn't count himself among such venerable lodgers. He had a feeling that he and Colter had been shown to such rooms merely as added incentive for them to accept the don's offer.

Prophet had a feeling that the don, in his illness and old age and with no sons to carry on after he was gone, so that Hacienda de la Paz had grown more than a little rough around its edges, no longer commanded the same attention and authority that he had at one time. Such rooms as those which Lou and Colter occupied likely rarely saw a human step through their doors, an opinion to which the pent-up air of Prophet's quarters had attested before Raoul had opened the large windows to the night's fresh breeze lightly tanged by the fruit trees.

The lavish furnishings, including the comfortable bed, didn't help Prophet fall asleep. When he'd first entered the room on the heels of Raoul, his eyelids had weighed ten pounds apiece, his head had been calling for a deep pillow, his bones crying out for a soft mattress.

But as soon as his head had hit that pillow, slumber slipped away from him like a shameless coquette who turned out to be nothing but a tease. He tossed and turned, trying to get comfortable. The problem, however, was that his body *was* comfortable. The culprits responsible for his lack of sleep were the thoughts swirling in his brain. Troubling, restless thoughts that had nothing to do with the don's offer. He might have told the don he'd sleep on it, but he'd already made up his mind. He suspected Colter had, as well.

How could either of them come down to Mexico, each chased down here with a posse nipping at his heels, and not help out an old man in dire need? The money wasn't bad, either. At the very least, it would finance the rest of Prophet's winter in Mexico.

Also, Lou Prophet was not a man of leisure. Oh, he enjoyed entangling himself in the limbs of a willing *puta* for a few nights here and there, but as much as he wanted to believe it about himself, he wasn't really one to bear up under days of inactivity. He always told himself that he came to Mexico for rest and relaxation, but that was rarely ever true. Every time he'd come down here, he'd gotten entangled in one misadventure or another.

He was, if he was anything, a man of action.

And so was Colter Farrow.

The kid was younger, and he hailed from a different world than Prophet's beloved prewar South, but they were both cut from the same cloth. They were brothers in many ways. Colter hadn't told Lou his decision before they'd parted for the night, but Prophet sensed that Colter had decided to go after Alejandra de la Paz and Ciaran Yeats, as well. He'd probably made up his mind as soon as he'd heard about the damsel in distress, as had Lou himself.

The job had it all. Adventure. A beautiful

woman. And gold at the end of the trail.

No, the decision had been made. That wasn't what kept Prophet from sleep.

The thoughts churning through his brain and making his heart thump had a face — the beautiful, beguiling, brown-eyed face of Marisol de la Paz . . .

What a heartbreaker! It might not have been so bad if it hadn't been a week since he'd last had his ashes hauled.

Six days!

He hadn't had a dry spell that long since the War of Northern Aggression. Then it was for a good cause. But this here . . . this was just torture. Especially with the beautiful señorita so close. Yet so far away . . .

Suddenly, before he knew it, his gun was in his hand and he was cocking it and extending it toward the open courtyard doors. As usual, he'd looped his Peacemaker and shell belt over the bed's right front post, within a fast, easy grab. Now, half sitting up in bed, he extended the cocked revolver toward the gauzy red curtains blowing back away from the doors in a cool breeze.

There was a large moon tonight, and the milky light had turned the curtains the color of softly glowing embers over there in the darkness of the large room.

Lou hadn't realized it until just now, but

he'd heard something. The sound must have slipped into his brain before he'd even known it. Now he knew it, though he couldn't say what that sound had been.

His heartbeat quickening, he tossed the covers off his long, lean frame clad in only his summer-weight longhandles. He rose from the bed and walked slowly toward the curtains dancing back away from the windows, like ghosts swaying to some music he couldn't hear.

He paused, listening. There were no sounds but the faint swishing sound of the breeze and the dry scuttling of dried orange leaves and seeds the breeze was shepherding along the stone walk ringing the patio just outside the doors.

What had his senses, honed from years of manhunting, picked up?

Quickly, he stepped between the doors, extending his cocked revolver straight out into the night. He stared into the courtyard, squinting, not seeing much but the silhouettes of trees and leafy branches and the occasional dry fountain and statue, most of which, Prophet assumed, were depictions of saints and deceased members of the de la Paz family. Not that he'd taken much of a gander at the courtyard, for Raoul had led him and Colter here to their side-by-side rooms in the twilight, when there'd been only a little more light than there was now.

Lou stepped forward, looking around more carefully.

He jumped when a female voice said softly, intimately, "Can't sleep, amigo?"

He recognized Marisol's voice before he saw her sitting there against the adobe wall to his right. At first, he could see only her vague silhouette, but as his eyes adjusted to the pearl light competing with the court-yard's shadows, her figure clarified some, so that he could see her hair spilling down her shoulders that were wrapped in a dark brown, striped serape.

The serape came down to just above her knees. She didn't appear to be wearing anything below it. Meaning below the poncho her legs were bare, as were her fine feet, which were resting one atop the other and pulled slightly under the wooden bench she was sitting on, her back against the wall.

Her bare skin glowed like alabaster in the moonlight.

"I sensed as much," she said, again in that soft, intimate tone that bit Prophet deep and that seemed to entangle his vocal cords. She lifted her hand. "Drink? It's pulque. A sleep tonic if there ever was one."

She rose gracefully from the bench and

moved over to Prophet, lifting the cup to her lips and taking a sip. She lowered the cup, swallowed, and the moonlight flickered in her dark eyes as she stared up at the big bounty hunter standing a full head taller than she. "If you want to know the truth, Papa's pulque isn't as good as that goatish dog One-Eye Acuna's. *Shhh!*"

She giggled. "But then, how good can any liquor be that takes only one day to ferment?"

"It does all right by me," Lou quipped. "But then I'm not the top-shelf brand of fella."

She smiled devilishly and placed a finger to those swollen lips of hers and which Prophet couldn't take his eyes off. "But it will help you sleep." She paused, blinked, then arched a brow speculatively. "If sleep is what you want . . ."

Prophet's heart bucked in his chest like a .45 revolver.

He lowered his own .45 to his side, depressing the hammer.

Slowly, he shook his head. "No," he said, reaching down and grabbing the serape's hem. "I don't want to sleep."

Marisol gave a sudden gasp of surprise then raised her arms, including the hand holding the cup, as Prophet brusquely lifted the serape up and over her head. He dropped it to the paving stones at her bare feet. Her hair spilled in a lovely mess across her shoulders.

Prophet raked his eyes across her naked body limned beautifully by the moonlight. Again, his heart bucked.

He reached down and picked her up in his arms.

"Careful, *pendejo,*" she laughed. "You'll spill the pulque!"

Prophet swung around and carried her into his room.

Later, they lay sprawled belly down across the bed, at last sharing the pulque she'd brought. The light from a single lantern perched atop the room's dresser tossed watery, umber light and shadows this way and that. It brought out the rich, earthy tones of the señorita's smooth cheeks to which several strands of her hair were sweat-pasted, attesting to the fury of their recent frolic.

"So," she said, having just taken a sip of the liquor and handing the cup back to Prophet, "did you take *mi padre* up on his offer?"

"You knew?"

"I suspected it was what he wanted to

speak to you and Colter about. I haven't had a chance to talk to him myself yet about Alejandra's kidnapping. About Yeats laying siege to the hacienda. He told me about it briefly in the letter he sent me asking me — instructing me, rather — to return to Hacienda de la Paz, because he needed me." She gave a slow nod, pulling her mouth corners down and staring at the pillow she was resting her forearms on. "So . . . finally the old reprobate needs me. But only after Alejandra left . . ."

"I take it it ain't exactly smooth sailing for you and the don?"

"No, it has never been smooth sailing for me and the don." Marisol gave a sarcastic laugh. "It is no secret around here that Alejandra has always been his favorite. She's the baby in the family. There was a son ahead of me, but he died in a fall from a horse. The fall didn't kill him — it was the nest of rattlesnakes he fell into that killed him. He lingered for days, suffering in the most awful way. I can still hear the screams when I close my eyes.

"I was the middle child. Alejandra had just been born when Salvador, named after our grandfather on our father's side, died. So all of Papa's attention went to the baby. It was almost as though he thought she was the

second coming of Salvador. Anyway . . ."
She shook her head and took the pulque
back from Prophet. "Don't mind me. I am
indulging myself."

"What were you doing in Mexico City, if I
may ask?"

Marisol took a deep sip of the pulque then
rolled onto her back, stretching like a cat
and giving Prophet a view that twisted his
heart one-quarter turn counterclockwise.
They'd gotten so warm they'd kicked the
covers down to the foot of the bed. "Señor,"
she said, "after what you just did to me, you
can ask me anything you want."

She chuckled, pushed up on an elbow, and
kissed him on the mouth. She brushed her
nose against his then rested her head back
against the pillow. "Papa sent me there to
get me married. I rented an apartment with
Tía Aurora, who acted as my chaperone, of
course, and arranged for me to meet suitors
suitable for a señorita of my class and sta-
tion. I felt a bit like Papa's *puta,* but where
else was I going to find a man except out in
society? Obviously, not out here. Our only
near neighbors were our blood enemies.

"Oh, I would have married Juan Carlos,
anyway, but . . . well, you know all about
that. Besides, in hindsight I realize that
either my father or Juan Carlos's father

would have had us both murdered." She gave a flippant sigh and continued with: "So the years passed, and suddenly I was twenty-seven with no prospects — we were getting fewer and fewer visitors way out here at Hacienda de la Paz, as my father's reputation as a businessman waned — so Papa thought it was time I moved to Mexico City. I'd been there less than a year when Yeats came and took Alejandra. And here I am . . ."

She rolled onto her side, facing Prophet, moving her hand up from her belly, caressing herself and smiling beguilingly. "So far, so good, if you ask me."

Prophet sipped the pulque, studying the earthily charming young woman over the brim of the cup. "You don't seem all that busted up about your sister being kidnapped. By a madman, no less."

"No? Oh well . . . you see, it's not easy to get busted up, as you say, about the misfortune of one I spent my life in savage competition with. As far as the gold and guns Yeats stole from the hacienda, Papa has been on a slow plummet for years, business-wise. It's not only his body that is crippled, but his mind is, as well. He has not hired the best men. Now he can rarely find anyone who is willing to work for him, since they never know if they'll be paid or not. I noticed the compound is practically deserted, and nothing is being kept up properly. There used to be a lot more men around the place. A small army of men who had their wits about them and who knew how to fight. You saw how easily Juan Carlos cut down my guards." She gave a caustic chuff. Prophet thought she would have spat on one of the dead men, if one were near.

Marisol looked at him as he lay on his own side, feasting his eyes on her. She smiled under his obviously admiring gaze. He liked how her eyes flickered when she smiled, the outside corners drawing up beautifully. He leaned forward and buried his head in her ripe bosoms for a time. She ran her hand through his hair, groaning as he pleased her.

Then she said, "You didn't answer my question, Lou."

He kept his head where it was. "I done forgot what it was. Distracted, I reckon." His voice was muffled.

"Did you accept Papa's offer to go after Yeats and Alejandra?"

"Oh, that." Prophet pulled his head up. "Not yet but I'm going to."

"I figured you would, knowing the man you are." She grabbed his ears in her hands, gave them a playful tug. "Be careful. The odds are stacked against you."

"I will."

"And do me a big favor, will you? When you see Alejandra?"

"Sure, anything."

Again, Marisol gave his ears a tug only it wasn't so playful this time. "Don't you dare fall in love with her, you *bastardo*!"

CHAPTER 19

Prophet woke up alone, which surprised him. He must have slept so deeply after his and Marisol's last frolic that he'd slept right through her leaving.

She'd probably left to avoid anyone finding out that the don's daughter had spent the night with a guest. Not any guest, either. A burly, unwashed, ex-Confederate bounty hunter from north of the border. Ye gads — the woman's reputation would have been muddied from hither to yawn!

Lou didn't blame her one bit. If he were she, he wouldn't have wanted anyone to know about him, either. He gave a wry chuckle at the notion while he took a whore's bath from the porcelain washbasin sitting atop the marble washstand. Lemony morning sunlight angled brightly through the open doors facing the courtyard. The air was cool and winey fresh, and it fairly bubbled with the piping of songbirds. Obviously, Prophet had slept far later than he normally did.

While he dressed, he reflected on the dreamlike night he'd enjoyed with Marisol de la Paz, and the reflection put him in such a good mood that he found himself whistling softly as he twirled the Peacemaker on his finger before dropping it into the holster thonged on his right thigh and donned his hat.

He left the room whistling, as well, and saw Colter just then leaving the room to his left. Colter didn't look nearly as well rested as Prophet felt. The younker's tattooed face was drawn and pale, and there were pouches under his eyes.

"Well, I'm glad to hear someone's happy as a well-tuned fiddle," the redhead quipped. He paused to gingerly set his snuff brown Stetson on his head after tucking his long, straight red hair back behind his ears.

"What's the matter with you, Red? You look like you just tangled with two rabid mountain lions in the back of a Pittsburgh freight wagon." Prophet smiled in sudden understanding. "Oh . . . one olla too much pulque."

"Too much pulque and too much wine. I swear the don's butler was bound and determined to get me drunk."

"It's tradition down here to never allow a guest's glass to get empty."

"Now you tell me. I was trying to empty my glass so I wouldn't look like a damn tinhorn, but every time I looked at the blasted thing, it was filled again!"

Prophet laughed.

"All the noise coming from the room next to me didn't help matters one damn bit," Colter groused.

"Huh?"

"I thought it was *you* wrestling wildcats in yonder. And — pardon me if the question is indiscreet — but do you *always cut loose with a blood-curdling rebel yell*?"

"I did that?"

"Several times. Not that I was counting. I was trying to drown out the sounds with my pillow."

"Jesus, if you heard . . ." Standing just outside his room, Prophet looked around warily, wondering if any of the rooms around them were occupied. He didn't think so, as this far-flung wing of the casa appeared to be virtually abandoned, but it was a risk he shouldn't have been taking, not that he'd known he had. The pulque must have turned him into a real animal last night.

Not that Marisol seemed to have

minded . . .

Colter chuckled then winced and pressed the heel of his hand to his forehead. "Ouch!"

"Sorry, Red."

"Oh well — at least one of us had . . ."

Colter let his voice trail off when sounds rose from the direction of the main compound. A couple of men were shouting, one farther away than the other. A horse gave a fierce whinny. It was answered by another horse farther away than the first.

Prophet and Colter shared a dubious glance then swung around and began walking along the stone path beneath the ramada encircling this rear courtyard. The sunlight bathed the courtyard in its harsh morning light, revealing the cracked and crumbling stone statues and dry fountains. Many of the trees back here appeared dead or nearly so.

Indeed, Hacienda de la Paz had seen better days . . . .

The two trail partners strode to the end of the courtyard, dropped down a short stone staircase, then walked through another outside corridor between two blocks of cracked adobe also comprising the casa before turning and dropping down yet another staircase.

They soon found themselves in the front

240

courtyard abutting the main compound, maybe a hundred feet from the main entrance. The don was standing outside the arched front doorway, leaning on his crutches, Raoul at his side.

The *hacendado* was yelling at someone in the yard beyond the adobe wall. Several men were yelling back frantically.

The don was asking what in God's name was going on out there and the replies seemed garbled — at least to Prophet's ears. The replies were also somewhat drowned by the clomping of horses and the squawking and rattling of tack.

Prophet and Colter shared another skeptical look then moved out across the courtyard and through a gate that led out into the compound. All the activity was happening to their right, maybe fifty yards away, between the far end of the adobe wall and a corral on the opposite side of the yard.

A half-dozen horses were milling around over there, stomping, bucking, and whinnying. Three vaqueros were trying to get the horses stopped while a half-dozen others watched from the side near the end of the adobe wall, the bunkhouse behind them. One of the vaqueros, a bandy-legged old man with a long gray beard, shook his head and crossed himself as he watched the commotion.

"What the hell . . . ?" Prophet muttered.

He walked along the adobe wall, frowning as he studied the horses and the three vaqueros running along beside them, grabbing at the reins. The horses were saddled and appeared to be carrying something across their backs. Something else looked odd about the mounts but Prophet couldn't see what it was until he'd walked another thirty feet.

Then he slowed his pace, muttering to himself, absently raking a thumb across his chin. "What . . . the . . . hell . . . ?" he repeated.

"Am I still addled from that Mexican panther juice, or am I seein' what I *think* I'm seein'?" Colter asked.

They both stopped and stared toward where two of the vaqueros finally got two horses settled down. Dust wafted up from the obviously terrified mounts' hooves, so for a few seconds the horses and men were somewhat obscured. Still, Prophet could see one of the vaqueros cry out and jerk back away from the horse he'd stopped.

The man wheeled, facing the others gathered near the casa's patio wall, and fell to his hands and knees. He violently aired out his paunch.

The other vaquero released his own horse suddenly and stepped back as the horse ran over to the corral, scraping up against the stone fence, wanting whatever was on its saddle removed. The other horses — there were six of them total, each carrying a dead man — were acting similarly, one bouncing on its front hooves and whickering.

This horse turned so that Prophet could see it more clearly, could clearly see that what lay across its saddle was a man's body. The body of a vaquero.

The *headless* body of a vaquero.

The head of the body was mounted on the horn of the horse's saddle, like some grisly trophy of a bloody battle. The head's eyelids dropped and the lips were stretched back from teeth gritted as though still in the throes of the man's barbaric demise.

Prophet hadn't noticed until now that Don de la Paz and his *mayordomo,* Raoul, had stepped out of the patio gate to stand where they'd been standing when Prophet had first met them. Slumped over his crutches, the don yelled, "Tomás, lead that horse over here!"

The vaquero holding the reins of one of the other Arabians, and scowling at the horse's grisly cargo, turned toward the don

243

and said, "Are you sure you want to see this, *patrón*?"

"Lead it over here!" the don yelled in his raspy voice before hacking up a gob of phlegm and spitting it into the dirt.

Prophet and Colter walked slowly over to the don and Raoul. They stopped near the older men and watched Tomás lead the smoky gray Arabian with white-speckled hindquarters toward the don, a look of extreme distaste twisting the vaquero's mouth. He was muttering, "Yi, yi, yi . . ." while shaking his head.

He stopped ten feet away from the don and regarded the old man gravely. "It is Miguel, *patrón*!"

Sure enough, the head of the *segundo* who'd led the contingent returning Juan Carlos's body to his father was now mounted on the horn of his saddle. That meant the headless body draped belly down over the bowl-like Spanish saddle likely belonged to the *segundo,* as well.

"Mierda," the don raked out, staring in wide-eyed fascination at the grisly spectacle.

For the first time, Prophet heard Raoul speak. "Good Lord in heaven, what kind of savage is that crazy demon, anyway?" he exclaimed in a voice nearly as raspy as the *hacendado*'s. The *mayordomo* crossed himself, muttering.

The old don sighed and shook his head as he stared at the head of his *segundo* mounted on the apple of the man's saddle. "Don Amador, that old lion, took Juan Carlos's death harder than I thought he would. Hmmm." Pensively, he drummed his index finger against his whiskered chin.

Prophet stared at the grisly scene before him, his heart thumping. If Don Amador did this to the men who were merely returning his son's body, what would he do to the man who'd actually killed him?

Nah, the bounty hunter decided. *Probably best not to think about that.*

"I reckon this means trouble for you, Don," Prophet said. "I mean more trouble than what Amador sent back with these horses."

Amador pursed his lips and shook his head. "I am not worried. Amador is even older than I, in even worse shape. So is his hacienda. We both have been pillaged and plundered by Ciaran Yeats. He doesn't have the men or the firepower to stand against my small army of vaqueros, which it seems has just grown smaller by six after being culled by seven more only yesterday!" The don gave a dry laugh and shook his head as though in response to his blood enemy's reply to the package Don de la Paz had sent to Hacienda del Amador. "He still has his sense of humor, though — I'll give the old lion that much!"

The don gave quick, sharp orders to bury the bodies then turned to Prophet and Colter Farrow. "Now, then, back to the business of the day. How did you sleep, gentlemen?"

Prophet and Colter shared uneasy glances. Lou had seen his share of carnage during the war and then over his decade-long hunt for the nastiest owlhoots in the West. Still, the savagery of Old Mexico never ceased to rock him back on his heels.

Colter gave his head a single wag of amazement.

"Gentlemen, I am sorry you had to witness such nastiness even before breakfast," the don said, "but as I was saying, back to the business of the day."

"Right, right," Lou said. "Back to the business of the day."

"How did you sleep?" the don asked him, gazing directly into his eyes.

Prophet scrutinized the don's regal, weathered features, looking for any indication the old man suspected that his daughter might have paid a visit to the bounty hunter's room. The old man's eyes appeared absent of guile, which was a relief. Seeing those dead vaqueros in such grisly states had left Lou feeling a little colicky. He thought he'd seen enough Mexican justice for one morning. He didn't feel like suffering any himself.

He smiled broadly. "Slept like a log! Just like a log, sure enough! Both of us did." He draped a thick arm around Colter's shoulders. The redhead pulled his mouth corners down. He still appeared a little green around the gills.

"Did you come to a decision?" the don asked hopefully. "Regarding my offer . . . ?"

Prophet looked at the don. How could he say no? The old man had few men left on his roll, likely even fewer with the salt to go after a man like Ciaran Yeats. The *hacendado* was in failing health, of both mind and body. His daughter had been taken from him by one of the evilest men to ever ride the western frontier, north or south of the border.

Besides, Prophet had just plain taken a liking to the proud old *hacendado* staring up at him plaintively.

Prophet looked again at Colter. The redhead looked back at him. He shrugged as if to say, *What else we gonna do for entertainment down here in Old Mexico, Lou?*

"We're gonna get your daughter back to

you safe and sound, Don," Lou said. "And we're gonna kick Ciaran Yeats out with a cold shovel, which is better than he deserves."

The old man gazed from Prophet to Colter and back again. He pursed his lips as though to check his emotion, but his eyes filled with tears. That forked vein in his temple bulged again, dangerously.

"I am most happy to hear that, gentlemen. Most happy!" The don looked at Raoul and stifled a sob. The *mayordomo* smiled at him tenderly. "Come in, come in," the don said, brushing a tear from his cheek. "Let's have a *gran desayuno* and discuss the finer points!"

CHAPTER 20

There were few particulars to discuss.

The don knew next to nothing about where Prophet and Colter Farrow would find Ciaran Yeats and the *hacendado*'s kidnapped daughter, Alejandra de la Paz. According to the don, the way Yeats had avoided capture for the nearly twenty years he'd been on the run was to keep moving through Baja's deserts and mountains, from the Sea of Cortez in the east to the Pacific Ocean in the west, a wild lobo by day, a ghost in the night.

All that he knew of Yeats's current whereabouts had come by rumors from passing strangers — that he was holed up somewhere in east-central Baja, near a fishing village overlooking the sea. It was said that as Yeats had grown older, he'd grown weary of moving around so much and preferred now to remain in one place longer than he'd been known to do in the past.

"Drift south, amigos. South and east toward the salty sea breezes. Follow the rumors. Eventually, those rumors and whispers on the night wind whistling through the ghostly *pueblitos* of this ancient land will either lead you to Yeats, or . . ." The old don gave a baleful half smile and a shrug, opening his hands over the remains of his eggs, frijoles, and roasted goat loin drowned in hot cactus syrup spiced with chilis.

"To a lonely death in a deep barranca," Prophet finished for him, wistfully, having come to know the sentiment of Old Mexico well enough not to deceive himself of his chances here.

"You two are right cheerful this morning," Colter grunted over the rim of his steaming stone coffee mug.

Again, the don shrugged. "It is Méjico. Go with Madre María, my friend. Travel with the blessings of the ancient ones. I will light a candle for you . . . one for every day that you are gone, beating the rocks and arroyos for my beloved Alejandra. If anyone can bring her back to me and kill the devil who took her . . it is you."

Prophet had glanced across the table to see Alejandra's older sister burning holes through him with her eyes, silently reminding him of her admonition of the night before: "Whatever you do, don't fall in love with her!"

So, drifting south and east, sniffing the air for the velvety, salty smell of the Sea of Cortez, Prophet and Colter rode, following one trail and then another, forsaking that trail for yet another for little more reason than the two partners' instincts instructed them to.

After three days' hard ride across mostly open desert rippling with small, isolated jogs of buttes and low mesas, they came to a *pueblito* spread out on a high, rocky plateau. It was late in the day, and the setting sun was a red blush in the western sky, between two towering mountain ridges. As they rode into the little village they passed a small wooden sign announcing the name of the place: LA BACHATA.

A dry wind blew, lifting dust and bits of moldy hay and goat dung and sweeping it up and over Prophet and Colter from behind and throwing it on down the broad main street of the adobe village laid out before them. The wind moaned and whistled softly between the small adobe structures standing back behind splintering boardwalks and brush ramadas from which the occasional clay water olla hung from a frayed rope.

A dog ran out from nowhere to bark and nip at Mean's and Northwest's hocks though Mean quickly discouraged the hound with a swift kick, which sent the mongrel squealing off through a break between a stock pen and a pepper shop.

At the far end of the darkling town, which smelled of goats and the spicy *ristras* hanging from viga poles, the two riders came to a large adobe brick structure, which a sign called LA PRINCESA. Out front a dozen or so horses were tied to three hitchracks.

Prophet drew rein. From inside the cantina came the low roar of conversation and the strumming of a mandolin. Weak lamplight shone beyond the sashed windows and the rotten chinking between the large adobe blocks comprising the stout, obviously ancient building. "We might hear a rumor or two here. What do you think, Red?"

"We might get a *cuchillo* in our backs in this place, too." Colter swung down from his saddle, drew his Remington, and checked the loads. "On the other hand — no risk, no reward." He spun the cylinder and returned the piece to the holster on his right hip but did not snap the keeper thong over the hammer.

"You're wise for your years." With a weary sigh, Prophet stepped down from Mean's back. He walked the mount up to one of the three hitchracks, giving the colicky gelding some room from the others tied there, and looped the reins over the worn cottonwood rail. He grinned ironically at Colter tying his coyote dun beside Mean. "Just please never lose that angelic innocence of yours, will you, Red?"

Colter grinned back at him. "Never."

Prophet looked at the big shotgun hanging by its lanyard from his saddle horn. He fingered his left earlobe, considering whether it would be a good idea to hang the gut-shedder from his shoulder. He might need it in such a place. This was Mexico, after all. On the other hand, the twelve-gauge could be as prone to attracting trouble as solving problems. It marked its owner as a bounty hunter, and more than one or two fellas in a place like this might have good cause to feel peevish around bounty hunters.

Lou gave a grunt, deciding to leave the Richards with his horse. Mean wouldn't let anyone steal it or the Winchester '73 jutting up from the scabbard on the saddle's right side.

He and Colter mounted the wooden-floored ramada and stopped just outside the front door — a rickety-looking panel with a rudimentary handle — that was propped open to the fresh night air with a rock. The partners paused, glanced at each other. It was a narrow opening, offering room for only one to pass at a time.

"Go ahead," Colter said, waving a gloved hand at the arched opening through which tobacco smoke wafted. "Age before beauty."

"Ain't you respectful of your elders, though?"

Prophet walked inside and paused to get the lay of the land. Colter walked in behind him and did likewise. Lou was surprised. He'd been expecting to find a smoky little hole with a crude plank bar upon which a couple of clay ollas sat and out of which some little Mexican not unlike One-Eye Acuna ladled sour-smelling tarantula juice spiced with strychnine and gunpowder.

This place was several rungs above old One-Eye's bullet-pocked pulque stand. There was whitewash on the walls, an actual wood floor, and a most impressive bar running along the rear wall — a sturdy one of varnished mahogany sporting a leaded back bar mirror. There was even a brass footrail running along the bottom. Brass spittoons were placed here and there about the broad room. The tables were draped with heavy white cloths.

The clientele — a dozen men or more — were drinking out of heavy glass mugs or cut glass goblets. Some even drank out of long-stemmed wineglasses. A man dressed sort of like a Mexican bullfighter — in a puffy silk shirt, red silk necktie, and tight black *pantalones* elaborately embroidered in gold — stood on the second-floor balcony overlooking the main drinking hall. He was the one playing the mandolin. He was also singing softly — too softly for Prophet to make out what he was singing beyond gathering it was something typically sad and romantic most likely involving ill-fated love and bloody murder.

Typical Mexican fare.

The gent hustling drinks behind the bar was a well-attired middle-aged hombre sporting a very wide, green silk necktie, a green silk sash, and a broad curlicue mustache. His short, coal black hair was combed straight back from a severe widow's peak, glistening with pomade. There were several serving girls clad in very little, and there were also *putas* working the tables, chatting and laughing with the clientele. They wore even less than the serving girls. In fact, a couple were wearing nothing above the waist except a few strings of pearls or colored beads.

Prophet smiled. Now, this was a watering hole!

He glanced at Colter. The redhead seemed to share Prophet's assessment. He was smiling also.

Prophet clacked his boots together to rid them of any goat dung they might have picked up on the street and then strode into the room, weaving around occupied tables at which various hombres were drinking and palavering and/or playing cards or rolling dice. At one, two men dressed as *campesinos* in white cotton trousers and tunics, with rope-soled sandals on their dirty feet, were playing a traditional Mexican bone game, betting prerolled cigarettes.

The clientele was composed of men from several different societal rungs — from businessmen to *campesinos,* or peasant farmers — and it was only when Prophet was three quarters of the way toward the vacant table he was heading for, near a square-hewn ceiling support post from which several *ristras* hung, that he saw a table near the front crowded with men clad in the dove gray uniforms of the Mexican rural police force, or *rurales,* as they were known.

His gut tightened slightly and he looked away quickly. He'd had run-ins with the *rurales* before, most of whom were actually just banditos in uniform. In fact, some were shrewder and deadlier than your average bandito, using their governmental power for personal gain.

Besides, technically, Prophet and Colter were in the country illegally. You couldn't just slip back and forth across the border at will; you were supposed to have written permission from the Mexican government. Hardly anyone ever sought out such permission, but the laws were on the books and the *rurales* would enforce them according to whatever state of grace they were in and how much money they thought you might be carrying.

As he reached the table he'd been heading for, Prophet glanced at his trail partner. Colter returned the look with a direct one of his own, telling Prophet he'd seen them, too.

Their table was near the wall on the room's right side. Prophet would have preferred having his back right up against the wall, but the table beyond his was occupied, as were most of them against the wall. Oh well, after nearly fifteen years of bounty hunting, he'd grown eyes in the back of his head. They'd have to suffice.

He and Colter had no sooner kicked out chairs and slacked into them than two pretty young *putas* appeared out of nowhere to drop into their laps, laughing and kicking their feet, which were bare beneath the short, colorful Mexican dresses they wore.

"There you are," said the little coquette who'd dropped, light as a feathery little angel, into Lou's lap to wrap her arms around his neck and brush her pert brown nose against his. "We've been waiting all evening for you two! *Americanos,* no? We're so glad to have you here. Now the party can really begin!"

Prophet laughed. "Darlin', I'd swear you don't know me from Adam's off ox!"

He doubted she'd understood the reference, but she laughed just the same. So did her friend writhing around on Colter's lap. She was a little plumper but even prettier than Lou's new friend. Colter's *puta* frowned at his cheek and placed her index finger on the *S* that so tragically marred it. "Oh no!" she cried, as though the assault had just occurred. "What a rotten thing to have happened to you, *mi amor*! Does it hurt *terribly*?"

Colter glanced at Lou, grinning. He laughed and turned back to the flirty little

258

puta and said, "It did until just now."

"See why these two right here are the second reason I come to Mexico, Red?" Prophet called across the table.

"These two right here are the *first* reason I come to Mexico, Proph!"

The girl on Prophet's lap was wasting no time. She was well trained. "What do you say we get a bottle of the good stuff and go upstairs — eh, amigo?" She brushed her nose against his again, then pulled her head back, smiling, showing that one of her front teeth was chipped. "I can take all the soreness out of your tired bones, amigo. I can make you feel very, very *good*! Huh? What do you say?"

Colter's *puta* appeared to be proposing a similar endeavor. Colter looked over at Prophet, one brow arched in question. They'd been on the trail a long time and, unlike Lou, the young redhead hadn't had his ashes hauled.

Prophet turned his head to look behind him at the *rurales*. None was looking his and Colter's way. They were playing poker. One appeared vaguely familiar to Prophet's eyes, but it was hard to tell, as their table was partly in shadow and badly obscured by a thick cloud of tobacco smoke webbing over it, in the weak yellow light of a low-hanging lamp.

It might be just as well the two trail partners depart to the whores' cribs. Besides, in the privacy of the girls' rooms, they might learn something about the man they were hunting, who had no doubt passed through this oasis in the desert mountains from time to time.

Hell, who wouldn't?

Of course, there were other reasons to vacate the premises with the pretty doxies, but for the time being, Lou preferred to keep his mind on business.

"I can't think of anything I'd rather do," Prophet said, laughing and climbing to his feet with the half-naked girl in his arms.

CHAPTER 21

Colter and his girl rose, as well. Prophet's girl wriggled out of his arms, grabbed his hand, and she and Colter's *puta* led both men over to the bar. They turned to their respective jakes and held out their hands, palms up, smiling up at them shyly, like sweet little street urchins selling roses.

Prophet laughed. "How much you need, darlin's?"

"Ten American dollars apiece," said Prophet's *puta,* her innocent smile in place. She shook her long, coal black hair back from her plump cheeks. "For Roselle an' me and a bottle."

"What's your name, darlin'?"

"Pilar."

"Ten dollars *apiece?*" Colter said in hang-jawed awe.

His *puta* playfully slapped his belly with the back of her hand. "Believe me, amigo — Pilar and I are worth every centavo!"

Prophet laughed again as he dug into his denim's pocket. "Pony up, Red."

When the girls had handed two gold eagles to the bartender in exchange for two bottles of likely cheap busthead he brewed in a barn out back, they took their jakes' hands again and led them around to the stairs flanking the bar. As Prophet and Colter climbed the stairs behind the girls, Colter leaned toward Lou and said, "Losing that eagle lightened my load considerable. I didn't come down here a rich man."

"Me, neither," Prophet said. "But in Mexico, it sometimes costs a feller to hear a rumor or two. If anyone knows about Ciaran Yeats in these parts, it'll be the *putas.* So, while you're enjoying yourself, don't forget to do some business, too, Red."

"For ten bucks, I sure as hell won't!" Colter exclaimed just before his doxie opened a door on the right side of the second-floor hall and pulled him into her room.

She hadn't closed the door before Lou's *puta,* Pilar, pulled Prophet into a room two doors farther down the hall, on the hall's left side. It was a small, cluttered crib with a brass-framed bed. There was no window, and the room smelled ripe. Several candles burned here and there around the room, offering a dim, intimate light.

Pilar turned to Prophet, smiling and raising the bottle. "Would you like a drink before or after?"

Her English was nearly perfect, telling the bounty hunter she'd had encounters with more than a few *americanos*. He hoped she'd encountered Ciaran Yeats or one or two of Yeats's men.

"How 'bout before?"

"*¡Sí!*"

Ever the coquette, she wheeled, letting her hair fly, and pulled two goblets off a cluttered shelf above an even more cluttered dresser. As she popped the bottle's cork and splashed tequila — or something akin to it — into the goblets, Prophet looked around for a place to sit. There were no chairs in the tiny room, only the bed. He sat down on the edge of the bed, removing his hat and setting it down beside him. He leaned back and hooked one leg beneath the other one.

Pilar turned to him, giving a smoky smile. Her eyes were nearly black. They and her hair and the deep brown of her face told Lou she probably had more than a little Indio blood, as did most folks in Baja. She knew her trade well, striding slowly over to the bed, chin down, a graceful little scamp making sure she was jiggling in all the right places.

Prophet felt the old male pull, which he tried to suppress.

"Drink?" she said, offering him one of the glasses.

Prophet accepted the clear liquid, whatever it was. *"Gracias."*

"Mezcal," Pilar said. "Drink up. It is very good. Señor Anaya has it freighted in from Mulegé." She took a sip, swallowed, and smiled.

"Later." Prophet wanted to keep his head clear for the time being. Sometimes Baja busthead could hit a man of even his formidable tolerance extra hard. "I have a question for you."

"Question?"

"Sí. Pregunta."

"I know what *question* means," she admonished, giggling, teasing.

"Of course you do. I'm just unduly prideful of my limited Spanish. You speak better English than I do."

The *puta* shrugged. "We get quite a few *americanos* down here. In the winter, mostly. They dig for gold" — she smiled — "or just enjoy the señoritas. There aren't too many watering holes in this part of the mountains, so Señor Anaya tries to make it

264

special for the men who visit here." Again, she smiled. "So that they will return."

Again, she sipped her drink, keeping her seductive gaze on Prophet.

"Smart businessman. But regarding my question —"

"*Sí, sí,* regarding your question. But first, you must drink." Pilar held her own goblet up to her lips. "I want you to enjoy this wonderful mezcal."

"Oh, all right." Prophet sipped. "Damn!" he exclaimed, genuinely surprised at its rich flavor but also at its smoothness. Definitely not the rotgut variety he was more accustomed to in back-trail Mexico. "That is good stuff." He threw back the rest of the shot. "Damn good."

"More?"

Prophet shook his head. "No, no." He ran the back of his hand across his mouth. "Now — regarding my question . . ."

Pilar gave a tolerant roll of her eyes. "*Sí,* regarding your *pregunta.*"

"Has an *americano* by the name of Ciaran Yeats ever passed through here? Some call him the Mad Major."

Pilar stared at him, expressionless, her lips ever so slightly parted.

"Big man, I think I was told," Prophet continued. "Thick mop of curly red hair,

265

curly beard, blue . . . eyes . . ."

He let his voice trail off because the girl's eyes had widened and glinted with emotion, her mouth opening until it formed nearly a perfect, wide circle. *"Shhh!"* She grabbed Prophet's arm to silence him and looked around as though certain she'd see someone eavesdropping, maybe poking his snooping head out from under the bed.

"Shhh!" she hissed again, turning to Prophet and pressing two fingers to her plump lips. "Don't you know that no one mentions that name around here? Not if they don't want their tongue cut out!"

Prophet's pulse quickened hopefully. "So, you have seen him."

Again, she squeezed his arm, as though it were his arm that was uttering the forbidden words. *"Shhh!"*

Keeping his voice down, Prophet said, "I'm pretty sure we're alone in here, Pilar." He glanced around the little, cluttered room. Every article of clothing in the girl's wardrobe appeared to be either on the floor or hanging from something. "If we're not alone, whoever's in here is pretty small. I bet I could squash him like a bug."

He'd meant to douse the girl's fear with humor, but she wasn't having any of it.

"Please, señor," she said, shaking her head

slowly, awfully. "I urge you not to mention el Mayor Loco's name down here. Not anywhere around here. He has spies everywhere. They will kill you in the most horrible ways."

"Please, Pilar," Prophet urged the girl, taking her hand gently in his. "I have to find him. He has taken another man's daughter. An innocent girl. Like yourself."

Pilar just stared at him with those round, fearful, dark eyes of hers and shook her head. "Don't be a fool. There is no finding . . . that man. If he gets wind you are looking for him, he will look for you. And he will find you."

Holding Prophet's gaze with a terrified one of her own, she slipped her hand back from his and made a slashing motion across her throat.

Again, he took her small, soft hand in his. "I won't mention his name again if you just tell me where he is."

Pilar looked around the room once more, her paranoia obviously acute. She looked at the door, stared at it for several seconds, pricking her ears as though certain someone was standing out in the hall, listening through the panel.

"No one's out there," Lou assured her. "We're alone. I won't tell anyone you told me. Just tell me where I can find him, and that'll be the last we speak of him."

She turned to Lou with a hard, shallow chuff of disgust. Keeping her voice just above a whisper, she said, "I don't know. How would I? But I do hear things."

"What have you heard?"

She drew a deep calming breath. So quietly that Prophet could barely hear, she said, "Baluarte Santiago."

Prophet frowned. "Can you . . ."

He stopped and lifted his head, listening.

He'd been so intent on the girl's words that he hadn't realized that the steady hum of conversation in the main drinking hall had fallen silent. So, too, had the strumming of the mandolin, which had been a steady accompaniment to his and the girl's conversation until . . .

When?

Just a few minutes ago?

He wasn't sure when the rest of the building had fallen silent, but it was silent, all right. Silent as church mice with the preacher on a holy tear.

The girl must have just then noticed it, too. She slapped a hand to her mouth in shock, her eyes wider and more terrified than before. Of course she was thinking that their little discussion of Ciaran Yeats had

268

caused it.

For a second or two, even Prophet thought so. But, no. There was no way anyone else in the building could have overheard his and the *puta*'s conversation.

His pulse quickening, he turned to the girl and pressed two fingers to his lips. Quietly, he rose from the bed and went to the door. He opened it a few inches, peering cautiously through the crack. Not seeing anyone outside the door, he drew it open farther, stuck his head out, and peered both ways along the hall.

Nothing.

Apprehension hung heavy on him. The cantina had gotten too quiet too quickly. It was so quiet he could hear his own heart beating.

He motioned for Pilar to stay where she was. She sat on the bed staring up at him with trepidation.

Prophet stepped into the hall and drew the door quietly closed behind him, wincing when the bolt slipped into place with a click that echoed in the silence. One hand on the horn handles of his .45, he moved up the hall in the direction of the stairs, the top of which he could barely see in the dim light. More light filtered up from the first floor, giving a watery glow. Under the circumstances it was an eerie sight — light sliding up from the forbidding silence below, like a poisonous fog.

Prophet stepped to his left and very lightly tapped on the door through which Roselle had pulled Colter. He could hear the murmurings of intimate conversation on the other side of the door. He didn't bother knocking. He turned the knob and poked his head into the room.

"Red . . ."

He stopped, staring into the room lit by three flickering candles. Colter was sprawled belly down on the bed, beside the brown-skinned *puta.* She lay on her back, head propped on two pillows. Colter was cradling her feet and chuckling as he counted off her little, brown toes. The girl was laughing and writhing as the redhead tickled her. They were both as naked as jaybirds.

Colter looked up at Prophet, scowling, instantly flushing with embarrassment. "Lou, what the — ?"

Prophet pressed two fingers to his lips. "Trouble!" he whispered.

"Huh?"

"Listen."

Colter raised his eyes to the ceiling, pricking his ears. "I don't hear nothin'."

"Yeah. I don't like the sound of it one bit."

Prophet glanced toward the stairs again then turned back to Colter. "Get dressed. We're pullin' foot. Fast!"

Colter scrambled off the bed as Lou pulled his head back into the hall and drew the door shut. He stood staring toward the stairs, keeping watch, listening, not hearing a thing. The silence was so heavy he should have been able to hear something down there on the main floor, but there wasn't even the sound of a man clearing his throat.

Prophet didn't mind silence. At least, most places he didn't mind it. Enjoyed it, in fact. Here, it meant trouble.

He remembered the *rurales* he'd seen when he and Colter had first entered La Princesa, and his heart gave a little hiccup and increased its pace.

Keeping his hand on the holstered .45, he stepped backward and to his right, moving lightly on the balls of his feet. He opened Pilar's door. Still sitting on the edge of the bed, the girl gasped with a start and clamped a hand over her mouth.

Prophet held up a placating hand. She stared at him from over the little brown hand she held over her mouth, a slight relief showing in her eyes.

"Is there a back door, honey?"

"Downstairs only," she whispered.

Prophet looked toward the window at the end of the hall, considering how far the drop to the yard would be. He didn't have time to think about it for more than a couple of seconds, because just then a creak came from the direction of the stairs.

CHAPTER 22

"Stay put," Lou told Pilar, though he doubted she needed the admonition.

He pulled her door closed again and, turning toward the stairs, slid his Peacemaker from its holster.

Another creak came from the stairs. It was followed by the very faint groan of a strained riser. He slowly clicked the Colt's hammer back. From behind Colter's door, Lou had been hearing the light thumps of the redhead stumbling around, hastily dressing. Now that door latch clicked.

As Colter began to draw the door open, a head slid into view at the top of the stairs. Prophet saw the red-trimmed gray collar of a *rurale* uniform and part of a sombrero dangling down the man's back by a neck thong. The *rurale*'s eyes focused on Prophet, and widened, and as he bolted up onto the second-floor hall, raising a pistol, Lou yelled, "Down, Red!"

273

The Peacemaker roared.

The bullet flew wide of the first *rurale* as a second *rurale* leaped onto the second-floor hall, inadvertently nudging the first man to one side. The first man fired, and then the second man fired, and then Prophet returned fire, and that bullet took the second man through the chest. Meanwhile, Colter had hurled himself onto the floor of the hall in front of Prophet, triggering his Remington and punching the first *rurale* straight back against the wall behind him.

The *rurale* cursed, dropped to his knees, and fell sideways down the stairs.

Yet another *rurale* leaped over the falling man and into the hall, extending two revolvers toward Prophet and Colter, who both fired at the same time, punching lead through the man's upper torso. He was thrown back against the wall, as well, triggering both pistols into the ceiling before falling sideways down the stairs, his body's heavy thumps joining those of the other man plunging toward the first-floor drinking hall.

"Let's go, Red!" Prophet ran forward, clicking his Colt's hammer back again.

"We gonna have to shoot our way out of here, you think?" Colter asked, scrambling to his feet and then running beside Prophet as they both made for the stairs.

"There's no door up here and the windows are a craps toss with the house rigged against us, so . . ."

"I reckon we'll be shootin' our way out of here!"

"No problem," Prophet raked out as they gained the top of the stairs. "There's only three left. At the most, four!"

He thought he'd counted around a half-dozen *rurales* gambling at the table near the saloon's front wall.

Crouching with their smoking pistols extended, Prophet and Colter started down the stairs. As they took the steps slowly, one at a time, their index fingers pressed taut against their triggers, Lou could see more and more of the saloon spreading out before them.

It was vacant.

At least, it appeared that way. All that remained of the crowd that had been gathered there was the tobacco smoke wafting in the ragged spheres of light cast by a half-dozen lanterns and bracketed wall candles trying feebly to shoulder away the stubborn shadows of the night.

Lou and Colter dropped lower into the saloon . . .

When they were halfway down the stairs,

Prophet saw that two tables had been turned onto their sides. One was on the room's left side, near the one he and the redhead had occupied. The other one was on the room's right side, near the back. At the same moment he saw the overturned tables, two heads jerked up above the one on the right while one more head darted up from behind the one on the left.

Three pistols flashed and roared, the bullets tearing through the air around and between Lou and Colter, hammering the steps and the rails to each side. Prophet crouched, extending his Peacemaker in his right hand, and returned fire.

Colter leaped over the rail to his right as two bullets ripped wood from it. He hit the floor beside the stairs with a thud. A second later, he was throwing lead toward the table on the room's right side while Prophet, dropping down the steps, peppered the table shielding the other two *rurales* on the room's left side.

He was nearly to the floor when his Colt clicked on an empty chamber.

He cursed as more bullets cut the air around him. He leaped down the last three steps to the saloon hall floor and dropped behind a table near the bottom of the stairs. Immediately, he flicked open the Peacemaker's loading gate and began reloading.

In the corner of his right eye, he saw Colter do the same thing behind a chair just ahead of the bar. The redhead knocked over another chair to add additional cover.

"Yep, should have brought the Richards," the bounty hunter chided himself.

As Lou quickly shook the spent cartridges out of his Colt's wheel, letting them clatter onto the floor, bullets hammered the top of the table behind which he crouched, throwing slivers onto his hat. They threw glass shards from the glasses and bottles that had been left on the table after the drinking hall had been hastily vacated, the other customers apparently realizing what had been about to happen and not wanting to get caught in a cross fire.

One of the *rurales* shouted in heavily Spanish-accented English, "You crossed over again, Lou! No, no, no — I told you not to do that!"

Prophet flinched as a sliver of glass cut into his cheek. Brushing it away, he said, "Well, well — Lieutenant Oscar Ruiz! Is it really you, you chili-chompin' old polecat?"

Ruiz must have gestured for the others to hold their fire, for the shooting died abruptly.

"It is me, Lou! Have you missed me, you

old Confederate?"

"I thought I recognized that ugly face of yours. You still look like an old rattlesnake that tangled with a rabid coyote!"

"I will give you that, Lou! And you yourself still resemble what the banker's sick dog leaves on a neighbor's porch!"

Prophet punched a cartridge into the wheel's sixth chamber, flicked the loading gate home, and spun the cylinder. "I been called that an' worse from better'n you!"

"You might as well give yourselves up — you and your tattooed friend — or I will nail your hides to the wall!"

"Go back to sleep and keep dreamin', Oscar!" Colter shouted, adding his own two cents to the palaver.

"Is that your tattooed friend, Lou?"

"That's him, all right!"

"What's his name?"

Colter jerked his left hand up and fired two rounds toward where Oscar Ruiz was poking his head up above his table. Ruiz cursed as he jerked his head back down behind the table. He cursed again, his voice shrill with fury.

"That's his name, Oscar," Prophet yelled with a laugh. "You think you can remember it?"

"He damn near shot my ear off!" Ruiz bellowed. "For that, I am going to cut both of his off — after I have killed him very slowly — and wear them both on a string around my neck for the rest of my life! I will be *buried* with them!"

"Careful, Oscar," Prophet warned. "Red's got a temper."

"I don't appreciate being bushwhacked," Colter yelled at the *rurale*. "Especially not when I'm funnin' with a purty *puta*!"

Prophet glanced at his partner, frowning. "What the hell *were* you doin', anyway, kid? Pardon my curiosity."

Colter blushed, shrugged. "How do you know this fella, Lou?"

"Oscar and I tangled over in Sonora a time or two. He don't like it when gringo bounty hunters cross 'his' border after bounties on 'his' Mexican cutthroats. Leastways, he don't like it when gringo bounty hunters balk at sharing said bounties on Mexican cutthroats . . . *with him. ¿Comprende?*"

"Is it so much I ask?" Ruiz said in a tone of mock injury. "To be respected by foreigners on my own soil?"

"See, it's 'his' soil," Prophet said. "Now do you understand why it's impossible to get along with this jackass?"

"Some folks are contrary that way," Colter said.

"What happened to your face, you ugly gringo shaver?" Ruiz asked. "Did your horse of a mother kick you after she dropped you?" He wheezed a high, mocking laugh.

"That tears it!" Colter bolted up from behind his table.

"No!" Prophet shouted. "That's what he wants you —"

His warning was cut off by Ruiz's own gunfire. The *rurale* lieutenant had been ready to spring, waiting for the kid to show himself, and now he did just that as Colter's shoulders cleared his covering table. Ruiz's first bullet punched into Colter's left arm, sending the redhead stumbling back against the bar, dropping his Remy and gritting his teeth.

Ruiz's second bullet punched into Colter's left thigh, making Colter give a sharp yowl of pain as well as anger.

Ruiz was about to put another bullet into the young redhead when Prophet, trying to ignore the bullets being thrown at him by the other two *rurales,* swung his Peacemaker up over his table, aimed hastily, and fired. He was happy to see Ruiz slap a hand to his neck, trying to stem the flow of blood from it, just before the man dropped back down behind his table.

He howled a curse that echoed even above the gunfire.

As a bullet fired by one of the other two *rurales* on Lou's side of the room seared a hot line across the outside of his neck, Prophet set his Colt down, grabbed an edge of his covering table, and pulled it over on its side. Broken glass from glasses and bottles came crashing down to the floor in front of him, spilled liquor soaking his trouser knees.

Bullets punched into the table with loud smashing barks.

Lou crawled to his left, pulled another table down, and crouched behind it as bullets hammered into it and the contents from its top crashed around him, glass and liquor tumbling onto his hat.

He bulled the table out ahead of him, using it for a shield as he crawled at an angle across the saloon floor, pulling down yet another table and using it, too, for cover as he crabbed even farther forward and toward the saloon's left wall. He pulled down another table, and another . . . until he'd worked his way around the left side of the two shooters. As the two *rurales* fired into his current covering table, Prophet snaked his right arm over the top of the table and aimed at the two men who'd turned toward him, eyes wide in shock.

They were both fully exposed, and they knew it.

They both swore and, aiming their pistols at him — they must have had at least two, possibly three, apiece — clicked the hammers back. They'd thrown all the lead they were going to throw for one lifetime, however.

Prophet had the drop.

Quirking a devilish grin, Lou let two bullets fly and then three, four, and five for good measure, making sure that both *rurales,* who were writhing on their backs, swinging their arms and kicking their legs, would never get up again. He saved the sixth pill in his wheel for Oscar Ruiz, who appeared to still be breathing where he lay on the other side of the room, head propped against the base of the far wall.

Lou rose heavily. He was wet from the drinks spilled from the tables he'd knocked over. He was also peppered with glass, and a few playing cards stuck to the wet spots on his clothes. He glanced at Colter, who sat back against the bar, clutching his left arm and wincing. The kid had lost his hat and his long hair hung over one eye.

"You still kickin', Red?"

"Just not so high."

"I'll be right over."

Prophet walked over to where Lieutenant Oscar Ruiz lay against the wall. The man had his left hand pressed to his neck. The hand was all red from the blood that had poured out of him. He held a Smith & Wesson New Model No. 3 revolver in his right hand, on the floor. The top-break gun was partway open and covered in blood. Apparently, he'd started reloading the weapon but weakness from blood loss had kept him from finishing.

Ruiz glared up at Prophet, flaring his nostrils. He flared them wider and squinted one eye as he began raising the Smith & Wesson, also called a "Russian." He pressed the barrel against the floor, closing the gun with a click, but before he could raise it any higher, Prophet pressed his left boot down on it, pinning it and the man's hand to the floor.

"*¡Bastardo!*" Ruiz yelled, though in his depleted state it was more of a rasp.

Prophet raised his Peacemaker, aiming down the barrel at the lieutenant's head. "Maybe see you down below, Lieutenant," Lou said with a grim smile.

Ruiz turned his head slightly, eyelids fluttering as he awaited the bullet with dread.

"There are more where I came from, Lou." He tried a mocking, satisfied smile to go with the faint singsong in his voice.

"Then you'll be in good company." Prophet's Peacemaker bucked.

Ruiz's head bounced off the wall then settled back at an angle against it, the man's eyes rolling up in their sockets, his tongue sliding to one corner of his mouth. His chest sank as his last breath left him, and he lay still.

CHAPTER 23

Prophet turned away from the dead lieutenant and walked over to where Colter lay against the bar. The redhead appeared to have been hit in his left arm and his left thigh. "How bad?"

"I just need to collect myself. Give me a minute."

"You hotheaded fool!"

Colter grunted, winced. "My ma . . . she died in a plague. Along with my pa. I take it personal when her name is mentioned unfavorably. It ain't a joke to me, ya see, Lou."

"Yeah, well, you just got a case of lead poisoning to go with your thin skin. Christalmighty, anyway — you're damn lucky you ain't dead!"

"Am I?" Colter seemed to find some humor in that, albeit a gallows humor. He smiled and his eyes glinted. He was no more afraid of death than Louisa was . . .

285

Prophet spied movement in the upper periphery of his vision. He jerked back from the bar while casting his gaze behind it. The middle-aged barman with the curlicue mustache and wide green silk tie stood facing him, quickly raising his hands to show he wasn't armed. *"Por favor, señor —* do not shoot me!"

Prophet had raised the Colt and clicked the hammer back — a benign gesture since the gun was empty. Realizing that fact just then, he automatically clicked the loading gate open and started emptying the spent cartridges onto the floor. "You spooked me, amigo."

"Señor," the barman said, "Lieutenant Ruiz was not lying. He rode into town with a sizable contingent. He and these men you killed came here to La Princesa . . . but there are just as many, maybe more, who rode over to Doña Fernando's *burdel* just up the trail to the west." He canted his head to his left. "They no doubt heard the shooting, which means they will be here to investigate quickly."

"Ah hell!"

Prophet punched the last load into his Peacemaker's wheel, clicked the loading gate home, and spun the cylinder before dropping the piece into its holster. He reached down and grabbed Colter's right arm. "Time to rise an' shine, kid. We got no time to shilly-shally."

Colter cursed as Prophet hoisted the young man to his feet. "I'm fine, I'm fine," Colter insisted, setting his hat on his head.

"The blood comin' out of you says otherwise," Prophet said. "Just the same, we gotta fog some sage."

The redhead was obviously in pain, so Lou looked at the barman and said, "Give me a bottle for the road — will you, amigo?"

"*Sí, sí,* That will be three of your American dollars, señor."

"Horse hockey — I left nearly a fresh bottle I paid ten dollars for upstairs. Hand me over more of the same. Damn good painkiller."

The Mexican scowled at Prophet then turned to pluck a bottle off the back bar. He set it briskly down on the bar and fingered the right curlicue of his big, ridiculous-looking mustache, giving Lou the woolly eyeball. Prophet grabbed the bottle with one hand and wrapped his other arm around Colter's waist, turning him toward the open door. "Onward, Red. Time to do-si-do — the girls is waitin'."

"I'm fine, Lou. Really."

He wasn't walking fine. In fact, he was

walking as stiff as a ninety-year-old ex–fur trapper with the chilblains in his knees. Prophet kept a tight grip on his waist as he led him through the door.

The crowd that had been reveling inside the saloon earlier was gathered in several loose groups out front of the brush ramada. The doxies who'd been working the floor formed a tighter group off the ramada's right end. They and the customers regarded the two *americanos* warily, stepping back away from the two men as though they were afraid to catch a bout of the same lead poisoning Colter had.

"All's well, amigos . . . señoritas," Prophet said as he led Colter over to where their horses were tied at the far end of the third hitchrack. "You can all go back to havin' fun now. Just a little hiccup is all . . ."

He chuckled dryly at that as he led Colter between Mean and Ugly and Colter's coyote dun, heading toward Colter's left stirrup. He paused to stare carefully west, happy not to see any more dove gray uniforms bearing down on him. Maybe he and the redhead would get lucky, and the other *rurales* were three sheets to the wind . . . or otherwise preoccupied . . . and hadn't heard the gunfire. He helped the young man into the saddle, Colter grimacing and shaking against the obvious pain.

"As soon as we can," Prophet told him, throwing him his horse's reins from the hitchrack, "we'll hole up and I'll tend them wounds for you, get some painkiller into you."

"Like I said, Lou," said the redhead, sitting straight-backed in the saddle, "I'm fine."

"Humor me." Prophet wrapped some burlap around his bottle, dropped it into a saddlebag pouch, then swung up onto Mean's back.

He neck-reined the mount out into the street. Again, he glanced west. Still, it was all clear. "Let's go!" he rasped, and booted Mean to the west.

Colter did the same to his coyote dun. As the horse lunged forward into a gallop, Lou heard Colter give an agonized groan.

They ran the horses hard for nearly a mile.

The trail was wide this close to the La Bachata where it was likely well traveled, and it was lit by the stars and the light of a sickle moon kiting about halfway up the lilac sky to the east. When the trail narrowed and grew rocky, Prophet pulled Mean off the trace, to the right, and headed south for the murky darkness showing between two milky buttes.

He glanced behind. Colter was behind him but not as close as before, and the kid was sitting sort of loose in the saddle, his head wobbling. He held his reins with one hand, but his chin was down. Prophet thought the redhead was mostly just letting Northwest follow the leader — Lou and Mean and Ugly.

Worry touched Prophet. He wasn't accustomed to worrying about anyone but himself. Sometimes Louisa. But mostly himself. He didn't like the way it felt, because worry fogged the mind and just plain didn't feel good. The truth was, he'd come to like the scar-faced redhead, and he'd feel even worse if the kid up and died on him. He'd probably feel worse about Colter Farrow's death than the redhead would himself.

They had to stop soon. Lou just wanted to make sure they were far enough off the trail that the *rurales* wouldn't find them if they came looking, that they wouldn't spy the fire he and Colter were going to need to get the kid's wounds cleaned and stitched properly.

The gap between the buttes doglegged first to the left and then to the right. When the gap ended, the buttes drifting off behind, Lou followed a sandy wash for another quarter mile or so between six-foot-high banks of crumbling sandstone. Finally, when he judged they were surrounded by enough cover in the form of rocks, boulders, and bristling desert chaparral that it would take a damn good tracker to find them in the dark, he drew rein and swung down from Mean's back.

He turned to look behind him. Colter wasn't back there.

Dread touched Prophet. He had a brief, imagined glimpse of the kid lying dead on the ground beside his horse. Lou began walking back the way he'd come but stopped when he heard a horse whicker. Hooves thudded softly. A shadow moved, growing until it became a horse and a rider. Colter was slumped forward across Northwest's neck. He looked bad as hell. He looked damned miserable.

Prophet hurried forward and met the horse about thirty feet from where he'd ground-reined Mean and Ugly. He reached up and placed a hand on Colter's shoulder. "Which side of the sod you on, Red?"

His voice must have startled Colter out of a semi-doze. He jerked, lifted his head. "You worry like an old woman!"

"Come on — I'll help you down."

"Quit mother-hennin' me, damnit. I'm fine."

Prophet pulled the younger man out of the saddle, eased him to the ground. "Yeah, I know you are. I've never seen anyone look so good. Just the same, why don't we set you down over here and you try to stay awake while I gather wood and build a fire?"

Prophet helped Colter onto the ground near the bank of the wash. He retrieved the new bottle from his saddlebags, removed the burlap, and brought the bottle over to the redhead. He popped the cork and handed the bottle to the kid. "Take a couple pulls of that."

"Are you kiddin'? I'm still sick from Don de la Paz's pulque."

"Hair of the dog that bit ya."

Weakly, Colter took the bottle, and then Prophet wandered off in search of wood for a fire. Fifteen minutes later, he had that fire burning a little too brightly. The wood he'd gathered was tinder dry, and he'd included some brush in it, just to make sure it went. It went, all right, so that now he looked out from the pulsating glow, hearing the windy, crackling sound of the flames, wondering how far away the conflagration might be visible.

"Christalmighty, Lou," Colter scolded.

"You roastin' a buffalo?"

"I admit I overdone it a little."

Colter scowled and leaned back from the heat. The horses whickered where they stood ground-reined and sidled away.

"It'll burn down soon," Prophet said, taking a knee beside his trail partner. "Now, let me see how much damage old Ruiz did to you, kid."

"Oh, leave me be, Lou," Colter complained. "I'm . . ."

"Yeah, I know, you're fine. Now, hold still or I'm gonna tattoo ya with my pistol butt!"

"Mother damn hen is what you are . . ." Colter took a pull from the bottle.

Prophet did a quick inspection of the younker's wounds, relieved to find that neither one was too severe. They'd be sore for a while, but they were mostly just bad burns, the one in the arm a little worse than the one on the thigh. Both bullets had punched out some flesh, but Prophet was able to clean the wounds with some cloth from his saddlebags with little problem.

He sutured the one in Colter's arm, only wrapped the one in his leg. The arm wound took six stitches, and the kid didn't even flinch when the needle went in.

Prophet had a feeling this wasn't the redhead's first rodeo. Colter Farrow couldn't hold more than a teaspoonful of alcohol, but he'd probably sported enough lead over the years that if all melted down would have supplied ammo for a small army. That might be a slight exaggeration, he opined with a wry chuff as he pulled the last stitch taut, but the kid had ridden the wild 'n' woolly — there was no doubt about that.

Too bad about that tattoo on his cheek. That was the wound that grieved him most and likely would till they fitted him for his wooden overcoat . . .

"Stop starin' at me, Lou," the redhead cajoled him, lowering the bottle after taking another pull.

Prophet jerked his head away. He was putting his sewing kit back together and hadn't realized he'd been staring. "Helkatoot."

"You know what hurts more than someone lookin' at me like I'm a dog with a dead snake in its teeth?"

"No, I don't, but I reckon you're gonna tell me."

"Someone lookin' at me with pity in his eyes."

"Hell, Red."

"There you have it."

Feeling about as low as a sidewinder, Prophet returned his sewing kit to his saddlebags. "Let me get these hayburners tended and staked out, an' I'll put some beans on the fire."

"Forget it." Colter set the bottle down and heaved himself to his feet. It was an awkward maneuver at best. Not only was he sore as hell from the wounds and then having them stitched, he'd chugged down a good third of the mezcal, by Prophet's estimation. Setting his boots under him carefully, the redhead strode over to his own mount and grabbed the reins. Slurring his words slightly, he said, "The day I can't tend my own corn grinder is the day they plant me."

"All right," Prophet said, stripping his saddle from Mean and Ugly's back. "It's your plantin'."

As he tended the hammerheaded dun, he couldn't help keeping an anxious eye on his wounded but defiant young partner, hoping he didn't get his feet entangled and fall and thus open those wounds. Colter managed all right, though. He was a picture of angry insolence and boldness, stripping the tack from his mount, thoroughly rubbing it down with a scrap of burlap from his saddlebags, then filling his hat with water and setting it on the ground where the dun could drink.

He stood a little uncertainly beside the

horse, patting its withers but also furtively steadying himself as Northwest drew water from the hat. When the horse had had its fill, Colter picketed the mount where grass grew up along the edge of the wash, tying its halter rope to a picket pin, giving it room to move around as it foraged.

Prophet was already back to the fire when the kid stumbled into the camp, looking drawn and weary, his hair in his eyes. He practically tripped over the toes of his boots, his spurs ringing loudly. He dropped to his knees where he'd piled his gear and unrolled his soogan, his hands fumbling with the leather straps.

Prophet had started to make supper, but he needed a drink first. He picked up the bottle from where the kid had left it, popped the cork, and held it out. "Need a little more painkiller?"

Colter shook his head, cursing as he continued to fumble with his soogan's straps. Prophet wanted to help the younger man, but he didn't want to offend him further.

Finally, Colter got the straps untied. He rolled out his soogan and then knelt, staring down at the bedroll for a moment before looking across the fire, which had burned down considerably, at Prophet.

"Sorry about snapping at you, Lou. I was just bein' a sorehead. I was feeling sorry for myself."

"You got a right."

"That was the busthead talkin'. Go easy on that stuff. It's got some pop to it. I'm seein' two of everything, and three of you."

"Hell, one's too many of me."

Colter plopped down on his soogan, resting his head back against the woolly underside of his saddle. He snaked his arm across his forehead and lay staring up at the fire's cinders that glowed until they turned to gray ashes against the black velvet sky.

Prophet took a long pull from the mezcal bottle. Good stuff. It instantly filed the edges off this trying day. He took another drink and then looked at the redhead lying there staring up at the sky. Colter was thinking about something.

Or someone.

Lou decided to play a hunch and risk sticking his foot in his mouth again. What the hell? He was used to the taste of boot leather.

"Say, Red, can I ask you a personal question?"

"Try me."

"Did you leave a girl back in them mountains?"

297

Colter continued to stare at the sky. "Yeah." In fact, it was she he was thinking about. But, then, Prophet likely knew that. Marianna Claymore was her name. "We were gonna be married. That was three years ago now. She married someone else. Has a little boy."

"That's tough."

"It's the way it is."

"Still, it's tough."

Colter turned his head to scowl at the big man lounging on the other side of the fire. "Damnit, I'm tryin' not to feel sorry for myself anymore!"

"Good night, Red."

"Night," Colter grouched, then rolled over and folded his arms across his chest. He must have fallen instantly asleep, for he started breathing deeply, slowly, each breath rattling in his throat.

"Still, it's tough," Lou repeated quietly to himself, and took another deep pull off the bottle.

He took another pull . . . and another. He looked at the bottle. There were two bottles now before him, along with two of his own hands holding it though he was sure he was holding it with only his right hand. So he was seeing two bottles held by two right hands before him.

"Damn good stuff," he repeated, his words garbled even in his own ears. "But the younker was right. Goes down smooth then kicks like a mule . . ."

He finished off the bottle but didn't remember even setting it down after his last pull before a thick veil of sleep closed over him. He woke with a dull ache in his head. His tongue felt like a dried-up snake in his mouth. He opened his eyes then quickly closed them again, for harsh sunlight assaulted him, feeling like miniature, razor-edged spears stabbing his eyes.

The sunlight reflected off the red desert sand and gravel only inches from his face.

Wait. Something was wrong. His face shouldn't be that close to the gravel, nor in the position it seemed to be in.

He slitted his eyelids, looked around against the painful assault of the bright desert light. He saw ants toiling in the sand around him, just inches away from his eyes. They were so close he could see their itty-bitty little heads and feet, their itty-bitty little threadlike bodies.

He tried to rise.

No doing.

He couldn't move his arms or his legs. They were weighed down, held taut against him. He couldn't even move his fingers.

He was dreaming, of course. It was one of those dreams where you try to talk but your tongue is too heavy, and you try to move but your limbs are too heavy, too.

As his eyes adjusted in small increments to the light's vengeful assault, his heart thudded and cold blood pooled in his belly. He was not dreaming.

A silent scream ripped through his head, deafening him.

The reason the ground looked so close, including the many little ants . . . and the reason he couldn't move a damn thing on his body . . . was because he'd been planted up to his neck in the desert!

CHAPTER 24

Voices rose around Prophet. He could barely hear them above the horrified screeching in his own ears. His lifted his eyes from the ground that was snugged up close to his chin and saw several men milling around him.

Several men in the dove gray uniforms of *rurales* . . .

Of all the rotten luck.

One was looking at him. This man turned and said something in Spanish to the others and which Prophet translated as, "Look over here — this one's awake." Or some such.

Several others turned toward Prophet from where they were milling around nearby, holding tin cups in their hands. Prophet saw smoke billowing around the *rurales* and then, sliding his eyes to his left, saw that some animal was spitted over a fire. It looked like a javelina. It smelled like one, too. The smell of roasting wild pig would have smelled more savory had Prophet not woken to find himself buried up to his pea-pickin' neck.

More men were sitting or lounging around the fire, and now they rose heavily to move in close to where Prophet's head stuck up out of the ground like a sandy-haired turnip. Squinting as he gazed straight out before him, he saw that his was not the only head poking up out of the ground. The red head straight out before him, facing him from maybe ten feet away, belonged to Colter Farrow.

As the *rurales* closed around Prophet, panic swept through him, his heart racing. He desperately tried to move his arms and legs, but it was as though he were swathed in cement.

One of the *rurales* walked up to him. He was tall with a thick salt-and-pepper mustache and goatee. His face was long and very dark and the deep-sunk eyes were small, black chips of obsidian. He was not wearing the traditional tunic in this heat but only a sweat-stained gray undershirt and red suspenders that held his gray wool trousers up on his broad hips.

"Ah hell," Prophet said, crestfallen. "Sergeant Casal . . . long time, no hear from.

You should write more. We were getting worried back home." He sounded much less anxious than he felt. Being buried alive was the stuff of nightmares. But wailing about it in front of these Mexicans would only add insult to injury, and probably even more torment, as well.

Sergeant Alonzo Casal usually rode with Lieutenant Ruiz. In the back of his mind, Prophet had wondered about Casal when he hadn't seen him with Ruiz. Now he knew that the man had likely been one of the group that had gone over to the hurdy-gurdy house to get their ashes hauled while the lieutenant gambled in La Princesa.

Casal tipped up the clear bottle in his hand and took a long drink. He pulled the bottle down, smacked his lips, wiped the hand holding the bottle across his mouth, and smiled at Prophet. The sergeant's eyes flashed drunkenly from the tarantula juice. "Lou, how are you, *mi amigo?*"

"Me?" Prophet tried to shrug but he couldn't move his shoulders. "Fine as frog hair split four ways. Yourself?"

"Well, to be honest, Lou, it would take some pretty sour luck for me to be in worse condition than you, my friend."

"Nah!"

Casal nodded soberly though his eyes

were far from sober. *"Sí, amigo.* I think so. A few more shovelfuls of sand and you'll be all covered up in *madre tierra."*

"Ashes to ashes, dust to dust," Prophet said. "I'm at home right here."

A whiptail lizard ran past Prophet, about four inches from his chin, and made a little trail in the sand before it disappeared in some brush to the bounty hunter's left.

Casal chuckled. The other *rurales* — there were around ten or so, by Prophet's quick, distracted count — looked on with the dubious expressions of men who weren't quite able to follow the English that Prophet and Casal were speaking. Maybe a couple did, judging by their knowing smiles, but most hadn't followed, Prophet thought, though he had far more important things to think about . . . worry about . . . at the moment.

"Can I ask you a question, Sergeant?"

"Sure, sure, *mi amigo.* Ask me anything. That is what I am here for — to answer your foolish gringo questions."

Things hadn't gone well lately for Lou and Colter Farrow, and it didn't look like they were going to get any better real soon. The sergeant's tone had been nothing less than peevish.

Prophet narrowed one eye as he stared up at the *rurale* scowling down at him. "How in the . . . how did you manage to . . ."

"Locate you and bury you?" Casal grinned, showing several rotten teeth. "As you slept like little babies . . . ?" He canted his head against his bottle and briefly closed his eyes, pantomiming a sleeping infant.

"I don't remember a damn thing last night, after . . . I . . ." Now it was starting to come clear. "After I finished that bottle of stump juice."

"Gringos should never drink Señor Anaya's mezcal, *cabrón!*"

"Now ya tell me."

"Spiked." The word had sounded like a croak. At first, Prophet thought it had been croaked out by one of the *rurales*. But, no. It had come from straight out in front of him. Colter had croaked out the single word. The redhead's eyes were open; he was squinting into the sun in the same way Prophet was.

"The barman," Prophet said. "Gave us a bad bottle."

"*Sí, sí,*" said the sergeant. "You see — Señor Anaya sells spiked liquor to gringos so that his *putas* can rob them after they pass out. The poison is Señor Anaya's dear mama's concoction. It contains all sorts of nasty stuff, including the oil of a rare poisonous mushroom, if I remember correctly. Men have been known to go blind before they die. You see, robbing gringos was a sideline for Anaya's *madre,* an old *bruja.* That stuff creeps up on you very slowly, but then — *wham*! — you are out like a blown lamp. The *putas* usually cut the gringos' throats and then Anaya carts them into the desert and tosses them to the pumas."

"Gee," Lou said, squinting over at Colter. "Pilar and Roselle both seemed so nice."

"You really angered Señor Anaya last night, Lou," the sergeant continued. "It was the mess you made. So much blood! *¡Tanta sangre!* As soon as we rode over after hearing the gunfire, he sicced us on you right away. He didn't even demand his cut!"

Casal laughed delightedly through his teeth. "When we rode up on you, your horses were going wild but you two were really sawing logs. When we got close, following your tracks, it was your snoring that finally led us to you. And then the whinnies of your horses as they tried to wake you two gringo fools!"

The sergeant threw his head back and laughed some more. The other *rurales* laughed, as well, though Prophet doubted they knew what they were laughing about.

When the laughter died, Casal stared

angrily down at Prophet again. He straightened, stepped to one side, then pulled his right boot back. He shot the boot forward, slamming its toe into Prophet's left ear.

"Ow!"

Casal turned toward Colter. He stared angrily down at the redhead for a moment, then walked over to him and kicked his right ear.

"Ow!" Colter said.

"There," Casal said. "That is what I think of you two!" He staggered around as he regaled his prisoners, shuttling his gaze between Lou and Colter, holding his bottle almost tenderly in the crook of one arm. "You come into my country without permission, and you shoot Lieutenant Ruiz and our fellow *rurales* and leave them in bloody piles on a cantina floor!"

Oh boy, Prophet thought. *This is going south fast . . . not that it was ever north.*

Casal squatted between the two men and to one side, where he could keep an eye on them both though neither was going anywhere. "Tell me, Lou, what are you doing down here, huh? Who are you chasing?"

"What makes you think I'm chasing anyone?"

"You're always chasing somebody, Lou. You are a bounty hunter!"

"I just came down here to enjoy your purty señoritas," Prophet said. "And to avoid that nasty weather we'll have up north in a month or two."

"No, no." Casal shook his head. "I don't believe you. If you were down here purely for the señoritas, you would either be over on the ocean or on the Sea of Cortez. That is where the purtiest señoritas are. And the most comfort. No, no. You are out here" — he looked around at the sun-blasted rocks and wiry brush and cactus — "on this blister on *el diablo*'s ass . . . and that means you are on the trail of someone." He paused, focusing his bleary, drunken gaze on the bounty hunter. "Who? And . . . how much is on his head?"

Greed flashed in the *rurale*'s eyes.

"Ciaran Yeats," Colter said.

Prophet looked at his partner. Colter looked back at him. Prophet thought that Colter might have shrugged if shrugging were possible in their current states, but instead Colter just stared back at him without expression.

Prophet supposed the kid had a point. What did they have to lose in their current unfortunate states for not telling the *rurales* whom they were after? Why keep getting assaulted by Casal's boot?

Casal looked for a moment as though he'd been slapped. He drew his head back sharply then frowned incredulously down at the redhead, who rolled his eyes up and to one side, to regard the man standing over him.

"Who did you say you were after?" the sergeant said.

"Ciaran Yeats," Colter said, a tad slower this time.

Casal stared down at him. He slid his frowning gaze to Prophet. "Yeats?"

Prophet didn't say anything.

Casal shuttled his gaze between Lou and Colter once more. "You two are after the Mad Major?"

Prophet gave a wooden smile.

"The two of you," Casal said as though not believing a word of it. "You two gringos . . . alone . . . are going after Ciaran Yeats . . ."

"You want us to draw you a picture, amigo?"

Prophet glared at the redhead. He didn't say anything, but his eyes were shouting, *Shut up, ya damn fool!*

"A picture?" Casal glowered at Colter. "Why would I want you to draw me a picture? Of Yeats?"

Apparently, while the sergeant's English

was nearly fluent, he didn't have a good command of sarcasm. Which was damned lucky for Colter Farrow, and likely for Lou Prophet, as well.

"You know the hombre, I take it?" Prophet asked, changing the subject.

Casal bunched his lips and tipped his head to one side in a shrug of sorts. "I know him well enough to know that you two are crazy to think that you . . . *just the two of you* . . . are going to capture Ciaran Yeats." Chuckling, he turned to his men, most of whom were standing around behind him now, trying to follow the conversation — to no avail, it appeared. For most of them, at least. In Spanish, he informed them what Lou Prophet and his scar-faced amigo were up to down here in Baja.

They all looked from Lou to Colter, and broke out in unrestrained laughter.

Casal laughed, too. When he stopped laughing, he drained his bottle then threw it against a rock, smashing it. The violent movement nearly caused him to trip over his own feet and fall. He regained his balance at the last second, and, wobbling around drunkenly, he turned to Prophet and said, "Do you know how many men Major Yeats has *around* him, Lou?"

"I'm betting quite a few."

"*Sí, sí.* Quite a few. Quite a damn few!"

"You know where he is, Sergeant?"

Again, Casal shrugged. "*Sí,* I know where he is. It is the *rurales'* business to know where *everyone* is . . . once they cross the border into Méjico." He'd added that last part loudly, with meaning, his eyes nearly crossing with disdain for his foreign visitors.

Prophet had a feeling that not only did Casal know where Yeats and his men . . . and Alejandra de la Paz . . . were holed up, but that the *rurales* were in league with Yeats's bunch. How else would an American army major survive so long in Mexico, running off his leash with his small army of American men, than by sharing the fruits of his nefarious doings with the *rurales* and the *federalistas* and anyone else in positions of power down here?

"You know what I think, Lou?" Casal asked.

"I got a feelin' you're gonna tell me."

"I think you are a very stupid man. I used to think you were shrewd and slippery and even smart in the way that you knew how to make money where most other men wouldn't see the slightest opportunity. But this . . . this tells me you are very stupid. To think that you and El Rojo over there" — he pointed at Colter — "are going to ride

311

into my country and capture a close friend of mine and — what? — take him back across the border and turn him in for any bounty he may have on his head? That tells me you are in fact *eres un pendejo de mierda*!"

"Oh, he has plenty of money on his head," Prophet said. But he was really wishing now that Colter hadn't brought up Ciaran Yeats. It hadn't occurred to him that the *rurales* were likely in league with the Mad Major from California, but he should have. It only made sense.

Yeah, this whole little mess just got a whole lot messier. This hole Lou was standing in was likely his grave. A few more shovelfuls of sand, and . . . *dust to dust.*

He doubted, however, that Casal was a close friend of Yeats. Ruiz, maybe. But not Casal. Not the lowly, dog-faced sergeant, a notorious tequila drunk even by Mexican standards. A man like Yeats wouldn't give the time of day to Sergeant Casal.

"You know what, Lou?" Casal said.

"I got a feelin' you're gonna tell me."

"I think I'm going to leave you right there to die slowly in the sun."

"I was thinkin' maybe we could discuss other options."

"No, no. I think I am going to leave both

you silly gringos right here in the sand. It is the just punishment for two gringo fools who have come down here seeking riches in such foolish ways, not to mention that you killed Lieutenant Ruiz." Casal clucked and shook his head, feigning sadness. "That was very unfortunate, Lou. Very unfortunate to kill such a wonderful man."

Prophet quelled the urge to laugh at the sergeant's poor acting. Casal wasn't grieving Ruiz's demise. Casal was the lowest kind of man there was — the kind that didn't give a damn about anything except lining his own pockets. He'd come after Ruiz's killers only because it was expected that he do so. And because doing so might get him promoted a rank or two.

"Hey, that's my hoss!" Colter yelled suddenly.

The redhead was staring off to his right, Prophet's left. One of the *rurales* was holding Northwest's reins and trying to climb onto the coyote dun's back. The horse wasn't having it, however. He was pitching and sidestepping. The *rurale* was furious, slashing the horse's snout with a leather quirt and cursing at the tops of his lungs.

"Stop it!" Colter bellowed though it didn't come out very loudly. There was something about being buried that kept a fella from being able to raise his voice. "Stop it, damn you! That's no way to treat a horse!"

Casal kicked Colter's ear again.

"Ow!"

"Who is this scar-faced gringo, Lou?" Casal asked Prophet. "He is as ugly as *el diablo*'s dog."

"That there is Colter Farrow."

Colter shouted — or at least tried to shout — "You tell that son of a bitch to stop beating my horse or so help me . . ."

Casal laughed. "He's got spirit doesn't he?"

"Yes . . . yes, he does," Prophet remarked. Then, seeing a man carrying Lou's own saddle out of the camp, intending to place it on another horse standing nearby, rage burned through the bounty hunter's veins. "Hey, that's my saddle!" The man carrying his saddle also had Prophet's Richards coach gun slung over his shoulder.

Yet another *rurale* was spinning Prophet's Colt Peacemaker on his finger and grinning mockingly.

More fury boiled through Prophet. "Thievin' devils!" he bellowed, or tried to bellow.

"Shut up!" Casal kicked Prophet's left ear.

"Ow!"

"You have no more use for your belongings," Casal said. "Not to worry. We will put it all to good use. Your horse, however . . ."

Casal had turned to gaze toward where Mean and Ugly stood a distance from camp. Mean didn't look happy. He stood glaring at the gray-clad interlopers. He resembled an angry bull, his bridle reins drooping, head down, his ears peeled back against his skull. His tail was arched. His large, copper eyes were ringed with white, and they flashed fire. Prophet thought he could even see smoke jetting from the enraged gelding's nostrils.

"Your horse, however . . ." Casal moved out away from Prophet and Colter. He slowly slid a long-barreled Smith & Wesson revolver from the holster hanging low on his right leg. "Your horse, however, is not only worthless . . . but quite dangerous."

"Leave that hoss alone, Casal!"

"What that horse needs is a bullet between his eyes," said the sergeant, raising the revolver and clicking back the hammer.

CHAPTER 25

"Don't you shoot my horse, you low-down pile of goat dung!" Prophet choked out.

Mean and Ugly glared at the drunk *rurale* staggering toward him. Casal dragged his heels across the gravelly ground, spurs ringing hoarsely. The sergeant extended the cocked, long-barreled pistol toward the lineback dun's head, the horse lowering his head still farther, crouching like a bareknuckle fighter, pawing the ground with his right front hoof.

"Casal!" Prophet wheezed.

As if echoing Prophet's own attempted yell, another voice bellowed, *"Casal?"*

The voice sounded like a frog's loud croak. It was amplified by the stony ridges surrounding the encampment where the pig still roasted, its juices popping and crackling where they dribbled onto the fire's flames. The single word, *Casal,* reverberated around the broad arroyo where it formed a bowl nestled between escarpments that Prophet hadn't seen in the darkness of the previous night.

Casal froze, looked around.

The other *rurales* did the same, looking up and around, trying to follow the echoing voice to its source.

"Casal, you dirty pig! You offal of a donkey and the afterbirth of a jackass!" The epithets, also croaked out in a loud, froglike voice in a dirty border version of Spanish mixed with English, were followed by the disembodied laughter of several men. The laughter came from several places amongst the rocks overlooking the encampment. The speaker laughed the loudest. It was almost an effeminate giggle punctuated by snorting guffaws. When the laughter stopped, the froglike voice said, "Put that gun down before I drill you a second hole through your hairy ass, Casal, and leave you sobbing for your mongrel cur of a mother!"

There was the loud, metallic ratcheting of a rifle being cocked.

"Prepare to die, you ugly dog!" the frog croaked again, this time more shrilly.

"Jack!" Casal wheeled, glaring up into the rocks, his eyes bright with rage mixed with fear. "Jack, is that you, you old man-turtle?"

Snorts and giggles drifted down from the rocks.

Casal wheeled again. "Jack!" he screeched, spittle flecking from his lips.

The other *rurales* had clawed pistols from their holsters or grabbed their rifles from around the fire and were looking around as wildly, as fearfully, as the sergeant.

"Jack!" Casal wailed.

Several fist-sized rocks tumbled down from a jagged rock wall. Casal swung his pistol toward them and fired, the gun's crack echoing loudly.

"Jack, show yourself, you little turtle!"

"Casal!" the froggy voice yelled again.

"Show yourself, Jack!" Casal wailed, dragging his spurs as he looked around in desperation, a thin tendril of gray smoke curling from his revolver's barrel. "Show yourself, you ugly little spider!"

More snorts and chuckles drifted down from the rocks.

"Prepare to shake hands with *el diablo,* Casal, you *hijo de puta*!"

"Jack!" Casal swung his revolver again and triggered another shot.

His shot was answered by another shot — this one from the rocks.

Casal's head jerked back. He staggered backward, his gun hand dropping to his side. He twisted around, spurs chinging. As he turned toward where Prophet's and Colter's heads sprouted from the sand, Lou saw a quarter-sized hole in the upper left center of the sergeant's forehead. Casal stumbled farther backward and then dropped to the ground and lay quivering about six feet to Prophet's left.

Prophet looked at Colter. Colter stared back at him, eyes wide.

Lou scrunched up his face in dread. *Ah hell . . .*

"*¡Mátalos!*" came a rumbling roar in Spanish from up high in the rocks. ("Kill them!")

The *rurales* began running in all directions, screaming. None took more than three or four steps, however, before rifles began crackling in the rocks around and above them.

Bullets peppered the scrambling *rurales,* punching through their gray tunics and spitting blood every which way. The *rurales* danced and hopped and skipped as though a band had just begun sawing a jovial tune, only this dance included tooth-gnashing screams and shrieks and shouted epithets as the dancers' legs crumpled and the dead men dropped in ragged, bloody piles on the ground around Prophet and Colter.

Because of his confined position, Prophet

couldn't see all of the *rurales,* but he could see enough to know that whoever was slinging lead at them from the surrounding scarps was doing fast, messy, but decisive work. Blood spurted past Prophet's left eye to stain the sand before him. Another spurt struck his left cheek and dribbled down his cheek to his unshaven jaw.

Ah hell . . .

A second later a *rurale* staggered toward him, holding both arms across his belly. He inadvertently kicked sand in Prophet's face. He dropped to the ground and rolled onto his back to lie belly up between Lou and Colter. He writhed, glanced at Lou, and lowered a bloody hand to the old Remington holstered on his left thigh. Keeping his pain-racked, angry eyes on Prophet, his lips stretched back from his teeth, the *rurale* slid the Remy from its holster. He cocked the weapon and extended it toward Lou's head.

"Nah," Prophet said, dragging the words out in a fateful drawl. "Don't do that . . ."

The *rurale* grinned and tightened his finger on the Remy's trigger. A bullet punched into the *rurale*'s right temple and tore out a fist-sized chunk of skull over his left ear as it exited and plunked into the now-bloody, brain-splattered ground. The *rurale* triggered the Remington, but the round flew over Prophet's head to spang off a rock behind him.

Prophet's ears rang. Beneath the ringing, he thought he heard the dwindling of the gunfire. He looked over the bloody carcass of the dead *rurale*. Colter was staring back at him, the redhead's lips pursed ironically. Colter also had a few blood splatters on his left cheek, over the Sapinero brand. Sand clung to it.

Prophet laughed. "You just can't beat Mexico for fun and adventure — can you, Red?"

Colter didn't respond. He was gazing at something over Prophet's head, something behind Lou and on his left. Because of the ringing in the bounty hunter's ears, he felt the reverberations of the approaching riders through the ground around him before he heard them. There must be a good dozen of them, judging by the mini shock waves assaulting his back and shoulders.

He grinned over the dead *rurale* again at Colter. "As they say in the opry houses, reload your pistols for act two!"

Colter kept his eyes on the riders approaching behind Prophet. Lou heard the drumming of the hooves beneath the slowly dwindling ringing in his ears. He saw the first rider in the corner of his left eye as the man rode up on that side of him, stopping his horse maybe ten feet away between the two all-but-interred gringos. Two then three then four then several more galloped into view, drawing back on their wide-eyed horses' reins and stopping abruptly to stare down at Lou and the redhead.

Prophet kept an eye on those frisky mounts' prancing hooves. A fella was never more vulnerable than when only his head was sticking up out of the earth.

His poor heart was drumming another frenetic rhythm.

Now, who have we . . . ?

The newcomers staring down at him were a rough-looking lot. About the only difference between them and the *rurales* was that these men weren't in uniform. As Prophet's sidelong gaze swept them, he thought he saw some gringos amongst them.

He shaped an affable grin and said, "How do!"

The newcomers looked at one another as they were still getting their horses settled down. A couple chuckled. One laughed loudly. Then one of them, chuckling, swung down from his saddle and dropped the reins of his whickering Arabian, called a *trigueño* for its three shades of brown. The mount was looking down skeptically at the two heads poking up out of the ground. Apparently, the horse had never seen such a bizarre spectacle as two heads growing in the desert.

Its rider ambled over toward Lou and Colter. The man was as odd a looking duck as Lou had ever laid eyes on. If he wasn't a dwarf, he'd missed being one by only an inch or so. Prophet doubted if the top of the man's head, beneath a black velvet, silver-trimmed, wagon-wheel sombrero, would come up much farther than the bounty hunter's belt buckle.

When Lou was standing aboveground, that was, and not inside it.

The short man was nearly as broad through the hips and shoulders as he was tall. He was severely bandy-legged. His boots must have been a size five or six; they were black and hand-tooled. He wore a fancily stitched bull-hide vest over a calico shirt, deerskin charro leggings, and a Colt .44 on his left hip, in the cross-draw position. The revolver appeared enormous on the man's round, child-sized body, which he must have had to have his clothes specially tailored for.

His face didn't go with his body at all. It was a buzzard face, with a long, hooked nose and two close-set, dark brown eyes.

323

Long, grizzled brown hair laced with gray hung down from beneath the sombrero, and a good bit of it poked out from the little man's ears, which were way too big for the rest of him. But, then, his head was also too big for the rest of him so maybe his ears didn't look so out of place, after all.

"What on God's green earth do we have here?" said the little man, stopping near Prophet and Colter, pinching his leggings up at the thighs then hunkering into a squat, leaning forward to rest his weight on the balls of his little boots. He'd spoken in fluent English though Prophet had a keen sense that he was the same man who'd spoken in fluent border Spanish from amongst the rocks overlooking the encampment.

The little man cut his amused, befuddled gaze between Prophet and Colter, chuckling. He was missing one upper front tooth. The other was crooked and brown.

Prophet's heart lightened a little as he gazed up at the little man and said, *"¿Americano, amigo?"*

The little man grinned down at Prophet. If his face was raptorial, his eyes were even more so, one of which was severely unmoored so that it listed to the inside corner of the socket. Both eyes owned the off-putting cast of unbridled lunacy. "In a roundabout way, I reckon. The name's John Brian Rynn-Douglas, don't ya know." He thumped himself in the chest with a thick little thumb. "Baja Jack, they call me down here!"

He gazed at Prophet, apparently waiting for recognition of his handle to show in Lou's eyes. When no sign of recognition came, the little man turned to Colter, who stared back at him with the skin above the bridge of his nose furled dubiously.

"Jack!" the little man said, throwing his hands out as though to indicate his own diminutive, bizarre-looking self. "Baja Jack! Why, everybody's heard of *Baja Jack*!" He paused. "Why, the bean-eaters down here run like frightened children when they hear the name!"

"We're new down here," Colter lied. At least, Prophet wasn't new down here. But Lou had never heard of Baja Jack, either.

"Oh, is that so? Hmmm." The strange little dwarfish man known as Baja Jack scrutinized Colter's head, since that's all there was to look at aboveground. He pointed at Colter's cheek as though he were the first one to come across the Sapinero brand on the redhead's face. "Say, that's a nasty tattoo you got there, Red!"

"Thank you."

"Say, Baja Jack?" Prophet said.

Baja Jack whipped around with a startled grunt. "Huh?"

"I don't s'pose you'd see fit to dig us out of here, would ya?" Prophet gave an obsequious grin. "Seein' as how we're fellow gringos an' all."

"Well, I don't know," Jack said. "I see no reason to rush into things. You rush into things in Mexico, you often find yourself just where you two done found yourselves, and worse!" He gave one of his odd, snorting laughs at that. "Why did Sergeant Casal and them other *rurale* vermin bury you in the first place?"

Prophet saw no reason to lie. Especially since it looked as though Baja Jack didn't favor *rurales* any more than Prophet himself did. "We killed several others, including Lieutenant Ruiz, back along the trail a piece."

"Oh? Really?" Baja Jack fingered the stringy, greasy goat whiskers hanging from his chin. He had more whiskers hanging above his thin upper lip, and they were just as stringy and greasy as those on his chin. "Ruiz, eh? Well, wouldn't you know Oscar Ruiz was a damn good friend of mine, you two sons of low-down dirty swine sons of

326

putas!"

Baja Jack fairly roared those last words, bent forward at the waist, his face swelling up and turning as red as a Mexican sunset. He grabbed the Colt .44 from the holster on his left hip, held it barrel-up, and, glaring down at Lou, clicked the hammer back.

Prophet's heart thudded. All hope in him died. Yep, this was his final resting place, all right. Right here near where that javelina was getting cooked down to black ashes.

"Good goin', Lou," Colter castigated him.

"Ah hell," Prophet said with a sigh.

He lowered his gaze to the blood-splashed sand in front of his face, awaiting the bullet. He winced, anticipating the .44's roar though he probably wouldn't hear it. He'd probably be dead by the time the report reached his ears.

Snorting laughter sounded.

Prophet rolled his eyes up to see Baja Jack's shoulders jerking as, still holding the cocked pistol barrel-up in his right hand, his odd, snorting guffaws bubbled up out of his lumpy chest, beneath the two cartridge bandoliers crisscrossed over his buckskin tunic. His raptorial features were crumpled like wadded-up parchment, and tears dribbled down his cheeks.

"Don't you realize I'm just joshin' with

327

you fellers?" Baja Jack threw his head back and gave a croaking, rasping yell at the sky, throwing both his stubby arms up and firing a slug into the sun glaring down at him. Lowering his arms, he turned to Lou again and said, "I always did hate that snake Ruiz, and Casal even more. In my book, there ain't no such thing as a good *rurale* lessen it's a dead *rurale!*"

Baja Jack holstered his pistol and waved toward the men sitting their horses behind him. Continuing to chuckle at his joke, which he'd taken such open delight in, as though it were the best prank he'd ever come up with, he yelled, "Dig 'em out, boys!" He repeated the order in fluent Spanish, ostensibly for those Mexicans in his gang who did not understand English.

Prophet was almost giddy with the prospect of being freed from his earthy confinement. Still, he eyed Baja Jack warily. He wasn't sure if he and Colter hadn't leaped from the frying pan into one more fire.

A half-dozen men grabbed the folding camp shovels of the dead *rurales* and three each set to work digging away the sand from around Lou and Colter. Prophet watched each shovelful as it was scooped up and tossed away. Each shovelful of sand was a stay of execution.

When he could work his arms free of the ground, he clawed at the sand. Baja Jack's men continued digging around him until he could, with deep grunts of exertion, pull each of his legs free of the sucking ground. He clawed as though out of quicksand away from the hole. So did Colter until they both lay side by side, breathing hard.

Prophet glanced at the sand-caked redhead. "Next time you see me headin' to Mexico, you might want to try a different direction."

"Duly noted."

CHAPTER 26

Prophet looked up from where he lay *on* the ground now as opposed to *inside* of it.

Baja Jack and his men had gathered around Lou and Colter's fire. They'd broken out their knives and were cutting meat from the charred javelina and eating hungrily, letting the juices dribble down their chins and onto their tunics, jackets, and vests, wiping their hands on their leggings.

Jack himself held a big, charred knuckle in one hand and, chewing, eyed Lou and Colter with his customary, cross-eyed amusement tainted with a discomfiting insanity.

"Feel good, now, partners? You feel better now, to be free of the earth? The earth — she can wait, huh, until you are much older men? The earth — she feels better when we're old and used up. Then, she's not so unwelcome."

Jack's shoulders jerked as he laughed and

continued to chew the knuckle like a hungry cur. "That's no place for a younger man. Come on over here and enjoy some pig. Casal was worthless in most regards, but he could cook a javelina — I'll give him that. Damn good stuff! Come on. Have some. Just cut off the charred parts!"

Prophet heaved himself to his feet. He felt suddenly very light but the sand still clung to him, as though death, that black specter, was reluctant to let him go. Old Scratch thought he'd called Lou's note due at last, and he was about to get some fresh help on the shovel line.

Lou wriggled around, swinging his arms and kicking his legs, dislodging the remaining sand. He walked over to a rock, sat down, rested his right foot on his left knee, and pried off his boot. "Can't tell you how much I appreciate the help, Jack."

Baja Jack chuckled as he continued feeding, his men standing close around the fire, chopping at the wild pig with their knives. Their horses stood around the perimeter of the fire, reins dangling to the ground. Idly, Prophet wondered where Mean and Ugly was. The horse had probably run off when the shooting had erupted. He was likely close. Lou didn't see Colter's coyote dun, either.

"It is my pleasure, amigo, to rescue two of my fellow Anglos from such a bitter end. The Mexicans — they do have a sense of humor, though, don't they?"

"I wasn't laughing," Colter said with a weary sigh. He was also sitting on a rock, prying his boots off and dumping out the sand. He kept grumbling, and Lou knew his wounds were grieving him though he was trying to suppress the pain. But, then, Lou was doing the same with all of his own sundry physical grievances.

Prophet peeled a sandy sock off his left foot and shook it out. "You been down here awhile — eh, Jack?"

"A while?" Jack laughed again, snorting as he continued chewing the knuckle. "Yeah, I been down here most of my life. My dear old pa was an Englishman, don't ya know?" He grinned, showing that missing tooth and the remaining, crooked, brown one. "Do I look English to you?"

"Not a bit," Prophet admitted. Most Englishmen were pale. Jack was nearly as dark as the charred javelina he was feeding on.

Jack finished off the knuckle then tossed the bone into the brush lining the arroyo. Using his big bowie knife he hacked off a large chunk of javelina and tossed it to

Prophet, who caught it against his chest then switched it from hand to hand, chuffing against the heat.

"Be careful," Jack warned. "It's hot!"

Laughing, he hacked off another chunk of meat and tossed it to Colter. "Careful, Red —"

"Yeah, I know," Colter said, juggling the meat like a hot potato. "It's hot."

Again, Jack laughed before hacking off another chunk of meat for himself. He waddled over — and there was no more fitting term for the way the thick, little, buzzard-faced man moved — to a rock near Prophet and sat down on it. His men were now lounging around the fire, sipping coffee from steaming tin cups.

"Yessir," the little man said, taking another bite of meat and chewing it tenderly with his rotten teeth, "my dear old pa was an Englishman. Edward Phillip Rynn-Douglas Jr. A dapper little man with short hair and big gentleman's mustaches, waxed an' all! Had him a walking stick topped with a silver horse. He was also an adventurer, Pa was.

"Came from a rich family, but he didn't get along with me dear old Gramps back in Newcastle, don't ya know. He was a reader, Pa was . . . and by way of reading he got the adventure bug. Had gold and silver . . .

El Dorado and the gold of Montezuma . . . on his brain. So he turned freebooter and hopped a steamer and came West . . . to good ole Mexico. Found just enough gold and silver to stay here, prospecting.

"Romanced a purty li'l gal — my dear ole mum. She was purty, all right. I reckon that's where I get my own good looks. Hah!"

Baja Jack had a good long laugh at that, shaking his head at the sad irony.

"Injun gal, my ma. From the Cocopa tribe. Purty people, mostly." Jack shook his head again, sadly. "Anyway, my ma died and Pa got rich and took me to live in Phoenix, where he started up a precious-metals geology trade. Hell, I lived my first twelve years runnin' wild with him right here in Baja. I didn't want to live in no damn city . . . *eatin' off china plates and goin' to school!* I misbehaved so Pa sent me to Mexico City to straighten me out. He wanted to make a priest out of me. Hah!

"He figured that's all I was fit for, me bein' scrawny and ugly as a spiny-tailed iguana. Who knows? Maybe it was the best thing. I didn't think so at the time. Besides, them other kids — them sky-pilots-to-be — they beat holy hell out of me! I was just like Pa, anyways — I wanted gold and silver and purty, smoky-eyed women. Hell, I wanted *adventure*!"

John Brian Rynn-Douglas held his stubby, crooked little arms out to both sides, throwing his head back as though offering himself to the sky. "So here I am . . . these fifty long years now. *¡Aquí estoy!* Here I am!"

Colter swallowed a bite of meat and said, "What do you do down here, Jack? Still looking for gold and purty women?"

"Nah, I've had my fill of gold and purty women. I led the outlaw life when I was younger. Killed many men, ravaged women, stole a lot of money. I reckon I softened in my old age. Lost the blood thirst. Now I'm a farmer."

"A farmer?" Prophet asked with an incredulous chuff.

"Sure, a farmer. A *campesino.* A humble man of the land. Now I tend my plants, drink tequila, read books, and write poetry by candlelight after dark and my chores are finished for the day." Jack frowned at Prophet before shunting his curious gaze to Colter. "Say . . . what're you two doin' down here? You're a mite off the beaten path, if you don't mind me sayin'. There ain't no gold in these rocks, and the señoritas — well, they're on either shore."

Prophet glanced at Colter. The redhead arched a dubious brow.

Lou was wondering if he should relay his intention to kill Ciaran Yeats to Baja Jack. Why not? He doubted Jack had any liking for the crazy gringo major running off his leash in the land Jack obviously considered his home.

"I'll tell you what we're doing down here, Jack. Then maybe you can tell me where we can find the hombre we aim to do it to." Prophet ate the last of the javelina meat and wiped his hands on his trousers. He swallowed and said, "We're down here to —"

"Ahh," Jack interrupted, looking off over Lou's left shoulder. "There are my beauties now! I was wondering where they were. They probably ran off when the shooting started but leave it to old Pepe to keep a close eye on my precious boys and girls . . . and of course the precious cargo on their backs!"

Prophet turned to see a withered old gray-haired man dressed in the ragged garb of a *campesino* including striped poncho and frayed straw sombrero riding a mule between two rock outcroppings to the east. The man was trailing four — no, five — burros on lead lines. The asses wore pack-saddles and bulging panniers.

"Hello, my pretty ones!" Jack called, grinning like a proud father. He proceeded to call out the names of each burro in turn — Rosalia, Joaquin, Piedad, Anselmo, and Escorpión. "I call this one Scorpion," said Jack, sandwiching the head of a spotted dun burro in his hands and giving it a brusque but loving pat, "because while he has the gentlest of eyes, he has a wicked temper. No, no, this one you do not cross, and you do not turn your back on him, amigos!"

That cackling laugh . . .

Jack had to rise up on the toes of his boots to plant a kiss on the docile-looking burro's head, between its jackass ears. The burro gave a friendly whicker then stomped a hind foot at a blackfly.

Jack beckoned to Lou and Colter. "Come, come and see the fruits of my labor, gentlemen. This is my latest enterprise, and oh, what a lucrative one it is!"

Prophet heaved himself to his feet. He was feeling better now after the javelina had padded out his belly, though his head still owned a dull ache no doubt owing to the tainted scorpion juice he'd been given by Señor Anaya in La Bachata.

Jack beckoned again, smiling like a proud groom about to sneak a forbidden peek at his bride. He walked over to the pannier strapped to the *aparejo* on Escorpión's left side. He unbuckled the pannier's straps,

337

opened the flap, and dipped his hand inside. Smiling dreamily, he pulled out his hand and sniffed.

The dreamy expression grew until his eyes drifted up until they were nearly out of sight in their deep, wizened sockets. *"Ahhhh!"*

He held the hand out to Prophet and Colter. The man's small, dark hand held what appeared to be a pile of dried weeds and pinelike buds. Prophet recognized it even before he sniffed it. Ganja. Cush. Locoweed. Marijuana. The Orientals he'd known in Tombstone called it the *magic dragon* or *dream spice.* The substance was plentiful in some parts of the West. Lou had seen an entire storeroom of the stuff drying from the rafters in a parlor house in Dodge City.

He'd enjoyed a few puffs but hadn't liked it much. It smelled like skunkweed to him and made him fall asleep and dream crazy. Under the locoweed's influence, it had taken him nearly a half hour to pull a single boot off. After he'd finally gotten both boots off, with the help of a kind doxie, it took him another half hour to remember how to make love to a woman. Even worse, it made him laugh like a cork-headed moron.

Give Prophet a bottle of medium-grade tequila any day over the giggle weed.

"This is what you farm?" Lou asked skeptically.

Baja Jack nodded. He sniffed the weed again then returned it very carefully to the pannier. "Oh yes. A wonderful crop it is, too. It makes one nearly as happy to grow as to smoke." He glanced at the men lounging around the fire. "Ain't that right, amigos?" He repeated the question in Spanish.

The men's replies ran the spectrum from knowing grins to affirmative laughter. They'd sated themselves on the pig and were now lying back, some snoozing, some drinking coffee, one strumming a small mandolin and singing softly, two playing poker, while the dead *rurales* remained in their own blood pools.

Baja Jack's men were a strange, ragged lot — most of them Mexican with a few Anglos. Even the Anglos appeared Mexican, though, as was often the case when an Anglo stayed down here long enough. They might have blue eyes and ginger beards, but there was an aloofness in their bearings that made them seem almost more Mexican than American. Or, at the very least, a strange hybrid of both that became its own separate race.

That was evident in Baja Jack himself, who couldn't look more Mexican, with a good bit of Baja Indio thrown in, but who acted and sounded *americano.* That he was also a little touched was obvious. Maybe that came from such a mixed heritage, from wandering from one place to another and then from living so long down here in Baja, a strange land, for sure.

Or maybe he was woolly-headed on his own weed.

"Where are you goin' with the locoweed, Baja Jack?" Colter asked.

Jack grinned as he secured the pannier's straps. "My men and I are taking our crop to market." He smiled again and poked his sombrero brim back off his bulbous forehead. "We have a customer. A very rich man who enjoys our special crop very much. His life depends on it, in fact."

Lou felt his lower jaw drop.

Colter looked at him. His own jaw was sagging.

Prophet licked his lips, cleared his throat. "Who, uh . . . who is this fella, Baja Jack?"

Jack shrugged a shoulder. "I see no reason not to say. Most in Baja have heard of him and his, uh, somewhat *strange* ways — at least judging by most men's standards. Most men have heard of him but few have seen him . . . or seen him and lived to tell about it."

That cackling, crowlike laugh again. "He is the Mad American Major himself — Ciaran Yeats of Baluarte Santiago!"

Colter whipped an astonished gaze at Prophet, whose heart kicked like a mule in his chest.

When Baja Jack sobered, he looked at Lou and Colter and arched a speculative brow. "Say, why don't you amigos throw in with us on the trail to Baluarte Santiago?" He grinned seedily. "Yeats throws a hell of a party!"

CHAPTER 27

"¡El país de Dios!" said Baja Jack about forty-five minutes later as his men, his precious cargo, Lou Prophet, and Colter Farrow were all riding the trail toward Ciaran Yeats. "God's country. Wouldn't you say, amigos?"

The little man threw out a stubby little arm to indicate the terrain around them — a vast array of rocky hills threaded with chalky dry arroyos rolling off toward slab-sided bluffs and high mesas partly obscured by the desert's heat shimmer and scored with deep ravines. Cirio trees peppered the landscape — tall, spindly, ocotillo-like growths that stretched their thorny stubs up to sixty feet above the ground. They were the area's most noticeable feature.

The rest of the flora was all small, twisted cactus and brittle tufts of saltbush. The only shade was that offered by the widely spaced hillsides and mesas, unless you counted the fingerlike shadows the cirio trees spread out across the sun-bleached rocks and sand, which was hardly enough to offer temporary relief to an overheated Gambel's quail.

The only living things beast-wise that Prophet had seen were a mangy-looking coyote, several rattlesnakes, a roadrunner, and the occasional *zopilote* — Mexican buzzards — swirling high on desert thermals, ever on the watch for carrion.

Prophet glanced at his new trail guide skeptically. "I reckon beauty's in the eyes of the beholder, Baja Jack."

"*Sí, sí,*" Jack said. "It is true. I reckon I'm partial to these sunburned hills because I spent so much time running around in them, chasing my dear old man for the first several years of my life. What a beautiful damn time that was for me. My halcyon days. Hell, I was barely out of rubber pants before Pa started taking me into the desert on gold-digging expeditions. Me and my ma, a beautiful woman." He flung out a stubby arm, this time pointing east. "See all that white over there?"

Prophet cast his glance in the direction the little man indicated. A gauzy white, like steam clouds, appeared far off over a stretch of pale, craggy mountains.

"That's the Sea of Cortez," Prophet said.

"You got it, amigo." Jack grinned at him

knowingly. "You've visited Mar de Cortés before — eh, Lou?"

Prophet grinned back at the man. "You got it, amigo."

"Some of the most beautiful women anywhere in Mexico, perhaps in the entire world, reside along those storied waters. *Mi madre* hailed from there."

"I'll vouch for that," Prophet said. "Er . . . I mean that the most beautiful women live along the Sea of Cortez. I didn't know your mother."

Jack laughed. "While this is a sacred land — at least to me with all the memories I bring to it — keep your eyes skinned, my friends. It's a ticklish country when it comes to maintaining a firm grasp of your ghost." He arched an ominous brow at Lou and Colter riding beside him as they crossed one of the many dry ravines and began climbing the shoulder of yet another rocky butte. "Banditos are as plentiful as sidewinders out here. Especially now that it has gotten around that I am supplying Ciaran Yeats and his men at Baluarte Santiago with their precious elixir."

"Are they after the elixir?" Lou asked. "Or the money you're paid for it?"

"Both. Many of them are addicted to the stuff. The *campesinos* around Guerrero

344

Negro grow a lot of it — inferior crap. Tastes like dried lizard dung. It's popular in this part of the peninsula where life offers so few other pleasures besides the obvious mattress dance now and then. But even the whores out here are fat! After it got around that my spice is favored by the mad old major, who knows the stuff better than almost anyone, they all wanted mine. Barring the weed itself, they'll settle for what I get paid for it.

"That's why I got all these gun-handy gents riding for me and a whole lot more guarding the *granja* where I grow my superior crops, though so far I've managed to keep the farm a secret, thank the bloody saints in heaven. I don't know what in hell I'm gonna do once the cat get outs of *that* bag . . . and it will eventually. Oh, it will. Nothing's a secret for long in Baja!"

Jack spat and shook his head in disgust. "Damn hard tryin' to make a living these days, in these more complicated modern times."

"I haven't seen any signs of trouble so far," Colter said, riding between Prophet and Baja Jack. The old man, Pepe, led the burros just behind Lou, Colter, and Baja Jack. "And you can see for a long ways out here."

"It *looks* like you can see a long way, Red," Jack warned. "But I guarantee you there's two or three groups of bean-eatin' vermin watching us right now, even as we sit here and chin like old-timers on a loafer's bench on the public square in Bahía de los Ángeles."

"I guess we'd best shut up, then," Prophet said, squinting against the glare as he looked around, draping one hand over his Peace-maker's grips.

Jack spat again, this time in disgust with himself. "Ah hell, I can't keep these old lips of mine sewn for long. Not even when my life depends on it. It's too damn seldom I see anyone new down here, anyone who can hold a conversation, that is."

Jack leaned out from his saddle to speak covertly to Prophet. He jerked his head to indicate the Mexican and Anglo pistoleros riding behind the old man on the donkey leading the burros. "Those hombres are right handy with their six-shooters and carbines, but I swear even the *americanos* are so damn stupid they can't find their asses with both hands. Not only that, but their vocabularies in both languages amount to little more than *yep*s, *nope*s, *pulque,* and *whiskey* and *whore* and puta!"

Jack slapped Prophet's shoulder and

wheezed out a violent cry of unbridled laughter.

Prophet laughed, too. Jack was a cutup, he purely was. One of the most colorful characters Lou had ever run into even in Mexico. And he'd run into a few characters down here as elsewhere. He would soon run into at least one more:

Ciaran Yeats.

The notion had him more than a little on edge even though Yeats was whom Lou and his redheaded trail partner were looking for. But Yeats was a formidable man surrounded by formidable men. And Prophet and Colter had promised Don de la Paz they'd kill him.

Lou vaguely wondered if Baja Jack sensed Prophet's unease when the little man asked, "Forgive me, Lou, but I interrupted you back at the camp. You were about to tell me who you'd drifted down here to find. You remember — when I was distracted by my burros . . . ? I gather it is a badman wanted up north, since you are a bounty hunter."

Jack turned another knowing grin on Prophet.

Lou stared at him in surprise.

"Oh hell, of course I know who you are!" Jack laughed. "Why, hell, you're right famous up north of the border and even down here in Old Mexico!"

347

"Damn," Prophet said, casting an uneasy glance toward Colter. "I didn't know I was *that* famous. I thought down here at least I could ride with a little amon . . . am-onym . . . somethin' or other."

"Anonymity," Colter helped out.

"Amonyitymite, thank you."

"Glad to help."

"Yessir," Jack said. "Tales of your ex-ploits . . . yours an' that purty blond girl . . ."

"The Vengeance Queen," Prophet said.

"That's the one! Tales of you two's exploits have even reached my old, hair-tufted ears. What I wanna know is how much is true an' how much is gildin' the lily."

"You'll never find out from my lyin' mouth," Prophet said with a grin, hoping that Baja Jack had lost his train of thought.

But he hadn't, galldangit.

"So who you down here lookin' to haul back across the border tied belly down across his hoss?" Jack gave him a boyish smile of delight in secret things. "You can tell me. I wouldn't tell a soul. Hell, who in the hell would I have to tell it to, anyways?"

He snarled over his shoulder at his ham-merheaded pack of marijuana guards.

"Oh, that." Prophet's ears warmed though he didn't think anything could make them much warmer than they already were in this unrelenting heat and sunlight. "Uh, well . . . the kid an' I are lookin' for —"

"Ciaran Yeats," Colter said.

The name was a sucker punch to Prophet's solar plexus. He whipped his head to scowl in astonishment at the kid riding between him and Jack. Jack cast the redhead that very same look while one blazing eye crossed nearly to his nose. The other eye was a shimmering coal directed right at him.

Colter looked at Prophet and grinned from ear to ear. He turned to Jack with the same grin.

Jack slapped his thigh so hard he startled his horse, and peeled out another roar of croaking laughter. "Hahhhh! Hahh-hahh-HAHHHHH!" He slapped his leg again. "You had me goin', Red, you purely did! Ciaran Yeats! My fat hairy ass, you're down here after Ciaran Yeats! Hahhh! Yeats has a whole army gunnin' for him, and they're all mean as rabid wolves, since they're all addicted to the elixir, same as Yeats himself. They wouldn't let nothin' happen to the mad old major. Nothin'. Hahhh!"

Again, Jack slapped his thigh. "You had me goin' there for a minute, Red. You purely did! Damn near gave me a heart stroke!"

"Yeah," Prophet said, glaring at Colter. "Me, too."

349

Colter looked at him and shrugged with his customary, Louisa-like insouciance.

One of those two — this kid or the Vengeance Queen — would be the death of him yet.

"Yep," Jack said, still chuckling and wagging his head. "You really had me goin', Red."

They stopped for water at a springs where Prophet never would have thought there could be a springs. Jack wasn't whistling "Dixie." He really did know this country.

To reach the springs, the party had to leave the faint trail they were following, an old trading trail threading the peninsula from the Sea of Cortez to the east and the Pacific Ocean to the west, and travel a good mile down into a boulder-strewn canyon to reach the water. The springs bubbled up out of rocks littering the side of a tall, slanting mesa. There were rocks all over this hidden place — so many that Prophet doubted that few other than some natives of the area, Baja Jack, and his "dear old pa" had ever known about it.

That natives had known about it there was no doubt, for there were colorful rock paintings all over — bright depictions of oddly shaped men hunting oddly shaped animals, some of which looked like deer but with very large, curled horns. Some of those men and animals drank at pools — likely the springs itself.

The paintings gave Prophet, always superstitious, an odd, haunted feeling.

Since the party was on the east side of the mesa, and the sun was angling on toward three in the afternoon, the party was in cool, refreshing shade. While the men let their horses drink from a natural trough that ran down through the sand and rocks, forming an old creek bed carved through ancient lava, and sipped the cool water themselves, Prophet wandered off to tend to nature.

He stopped to unbutton his pants but stayed the motion when he heard something to his right. He lowered his right shoulder, sliding the Richards down off that arm and dropping it smoothly into his hands. As he did, he turned to his right.

A man had been moving stealthily toward him, shoulder brushing a wall of rock, a bowie knife in one hand, a bone-gripped revolver in the other. He wore a big straw sombrero and ragged cotton tunic. Black mustaches hung down both sides of his mouth.

His eyes widening, he lunged toward Prophet, who'd brought the Richards around and now tripped the right trigger. The shotgun roared, the double-ought buck turning the assailant's belly into a bloody mess as it threw the man straight backward and down a gravelly hill.

Another man lunged toward Prophet, this one to the left of the first man. He'd been brushing his shoulder against another wall of rock. The Richards thundered once more and sent the second assailant the way of the first with an ear-rattling, agonized shriek.

"Trouble, amigos!" Prophet bellowed though he realized the others in his party might have figured that out now after having heard the cannonlike roar of the twelve-gauge.

His instincts told him to wheel a one-eighty and he was glad he did.

Another bandito was rushing toward him between two boulders, extending a Colt straight out from his right shoulder. Prophet threw himself forward as the man triggered the Colt. Lou hit the ground on his belly. Since the Richards was empty, he flipped it around, grabbing the barrel, and made a slashing motion from left to right, clubbing this third assailant's legs out from beneath him.

As he heard yells and shooting from the direction of the others in his party, and the whoops and yells of who he assumed were more banditos storming down out of the rocks surrounding the springs, he rose to his knees. The third assailant had fallen hard on his face but he was pushing up onto his hands and knees, stretching his lips back from his teeth.

His sombrero hung down his back. His chin was bloody from where it had smashed against the rocky ground. As he lifted his oval-shaped, bearded face toward Prophet, clawing around for the old-model Remington revolver he'd dropped when he'd fallen, Lou slammed the butt of the Richards against the man's lower left cheek. The man's lower jaw made an ominous cracking sound and fell to one side.

The man gave a garbled wail.

Prophet silenced the wail with another savage assault with the Richards's stock, bashing in the Mexican's left temple. The man's head dropped to the ground, and he lay rigid, quivering as he died.

Lou wheeled to see another figure barreling toward him, this one aiming two .45s straight at him and grinning the devil's own grin of bloody murder.

CHAPTER 28

Prophet threw himself back behind a boulder as his fourth assailant's .45s roared. The bullet curled the air a cat's whisker off the end of Prophet's nose and then slammed into the boulder just as Prophet pulled his face back behind it.

Lou flipped himself around and into a better position to confront his attacker. He shucked his Peacemaker from its holster, clicking back the hammer.

His fourth assailant, a short old man with a red face and a white beard parted in the middle, continued hammering the rock with his .45s and then lunged into Prophet's field of vision, barking Spanish epithets and narrowing his brown eyes as he aimed down his Colt's barrels at Lou.

He didn't get off another shot as, hunkered on his heels, Prophet triggered two shots and then a third, sending the old peon in a ratty red serape flying back against another boulder. He shot himself in the knee, gave another shrill, howling wail as he stared at his ruined leg, then dropped to both his knees before falling sideways onto a shoulder where he expired with a heavy sigh.

The thunder of another near gun assaulted Prophet's ears, momentarily disorienting him.

Where in the hell had that one come from?

Then a shadow — a slender gray flicker of movement within the shadows here on this side of the mesa — slid across the ground to his left. He wheeled as another blast assaulted his ears. That bullet, too, came very close to punching his ticket and would have done so if he hadn't turned at that very instant.

He looked up to see a big, broad-shouldered man in dirty cream *pantalones,* high-topped deerskin moccasins, and a beaded deerskin serape standing on the boulder above him and extending an ivory-gripped Schofield at Prophet's head. Lou swung his Peacemaker up and fired twice, fouling the big man's aim as the bullet smashed into the man's left shoulder.

The man screamed as he fired a bullet into the ground just left of Prophet's left boot.

Lou fired another round, aiming for this

would-be killer's heart. The man had jerked sideways just in time to avoid a deadly bout of indigestion, instead taking the bullet in his upper-right chest. He screamed angrily, his broad, ugly, mustached face crumpling and reddening. He dropped the Schofield then stepped off the edge of the rock.

Prophet's heart hiccupped when he saw the big man hurling toward him, swinging his arms out and looking every bit like black, winged death.

Lou clicked back the Peacemaker's hammer but did not get off another shot before the big Mex smashed into him like a half ton of dry goods thrown from a freight wagon, slamming Lou backward off his heels and driving him to the ground while closing his big hands around Lou's neck.

Lou tried to smash the Peacemaker against his attacker's big, granitelike head matted with black hair peppered with lice and other vermin. But then he realized his right hand was empty. He'd lost the revolver when the man had smashed into him from above.

His knuckles merely glanced off the big man's left temple as the big man himself rose onto his knees and, snarling like an enraged puma, dug his thumbs into Prophet's throat, intent on busting his windpipe and smashing his Adam's apple back against his spine, a task which it felt to Lou he was accomplishing, despite the blood the man was losing.

In desperation, Prophet slashed up with his arms, ramming the man's hands free of his neck. He smashed his right fist against the big man's left jaw and then they were snarling and rolling together — over and over to the left . . . over and over to the right . . . exchanging grips on each other's necks and growling like two raging wolves in a struggle to end all struggles.

They broke their grips on each other's necks to exchange punches — savage, smashing blows. Prophet could feel the man's assault all the way down to his toes.

Then they went rolling and rolling again to the right . . . rolling and rolling again to the left, smashing each other with their fists, digging at each other's eyes, trying to get the other's neck in a death grip.

The Mexican brute grabbed Prophet's head up off the ground in both his massive hands and smashed Lou's head back against the ground so hard that for a second or two the bounty hunter lost consciousness. When he was aware again of who and where he was and of what was happening, the big Mexican was again trying to strangle him.

Prophet felt his eyes bulge. His head

swelled from lack of oxygen. He'd grabbed the man's big arms, even bigger than his own, but the Mexican brute had the high ground and a better angle. Prophet was addled from the savage blows to his head. He couldn't get his opponent to release his choking, death-dealing grip.

The big Mex grinned maniacally down at Prophet, his green-brown eyes glinting devilishly. His broad, Indian-dark face was so badly pocked and pitted, it looked like he'd been mistaken for a coyote and taken two loads of buckshot point-blank. He smelled like something dead that had seasoned too long in the hot sun. Vaguely, Prophet wondered what was going to kill him first — the man's thumbs grinding into his throat, or his smell.

The bean-eater's eyelids drew down as though in ecstasy, and in a soft, seedily intimate voice he said, "Can you feel the devil tickling your *escroto,* señor?" He grunted out a girlish laugh.

Prophet's vision was dimming and his brain was starting to die from oxygen starvation. In fact, he thought he could feel the devil's long-nailed finger tickling him down low.

The fast-expiring cells in Lou's brain were getting desperate. Suddenly, realizing he'd run out of all other options, he decided to slam his forehead up hard against that of the brute's. He didn't have enough room to build up much momentum, so he was pleasantly surprised when the man's head snapped back and he momentarily eased his pressure on Prophet's throat.

That gave Lou the half second he needed to reach down to his right hip with his right hand and shuck his big bowie knife from its sheath.

He lifted the knife just as the brute began grinding his thumbs into Prophet's throat once more, grinning girlishly, the tip of his tongue poking out one corner of his mouth. Prophet's vision was dimming again, as though an even deeper shadow had passed over this side of the mesa.

He probably would have passed out in another second or two if he hadn't managed to poke the razor-edged tip of the bowie through the brute's smoke-stained javelina-hide serape and into the man's left side, just beneath his ribs.

The man's eyes suddenly widened. He gasped, lower jaw loosening.

He shivered as if chilled.

Instantly, his hands fell slack against Prophet's throat.

Lou had gotten the bowie into the big

359

man's body only about six inches, but now as he sucked a strength-replenishing breath into his starved lungs, and the shadow of unconsciousness began to lift, he gritted his teeth and rammed the knife several more inches into the big bean-eater's body.

"*¡Dios!*" the brute cried, staring down in horror at Prophet's large, gloved wrist wrapped around the bowie's hide-wrapped walnut handle, between the handle and the brass hilt. Dark red blood bubbled up over the blade.

The brute raised his right fist, cocking it up near his shoulder, but before he could ram it down against Prophet's face, Lou slid the bowie even farther into the man's brisket, twisting and turning the blade, angling the savage point, curved like a wolf's fang, up to the heart. Lou felt the point glance off a rib just before perforating the thick, beating cardiac muscle itself.

"*Ach!*" the brute screamed. "*¡Mierda! ¡Estoy muerto!*"

His right fist dropped slack to his side.

Prophet grunted and lifted his head and shoulders up off the ground, funneling more strength into his right arm and hand, driving the knife up even deeper into the man's heart until Lou could feel the organ spasming desperately before it stopped beating.

The brute gave a choking, strangling sound as blood bubbled out between his lips. He fell straight back between Prophet's spread legs. Since his legs were still straddling Prophet's torso, it was a bizarre sight. Only the handle of Prophet's bowie protruded from the big man's side, drenched in blood. Prophet tried to pull himself out from under the lug, but he was too weak from the choking and the effort it had taken to kill the beast.

He lay back against the ground, breathing hard.

"Now that was somethin' to see!"

Prophet whipped his head to his left. He blinked incredulously.

Baja Jack stood about ten feet away, smiling in amazement. Colter stood behind the little man, two heads taller. The other men in Jack's gang, including old Pepe, stood in a ragged semicircle flanking Jack and Colter.

"It purely was at that," Colter agreed with the smaller man. He was smiling at Prophet and slowly shaking his head.

Prophet scowled at them all. "How long you been standing there?"

"Only a couple minutes," Colter said.

"You been standin' there a *couple minutes* and you didn't offer a hand?"

"It was a sight to behold!" Jack clapped

his fat dark hands together, stretching his lips so far that if he'd been wearing dentures he would have lost them. "Two rogue grizzlies going head-to-head! Truly a sight to behold, partner!"

Colter walked forward, holstering his Remington. "Don't worry, Lou. If I didn't think you'd get the better of him, I'd have helped you out. It looked like you were doing all right, though." He extended his hand to Lou and helped Prophet crawl out from beneath the dead brute.

"It looked like I was doing all right?" Prophet was out from beneath the big man now. He released Colter's hand and heaved himself to his feet. "He was *that* close to snuffing my lamp! If I hadn't had the bowie on me, I'd be a goner . . . while you stood there enjoyin' the entertainment!"

"Ah, don't be a sorehead," Colter chided him.

"Yeah, don't be a sorehead, Lou." Baja Jack walked over, took Prophet's right hand, and shook it, tipping his head back to smile admiringly nearly straight up at the taller man. "That was one hell of a show. Purely it was. We was all gonna help you out, but when we got up here and saw you two big fellas goin' at it so hard and savage-like . . . two wild bruins goin' at it tooth and claw . . . I reckon we didn't have the heart to interrupt!"

"Well, thanks a whole damn bunch for bein' so considerate!" Prophet glanced over at the other members of Jack's gang. They were exchanging money, some laughing victoriously, others grumbling curses. Prophet glared at Colter and Baja Jack. "You mean, you took the time to *bet on the outcome*?"

Colter held up both hands, palms out, and shook his head. "Not me. No, sir. I'd never bet on a friend in such a dire situation, and I'm hurt that you'd think I would."

Jack shrugged then planted his fists on his broad hips. "I admit I would have wagered, but I was transfixed." He loosed a croaking laugh and shook his head again in amazement.

Prophet looked down at himself in disgust. He was covered in blood. At least, it wasn't his own. That was something, anyway. He crouched over the dead man, planted a boot on the man's hip, and yanked the bowie knife free.

Cleaning the knife off on the man's deerskin leggings, he turned again to Colter and Jack.

"What about the other robbers?"

"Oh, there was only two more," Colter

said. "When we heard your gut-shredder thunder, we knew trouble was afoot and dispatched the only two that threatened us in no time. You cleaned out the whole rest of the gang yourself, Lou."

"Too bad a scribbler for one of the eastern newspapers ain't here," Jack said. "Why, he'd have some ink to spill!"

"I gotta admit," Colter said with some chagrin, "I was beginning to think you was old and washed up or maybe the scribblers was exaggeratin' about you. But, no. You still got it, Lou, and I'm just proud to know I was here to see it on full display!"

Jack and Colter started heading back toward the springs, which is where the other men must have vanished to, as well. Having settled their bets, they were no longer in sight.

"Hurry up, now, Lou," called Baja Jack. "We can't linger here much longer. It'll be gettin' dark soon. There are many more banditos where those *pendejos* came from!"

Prophet stared after both men — the slender redhead and the bandy-legged little buzzard of a sombrero-clad mestizo. He gave a caustic chuff. "You mind if I take a piss?"

That was what he'd stepped away from

the springs to do in the first place. His bladder was fit to bust.

CHAPTER 29

Prophet did his best to clean the blood out of his tunic at the spring.

There was a lot of blood, so it took a while. He got tired of hearing the others grumbling impatiently while they waited for him, so he told them to head on up the trail and he'd follow when he'd rid his duds of the Mexican brute's bodily fluids.

Colter offered to wait for him, but Lou told him to ride on ahead. He was feeling owly and he was aching from the beating. One eye swelled up only a little, but he'd be surprised if by the next morning he wasn't sporting two big shiners. Sundry cuts and abrasions on his cheeks and lips oozed blood. Not a lot but enough that he could feel the sting of each one. A loose tooth added to his laments.

"Sorry sons o' Satan," the bounty hunter grumbled as he scraped the soaked tunic on a rock beside the spring. "Bettin' on the outcome, my ragged rebel behind . . ."

He donned the tunic, which felt refreshingly cool against his hot, sweaty, trail-grimed skin, and mounted Mean and Ugly. The horse had also been eyeing him and whickering impatiently, as though he too were saying, *Stop bein' such a sorehead, Lou. Stop bein' so prissy about a little blood, fer cryin' in Grant's bourbon. Let's haul our freight and get to our destination. I want a good roll in the dirt, a slow rubdown, and a hefty feed sack.*

"Ah, shut up," Prophet grunted out as he booted the horse up the trail.

After fifteen minutes, he caught up to the others just as they were descending into yet another boulder-choked canyon. This one was even harder to negotiate than the first, because by now it was around five-thirty in the afternoon, and the shadows were growing longer and darker.

The trail was narrow and winding as they descended still farther into the canyon, which was a dinosaur's mouth of jagged rock outcroppings and boulder-choked arroyos. Ahead of Lou, he could see the others riding Indian file along the twisting, turning trail. He held back, riding drag, moving slowly now, for the canyon was a treacherous place to travel, given the fading light, all the rocks, and the trail pocked with deep holes his horse had to negotiate around or over.

He and Mean and Ugly traveled along the floor of the canyon for a good half hour before, as he followed a bend in the canyon's high wall, he drew back abruptly on Mean's reins. Ahead, the others had disappeared. He stared, squinting into the canyon's deepening shadows.

Nothing. No sign of them. It was as though they'd vanished into thin air.

"Come on, boy." Prophet nudged Mean forward, frowning, curious, growing more and more concerned.

He'd ridden another fifty yards before a soft whistle sounded on his right. "Lou! Over here, amigo!"

He turned to see Baja Jack poking his gremlin's head out from behind a pillar of pale rock. The little man almost seemed to be embedded in the canyon wall, but of course that wasn't the case. It was a trick of the dim light or the stone wall or a combination of both.

Grinning, that one eye crossed like that of an impish boy full of devilish secrets, Jack beckoned. "Come on, come on!"

Prophet swung Mean off the trail's right side. As he approached Jack and the canyon wall, he saw that Jack was standing in a natural stone foyer of sorts, one that blended so well with the wall that you had to scrutinize it pretty closely before you recognized it . . . and saw the dark opening beyond it.

Again, Jack beckoned.

Prophet swung down from Mean's back. He studied the natural portico of rock protruding from the face of the cliff wall and partially hiding the almost triangular-shaped opening in the wall flanking it. The ground dropped severely to what was apparently a cave opening. Down this decline Jack ambled in his bandy-legged fashion, teetering from side to side, little arms angling out from his sides like a penguin's flippers.

Prophet looked at Mean. The horse looked back at him, laying one ear back flat against his head. Lou shrugged and stepped forward, leading the horse by the reins.

He and the mount dropped down the inclination paved with red and black gravel and passed through the opening, which was around ten feet high at its pointed apex and roughly that wide near the ground. Jack had disappeared from his view when the little man had entered the cave but now as Lou stepped into the darkness, which was refreshingly cool, he saw the little man again, lit by the light angling through the opening behind him and the horse.

Baja Jack smiled up at him, his crowlike eyes flashing.

Prophet looked beyond him, surprised to see the others standing so far away from him — a good twenty feet, at least. Jack's men formed a ragged cluster. They dismounted and were unsaddling their horses. Old Pepe, the burro wrangler, was removing the panniers from the pack of one of his burros. Colter stood off to the left of Jack's men. He was holding his horse's reins and looking around in amazement. Prophet could see only the kid's back from his vantage, but he knew Colter was looking around in amazement, because he was looking at what Prophet was looking at, and it was truly amazing.

What they were standing in was not a cave but a canyon. At least, it was technically a canyon from about fifty feet back away from the entrance, because that's where the "roof" opened, showing the dimming light of the desert sky. The canyon was maybe a hundred yards wide by a hundred yards long. The ridges forming its walls were honeycombed with what appeared to be mud dwellings stacked atop one another halfway to the crest of the ridge. They looked like the nests of giant mud swallows.

The ridges were not sheer but sloped at maybe a thirty-five-degree angle, leaning back away from the canyon floor. Each level of the swallowlike homes was separated by a ledge of maybe ten or fifteen feet. Steps had been chiseled into the canyon walls, like the steps of an amphitheater, giving access to each level of the dwellings.

Prophet had seen such cliff dwellings before, for there were many all over the Southwest. An old prospector had guided him out to a vast one tucked away in southwestern Colorado, which was the only one he'd ever seen that was more extensive and elaborate than the one he was getting a neck ache gawking at now.

The floor of the canyon appeared to be the bed of an ancient river — likely the river that had carved the canyon, offering a well-hidden fortress home to some ancient people who'd likely lived and died thousands of years ago, even before the Aztecs and the Quill. They might have been dead, but their ghosts lingered here. Prophet could sense them. They were almost as real as they'd have been if he'd seen them. There was no imagining the flesh rippling between his shoulder blades and along the backs of his arms and legs, as though chilled by the ghostly breath of those long-lost souls who'd lived, loved, fought, mourned, and died right here.

"Pretty damn impressive — eh, amigo?" Jack ambled up to stand between where Prophet and Colter stood, turning their heads this way and that, scrutinizing the dwellings.

Colter whistled. "Right nice digs, Jack."

"I wish I could take credit for it." Jack chuckled. "I stop here on every run to Baluarte Santiago."

"You ain't worried about getting trapped in here?" Prophet asked. "Looks like there's only two ways in or out."

"Nope. Ain't never been worried one iota about that. You see, I don't think another soul knows about this place. At least, I've never seen sign of anyone living or even overnighting here in all the years I've known about it, and that's been a long spell."

"How'd you find it?" Colter asked, still admiring the ancient folks' handiwork.

Birds flitted through the canyon, flashing golden up where the sunlight reached, flicking like shadows nearer the canyon floor.

"My pa and I found it on one of our gold-hunting excursions, don't ya know! I was maybe ten years old. A little shaver. Even littler than I am now. Hah! A storm chased us and our pack burros into the main canyon. We needed shelter fast. Pa and I made camp just outside that entrance over there. We was lounging around the fire that night, roasting a pair of jacks under the overhang of a boulder, and Pa got to staring at the canyon wall while he smoked his pipe. He noticed something odd about how the light played across the side of the ridge. He got up and walked over to the wall and gave a yell. I jumped near a foot in the air. Pa — well, he damn near fell down that drop to the canyon's front door!"

Jack croaked out a long, snorting laugh.

"The next day we explored this canyon. Whoever lived here long ago had 'em a good fortress hidden away from their enemies. The Injuns all over Baja was fierce folks, don't ya know. Just like ole Baja Jack himself — *fierce*!" More laughter. "They'd fight each other at the drop of a hat . . . er, tomahawk. What have you. They knew what they were doin', too, because in all the years I've known about this place, I've never seen a single sign that anyone else knows about it. I've talked to a lot of desert rats. No, sir — not one word about it. I never let the cat out of the bag my ownself, because I had a feelin' someday I might need the hidey-hole, too. It makes a right fittin' place for me and my guards to hole up, safe from banditos, on the trail to Baluarte Santiago."

Jack whipped around and pointed toward the canyon's far end, which was a small, gray-blue oval from this distance. "It lets out on another canyon. Beyond that canyon, another day's ride, is Baluarte Santiago."

And Ciaran Yeats, Prophet added silently to himself.

Prophet glanced at Jack's men. "What about them? You sure they're gonna keep your secret."

"And what about you and El Rojo here?" Baja Jack looked cunningly up at Lou and Colter. "How can I be sure you two will keep the secret?"

"I reckon you can't be sure," Colter said.

"What good's a secret canyon lessen you can't use it when you need it most? Am I right?"

"I reckon you're right, Jack," Prophet allowed. "And for what it's worth, your secret is safe with me."

"Me, too," Colter agreed.

"What's that rumbling sound?" Prophet had been hearing it since he'd entered the canyon. It was so soft that he hadn't realized he'd been hearing it until just now. He could feel a faint vibration in the ground beneath his boots, like the reverberation you feel with the passing of a train.

Baja Jack grinned up at him, delighted by another secret.

He lifted his thick little right hand and hooked his index finger. "Come on. I'll show you something." He started to turn away but then turned back toward the men who were tending their horses. He ordered one of his men, Tío, to unsaddle his horse then added with an afterthought to unsaddle "his guests' " mounts and tend them, too.

Tío, a long-haired Mexican with mare's tail mustaches, gave Prophet and Colter the woolly eyeball through the smoke wafting up from the corn-husk cigarette he was smoking. That seemed to amuse Jack, who chuckled, gave a tolerant sigh, then glanced at Lou and Colter before turning away again, saying, "Right this way, *mi amigos.* Jack'll give you the grand tour."

He hitched his deerskin leggings up his broad hips then ambled off up the canyon between the looming dwellings that ever so vaguely resembled piled human skulls, their open doorways like empty eye sockets looking forbiddingly, maybe a little malevolently, down at the living intruders in their sanctuary.

CHAPTER 30

Jack inadvertently kicked a stone as, walking in his awkward, bandy-legged fashion, he said, "Pa and I had one helluva time figuring out what that sound was. We didn't even recognize it until our second visit to the canyon. I guess at first we thought it was the wind blowing over the tops of the canyon walls. But, no, no . . . that wasn't it."

A little breathless, kicking another rock and stumbling, Baja Jack continued on up the canyon, along the base of the dwellings on the canyon's left side. Prophet and Colter were dogging his heels.

Lou looked around, intrigued by the mystery of the place, trying to imagine what it had looked like here maybe a couple thousand years ago when those who had built the mud homes into the cliff walls still lived here in this little Indian town, working together. They likely ran out through the openings at either end to tend whatever beasts they tended, or maybe to hunt and bring back meat and skins they'd probably stretched and dried and turned into clothing right here on the canyon floor or on the ledges separating the various levels.

Both sides of the canyon were peppered with circular stone formations, black from charring, that had most likely been fire pits. In his mind's eye, Prophet watched the smoke from all those breakfast and supper fires roll up the canyon walls to turn to lazy wisps when they reached the open sky above. Maybe even a faint tang from the food that had once been cooked here, likely by the women to whom young children clung, had permeated the place so deeply that Prophet could still detect it.

Pshaw. That was just his imagination running wild.

All that remained here of the people who'd once lived here, maybe for many generations, were their ghosts. He didn't have to imagine them. He thought he could see them at the periphery of his vision, copper faces with mud-black eyes watching from the shadows. Lou gave a shudder.

Colter glanced at him skeptically. "You all right?"

Prophet glowered at him. "Hell, yeah."

"All right."

"All right, what?"

"Just *all right,*" Colter said with an ironic snort.

Jack stopped and pointed up to a stretch of crudely chiseled steps that rose toward a dark opening in the cliff wall, maybe fifty feet up from the canyon floor. "Up there," the little man said, breathless. "You two go up ahead of me and give me a hand. My legs is too short to make fast work of them steps. If I blow out a knee, my goose is cooked."

Lou and Colter mounted the steps ahead of Jack then reached back, each taking one of the older man's hands and half leading and half hoisting him up the staircase, the risers of which had been whittled down to near nubs in places by time and — what? By the many feet that had negotiated them over the long years this hidden, cliff-clinging village had been occupied?

Lou suppressed another shudder, this time at the incomprehensibility of so much time past.

They led Jack up the stairs and through the oval portal and into what appeared to be a room of sorts. It was impossible to tell just exactly what it was because it was nearly pitch-black in here. It smelled like rodent dung and cool, ancient stone.

"One of you got a match?" Jack asked. He was so breathless from the climb his chest rasped like sandpaper with each inhalation, and he could barely get the words out.

Prophet reached into his pocket for a lucifer and popped the sulfured tip on his thumbnail. The match flared, spreading a weak, brassy radiance. Baja Jack crouched with a grunt. Straightening, he held up a ten-inch-high lantern with a drop-away bottom.

He handed the lantern to Colter, then crouched again. When he straightened this time, he held a small box of short, wide candles. His face was swollen and red, his eyes dark as coals in their deep sockets.

"Stick a candle in the sumbitch and light the feller," he instructed Lou.

Prophet poked one of the candles into the lantern, attaching it to the spike at the bottom. He lit the candle with the match then tossed the match away.

Baja Jack grabbed the lantern's bail, swung around, and rasped, "Thisaway, pardners. Thisaway here!" Raising the lamp before him, he chuckled and walked straight out away from Lou and Colter, who stood regarding the little man dubiously.

Where was he going?

"Come on, come on!" Jack grinned tauntingly over his shoulder at Prophet. "Lassen yer yaller!" He winked and wheezed out a mocking laugh.

"I ain't yeller," Prophet grumbled, casting the grinning Colter a quick, indignant glare.

They followed the little man — where, God only knew. Maybe God didn't even know. Baja Jack seemed to be heading straight back into the ridge, beating back the shadows with his candle lamp. The rough stone floor, which appeared to have been chipped away with tools, dropped gradually.

As he followed Baja Jack and the soft yellow sphere of light with which the little English mestizo assaulted the thick velvety darkness before him, Prophet glanced at the stone walls passing on each side of the corridor. The walls had been decorated with crude paintings similar to those he'd seen before all across the West and which he'd attributed to ancient peoples.

Stick figures were walking along the walls — some taller than others, some holding spears. There were wavy blue lines upon which small stick figures reclined, extending their arms and legs, their mouths forming wide dark circles. Absently, Lou reached out and brushed his fingers across them.

The stone floor continued to drop.

The rumbling, which had been growing incrementally louder, was like muffled thunder now. The air had become humid and rife with the smell of mushrooms. It had also grown cooler.

The walls passing to each side were beaded with moisture.

Walking behind the seesawing, hard-breathing Baja Jack, Prophet and Colter exchanged a curious glance.

"Almost there now," Jack said roughly five minutes after they'd started out through the back of the room in which they'd found the lamp.

Beyond Jack and his sphere of weak light, Prophet thought something was moving. The rumbling grew louder . . .

Finally, as the rumbling became a roar above which Prophet could no longer hear his and the other two men's footsteps and spur chings, the walls pulled back away from him. Baja Jack stopped.

"This is far enough, gents," he yelled above the din.

Prophet stepped up to stand on the man's left side while Colter did the same to Jack's right. Lou gaped as he stared straight ahead and down at what was obviously an underground river roaring through yet another canyon.

Cavern, rather. It was fully enclosed.

The light from Jack's candle lamp shone like gold dust on the skin of a blacksnake, which was the river rushing past them from their left to their right. It appeared to curve toward them on their left, following a sharp bend in the cavern about thirty feet away.

It hammered violently past the spectators, thumping and throbbing, drumming against rocks and flailing against the stone banks, including the one on which Lou, Colter, and Baja Jack stood. Lou felt the river's drumbeat through his boots. It beat like a giant heart in the walls around him, in the stone ceiling arcing over him.

He felt the fine, cold spray of water against his face, dampening his clothes. It smelled vaguely of rotten eggs.

The river dropped sharply before him, on his right, the water foaming as it chugged and sprayed and tumbled away out of sight around yet another bend in its tomblike cavern.

It was a formidable sight, this underground stream. It seemed alive, like some ancient, forever-raging beast confined forever to the earth's bowels and not liking it one bit, struggling to free itself. Lou licked the moisture from his lips. It was cold and it tasted fresh but also a little sour, with that rotten-egg tang, like water he'd tasted from limestone *tinajas*.

Colter turned to Baja Jack, who stood staring dreamily out at the tumultuous water thundering through the gorge before him. The little man was thoroughly mesmerized. "Where does it come from?" Colter asked. "Where does it go?"

Baja Jack looked up at him. "I got no idea where it comes from. Probably deep underground. My pa figured it's part of some aquifer. Same one that carved out all these canyons and mountains in this part of Baja." He shook his head. "I can't tell you for sure where it comes from, but me and the old man tracked it to where it flows out of the mountains, about a mile downstream. Comes out nice, purty as you please, in a deep green valley. Flows on east to the Sea of Cortez."

Prophet turned to the stone wall to his left and yelled above the river's thunder. "Swing the light over this way, Jack."

Jack swung the light around, turning, revealing some of the paintings Prophet was staring at, absently tracing one in particular with his fingers. It was another small stick figure riding the tops of wavy lines. The figure's mouth was open, as though it were screaming.

"Bloody savages!" Jack cried, shaking his head and turning his mouth corners down.

"What?" Colter yelled, frowning down at the little man.

Baja Jack nodded at the figure beneath Lou's right index finger. "Poor little baby," he said, again shaking his head. "They musta took certain ones down here and threw 'em in. Some sort of sacrifice to the river gods rumbling beneath their town."

"You really think so?" Colter asked, incredulous.

"That's what the old man thought, and he was learned in the ways of the ancient folks. He figured the ancient ones who lived here was worried the water would rise and flood their town. Maybe it had in the past. To make sure it didn't do it again, they'd offer up the wee little ones — maybe the sick little ones and the old ones."

Jack paused to indicate a stick figure with long, white hair riding the wavy lines that were the river flowing through the gorge. "They'd throw 'em to the river gods to keep 'em happy and to keep themselves high and dry. Savages!" Jack shouted, shaking his head in anger. "Imagine all the poor little screaming wee ones and the old ones that got thrown into that river. You can see their bones — little white pieces here and there — sticking out of the riverbank where the stream flows out of the mountains."

Again, Jack shook his head and yelled, *"Savages!"*

Prophet stared at the figures blazed on the wall. They shone behind a layer of moisture on which Jack's lamp glistened like gold dust. He gave a little start when the light moved and a shadow passed through it, entering his field of vision on his right.

Baja Jack stared gravely up at him, his eyes wide and round, even the crossed one, which looked especially loony all of a sudden. "You can bet the seed bull this place is haunted. By the ghosts of the wee little screamin' ones and the poor defenseless old-timers who were thrown into that river to drown and get their bones spit out in that valley yonder!"

"I don't doubt it a bit," Prophet vaguely heard himself mutter. He hadn't meant to say it. He didn't think he'd said it loudly enough for Jack to hear. Maybe Jack only read his lips. Whatever the case, Baja Jack had understood. He gave Lou a crisp nod of agreement, winking his uncrossed eye.

Lou felt his ears warm a little with embarrassment. Sometimes he surprised even himself with his superstitions, his other worldly hauntings that were part and parcel to his Old Southern heritage.

He turned his gaze back to the roaring river. For just an instant, he saw a child riding those black, foam-frothed waves. For just that one second, he could hear the poor babe's wailing cries. Chicken flesh rose all over his body, and his intestines writhed.

He turned to Baja Jack, no longer caring one whit about showing his fear. He'd rather face twenty blood-hungry Apaches than ghosts any day of the week. "Let's get the hell outta here, Jack. I for one done seen enough of this place!"

Baja Jack smiled up at him in frank understanding.

"Come on, fellers," he bellowed, ambling back into the dark corridor, the weak lamplight waging a halfhearted war with the far more powerful darkness. "Come on, fellers — let's done get us a drink. My throat's drier'n the last button on a rattlesnake's tail!"

CHAPTER 31

Lou woke with a start.

He sat up, staring into the darkness of the canyon beyond the cold ashes of his and Colter's fire.

"What is it?" He'd awakened the redhead, who'd lifted his head from his own saddle on the other side of the fire. Colter already had his Remington in his hand; he'd already cocked the hammer.

Beyond him, Baja Jack and the little man's men snored around their own dead fire maybe fifteen to thirty feet away. Lou could barely see them in the canyon's penetrating darkness. He could, however, see the ridge looming on the canyon's north side. The stacked mud houses seemed to radiate a very soft, gray-blue glow. The light was probably a reflection of the starlight, for the sky between the ridge walls was peppered with those flickering lights, like snow smeared across black velvet.

387

"Lou?" Colter said.

"What is it?"

"You hear somethin'?"

"Yeah." Prophet shook his head. "I mean, no. Go back to sleep. Everything's all right."

"Good." Colter depressed his Remy's hammer and returned the pistol to its holster. "I was havin' a nice dream about one very talented young lady."

He lay back against his saddle, curled onto his side, and in seconds he was breathing deeply again.

Prophet stared up the ridge at those ghostly hovels fairly radiating with unearthly power. A malignant presence, like one of the demons his widowed great-granny used to mutter about and pray against, especially in her later years, when she'd ring her cabin in Dogwood Holler completely with salt, hang goat heads over her door, and lay strings of dried snake skins on her window-sills.

Prophet had heard something. But what he'd heard had been in his head. He'd known it even as he'd heard it, but it had awakened him, anyway.

It was the scream of one of those small children being carried down that stony corridor to the river snaking through the earth's bowels — a diabolical giant that eats children and old people. He'd heard it, all right, and it had sounded real. So real that he couldn't help wondering, a little sheepishly, if he hadn't so much heard it as *remembered* it . . .

Wait. *Remembered* it?

"Jesus, you're gettin' all woolly-headed, old son." Lou tossed his bedroll aside and rose. Colter muttered something in his half sleep, and Lou reassured him with a whispered: "Just gonna take a stroll. Go back to that sweet-smellin' señorita, Red."

Colter groaned as though in the affirmative, and his breathing was once more slow and regular.

Lou pulled his denims and boots on quietly, buckled his Colt and shell belt around his waist, donned his hat, and trod off down the canyon, toward the mysterious doorway through which he'd been introduced to this mysterious place. He wasn't sure he was glad to have been introduced. The chasm pestered him something awful. He'd felt a dark force at work here even before Jack had shown him that river, far less peaceful than the one in the Bible he'd heard about, and told him about the little tykes and the old people.

Sacrificial lambs.

"Oh, stop your fool-headed thinkin'," Lou

scolded himself as he walked out through the canyon's front door, so to speak. He climbed the rise and walked into the main canyon. A cool night breeze blew against him. He turned to face it, removed his hat, and tipped his head back, fully accepting the cool, refreshing air against his cheeks and forehead.

"There, now . . . that's better."

He chuckled at his superstitious nature, leaned back against a high rock, and dug his makings out of his pocket. "Much better," he said. "I'm all through with that crazy thinkin' now. I'm ole Granny Brindle's wild child, I am at that, but I gotta resist them crazy thoughts, I purely do, or I'll go as crazy as she was, and that was as crazy as a tree full of owls!"

He chuckled as he troughed a wheat paper between the index finger and forefinger of his left hand. He'd just started to sprinkle chopped tobacco onto the paper, when a hushed female voice said, "Lou!"

Prophet jerked with a violent start. He dropped the paper and the tobacco he'd sprinkled onto it and looked up, stifling a terrified yell. He looked around wildly, pushing away from the rock and sliding the Peacemaker from its holster, clicking the hammer back.

"Holster the hogleg," the woman's voice said as footsteps sounded to his left, accompanied by the soft ring of spur rowels. "I'm not going to kill you. At least, not now."

"Louisa?" he said, squinting doubtfully into the darkness.

She moved out of the rocks, a slender figure topped with gold-blond hair that glowed softly in the starlight. It hung down from beneath her tan Stetson, the chin thong dangling against her chest clad in a striped wool serape.

Lou could see the pearl grips of her fancy silver Colts holstered on both her narrow but womanly rounded hips, the serape tucked behind the pistols, making them available at a moment's notice. Her sun-faded denims were tucked into the tops of her brown riding boots.

Louisa Bonaventure stopped before him. She was a head shorter, so she tipped her head back to gaze up at him, lifting the corners of her beautiful, tender mouth with a wry smile. "Surprise, surprise."

Lou looked her up and down. "This ain't you."

Louisa scowled beneath the broad brim of her Stetson. "What?"

"This. This here." Prophet waved his hand

at her, indicating her delightful figure before him. "This ain't you."

"What ain't me?" she asked, mocking his poor grammar. Hers was perfect, of course. And she rarely cursed but when she did, it was usually at him.

Lou gestured again. "This ain't you. You ain't standin' here. Either I'm dreaming, or . . ." He turned toward the door to the secondary canyon in which the cliff dwellings lay. "It's this place . . . this crazy haunted place . . ."

"What crazy haunted place?"

"The place . . . in there . . ."

"Oh, for Pete's sake!" Louisa stepped up in front of him, grabbed his shoulders, rose onto the toes of her boots, and pressed her lips to his.

When she pulled away, she dropped to her heels and smiled up at him.

"Well, I'll be damned," Prophet said, astonished. "It *is* you!"

"It's me, all right."

"What are you doin' here? How'd you get here? How in the holy blazes did you know where I was? Baja Jack said no one but him . . . and now his men and me and Colter Farrow . . . know about this place."

"I followed you."

Lou scowled down at her in disbelief.

"Followed me? How far?"

"Ever since you left Silver City." Outside Silver City was where they'd had their falling-out over his snoring. Not just his snoring. The argument had multiplied the way arguments usually do, to include her slurs against his hygiene, his horse, and his ancestors and a few more things.

Lou continued to scowl down at her in disbelief.

Louisa shrugged. "I had a premonition about something bad happening to you down here. About you getting yourself into a situation that . . . well, a situation you didn't have full control of." Her right eye glistened wetly. "I had a dream that you came down here to Baja, fouled up, and got yourself killed, you big galoot!"

She gave a rare sniff of sadness.

Again, she shrugged — a single shoulder this time. "So I followed you. I stayed back because I was still angry. Besides, I knew you were still angry with me . . . and didn't want you to see me . . . so . . . I held back."

"You been shadowing me ever since Silver City?" Prophet couldn't believe it. Had he gotten so old and feeble that he didn't know when he was being trailed? What if she'd been someone out to snuff his wick . . . which she had been a time or two in the

393

past . . .

"Don't get your neck in a hump," Louisa scolded him in his own colorful language. "I kept well back. An Apache wouldn't have known I was back there."

"I doubt that." Prophet renewed his accusatory scowl. "Hey, what about when them *rurales* buried us up to our necks in . . . ?"

"I was about to take them down when your little friend and his mongrel cutthroats stepped in and saved your bacon."

"Ah, I see." Prophet raked a pensive thumb along his jawline then fired off another accusing glare. "Boy, you were close then, weren't ya?"

"Well, you were a little distracted by that time. Really, Lou — drinking hopped-up mezcal and letting *rurales* waltz into your camp to bury you neck deep in the desert! You see why I followed you?"

"We all make mistakes, Miss Persnickety Bloomers!" Lou leaned back against the rock he'd leaned against a moment ago, when he'd thought he was alone out here. He pulled out his makings sack again and started to build another quirley.

Louisa moved up close to him again, spread her feet, and crossed her arms on her chest, confrontationally. "Where are you headed, Lou?"

"Don't you know?"

"Ciaran Yeats?"

Again, he scowled with deep annoyance. "You've gotten close more than a coupla times. Close enough to overhear me and the younker gassin' over our plans!"

"Everyone in this part of Baja knows that Alejandra de la Paz was kidnapped by Yeats. After you visited Hacienda de la Paz, I figured you were after Yeats . . . sicced on him by the don." Louisa paused, canted her head to one side with even more accusing. "By the way, how was your evening with Señorita de la Paz? The beautiful Marisol . . ."

She tapped the toe of one cocked boot against the ground and wrinkled her nose at him.

Prophet looked at her again angrily, ready to cut loose with another tirade. But he stopped himself, poked the quirley into his mouth, and sealed it with his spit. He popped a lucifer to life on his thumbnail, touched the flame to the quirley, and said, "Wouldn't you like to know."

He blew smoke at her.

She waved it away. "You're an animal."

Lou smiled smugly as he puffed the cigarette. "That's what she said." He frowned.

"Say . . . what were you doing while I was . . . you know . . . otherwise involved at Hacienda de la Paz?"

"Never mind that. What I want to know is how in the world do you think you're going to be able to kill Yeats and squirrel his daughter out of that old Spanish fort? You do know how many men he has riding for him, don't you? And how savage they all are?"

"Yeah, I know a few things, Miss Smarty. What *I* want to know is how do *you* know all this about Yeats?"

"I've known about Yeats for years. He kidnaps young women . . . young peon women, mostly. He takes them from their families and turns them into slaves for his and his men's diabolical desires. When he tires of them, or they get sick or pregnant, he sends them across the Sea of Cortez to work for pimps in the slums of Mexico City where they cater to the ugly needs of men even more squalid than himself."

"Yeah, you would know about him, wouldn't you?" Louisa specialized in such men as Ciaran Yeats, who committed crimes against girls and families, similar to the way the Handsome Dave Duvall bunch had devastated Louisa's own family, leaving her an orphan. Now she rode the long lonely bloody western trails, scouring the frontier of men just like Handsome Dave . . . and Ciaran Yeats.

"I reckon it's right surprising you haven't hunted Yeats down by now," Prophet remarked, then took another deep drag off his quirley.

"Oh, I've thought about it. Unlike some, I make use of my winter vacations." She'd spouted that out in true Vengeance Queen–uppity fashion.

"I ain't exactly whistlin' 'Dixie' down here, you know."

"No, but you're going after Yeats for money."

"Yeah, well, I'm sorry not all of us are bleedin' hearts. I do like to eat a meal now and then, and so does Mean and Ugly."

"That horse should be fed a bullet."

"Be that as it may, you gonna shadow me to Yeats or do you wanna ride along?" Prophet smiled ironically at the pretty blonde. "Shall I introduce you to my pards in yonder?"

"I'll make my own friends, if you don't mind."

"Uppity!"

"Besides, I don't trust Baja Jack and neither should you."

"How do you know Jack?"

"Like I said, I make use of my winter vacations. Nasty little bandito. He grows locoweed for Yeats. Everybody knows that, and you would, too, if when you came down here you didn't just —"

"I'll do what I want on my own time, if you don't mind! And get your snooty tongue off Baja Jack. He pulled me and Colter out of a bad situation."

"Yes, didn't he?" Louisa gave an ironic snort.

Prophet studied the coal of his cigarette, which had burned down to a nub. "What don't you trust about Jack?"

Louisa gave a weary sigh, doffed her hat, and ran her hand back through her long, thick, gold-blond hair. "Think about it, Lou. He grows that vile weed for Yeats."

"I hear it keeps him alive."

"It's turned him into a madman. Him and his army of degenerates. They're all addicted to the stuff."

"You can't blame Baja Jack for turnin' a nickel."

Louisa stuffed her hat back onto her head, gave another tolerant sigh, and crossed her arms on her chest. "Do you really think he's going to let you and your redheaded friend just waltz into Baluarte Santiago and drill a couple of rounds into Yeats, his best customer?"

It was Prophet's turn to give an ironic chuff. "He doesn't know that's what we're gonna do, silly child!"

"Oh, please!" Louisa threw her pretty head back and trilled out a sarcastic laugh in true Louisa fashion.

Prophet stared at her. Chagrin buzzed around his ears like a pesky fly. He didn't say anything but only studied on the notion she'd planted in his brain.

"He knows you're a bounty hunter, doesn't he?" Louisa asked though it was obvious she knew the answer.

"Of course he does. I'm right famous, don't ya know." Of course, Louisa might even be more famous but he wasn't about to remind her of that.

"Lou, do you really think Baja Jack, who knows you're a bounty hunter, doesn't at least *suspect* that you're in this part of Baja because you're out to kill Ciaran Yeats, a man with multiple, high-dollar bounties on his head north of the border?"

Again, Prophet just stared at her. That pesky fly was joined by another . . . and another.

Louisa said in that annoyingly confident way of hers, "I have a pretty good notion that Baja Jack is leading you to Ciaran Yeats to —"

"Kill me?"

"Or to let Yeats do it."

Prophet flicked the quirley stub away. It bounced, red cinders flying before glinting out. He stared at where he'd thrown it, suspicion building in him, poking at his belly like a dull stick.

Louisa placed a hand on his right cheek, near his jawline. "You're bleeding, you idiot.

"Huh?"

"Your face looks like ground beef left out in the sun."

Lou fingered the cut over his swollen right eye. It left a faint smear of blood on his index finger. He shrugged. "It's been a hard ride." He gave a droll chuckle. "I think I'll spend next winter in Dakota."

Louisa pulled a lace-edged pink hankie out of her back pocket then rose up on her boot toes again. She dabbed the hankie at the cut over his swollen eye. She touched it to her tongue, gave him a vaguely coquettish sidelong glance, then went to work on the cut again.

"I swear," she said as she worked, "I don't know how you get along without me."

"I manage."

"Yes . . . the lovely Marisol."

"Jealous?"

"Not at all. I just feel sorry for her. There's obviously such a paucity of men around Hacienda de la Paz that she —"

Prophet grabbed her, drew her to him, and kissed her. She resisted at first then returned the kiss, groaning as they ground their lips together.

Finally, she pulled away from him, staring up at him, breathing hard.

"I've missed you," he confessed.

"I know." Louisa smiled, already back to her old tricks. She looked at the blood-stained hankie, wrinkled her nose, and held it out to him. "Here. You can have that."

Prophet took it without looking at it. He stared at her, desiring her the way he always desired her — with a surging, hammering, nearly overpowering need.

She backed away from him, smiling.

"Where you going?"

"Back to my camp."

"Why don't you ride with us?"

"Into that trap?" Louisa shook her head. "No thanks. I'll keep an eye on you, though, you big galoot — for all the good it'll do you with as many men as Yeats has riding for him."

She shook her head, giving a dark sigh.

She blew him a kiss, swung around, and

tramped off into the night.

Just like that, she was gone, and Prophet stood staring after her. As though to reassure himself she'd really been here, and he hadn't just dreamed her, he looked at the pink handkerchief in his hand.

He clenched it in his fist then started back to his bedroll. "Miss Uppity Bloomers!"

CHAPTER 32

"We'll be meeting our friend today — eh, Lou?" Colter said the next morning after they and Baja Jack and his men had enjoyed an early breakfast of tortillas, frijoles, and coffee.

Now they were all saddling their horses. Old Pepe was placing the *aparejos* and panniers on the burros while singing a typically forlorn Mexican ballad and smoking a cornhusk cigarette that dribbled ashes as the old man worked.

Lou was reaching under Mean and Ugly's belly to tie the latigo straps. "Sounds like we'll get there today, yeah. According to Jack."

Colter had finished saddling Northwest. Now he moved up close to Mean and stared over the saddle at Lou, frowning curiously. "Somethin' botherin' you, Lou? You ain't said much so far this mornin'. That ain't like you."

Prophet cast a quick, furtive glance toward Baja Jack, who was dressing down one of his men, whom he'd apparently caught spicing his morning coffee with tequila. His rule was only a couple of sips of tarantula juice during lunch, to wash the beans down, and a few more at night, excluding those men on first guard duty, of course.

Last night no guards had been posted since Baja Jack was fully confident that no one but him and his present company knew about the ancient mud dwellings in the secondary canyon.

Baja Jack strictly forbade morning libations, wanting his men to be as clear as "Baptist preachers and Madre María on Easter Sunday her own damn self" at the start of the day. It was a somewhat comical sight — little, squat, bull-legged, hawk-nosed Baja Jack remonstrating a man who was easily twice as tall as he was and who could, if he'd wanted, have squashed Jack like a bug without trying. The bigger man just stared silently down in chagrin at Jack, however, absently rubbing his hands up and down on his serape.

Lou was glad to see Jack preoccupied at the moment. He wanted to have a quick, secret palaver with his trail partner. He hadn't slept much after talking with Louisa last night in the main canyon, because he knew she'd been right, and he felt like a fool for not having considered the possible problem himself.

Lou gazed over his saddle at Colter. "Keep an eye on Jack, Red."

Colter frowned. "Huh?"

"Just keep an eye on him."

"You don't trust him?"

"Uh . . ." Prophet cleared his throat. "Somethin' sort of occurred to me last night, after I walked out for my stroll and had me a ponder." He saw no reason to mention that his female partner was shadowing him. At least not yet. It was damned embarrassing, his getting shadowed by his female partner and not even suspecting she was back there. And then her informing him of what he should have recognized as an obvious threat.

No, it was just too much to admit to right off . . .

"What occurred to you last night, Lou?"

"Jack might be onto us."

Colter frowned. "Onto us?"

"Yeah. You know . . ."

Prophet glanced over at Jack. The little man had finished dressing down the morning tequila-imbiber and had gone over to palaver with old Pepe. His mood had changed suddenly, like Mexican governments that came and went with the wind, and now he was laughing and sharing dirty stories in Spanish with the old burro wrangler while the other men finished saddling their horses.

Lou continued with: "I'm thinkin' Jack might have figured out we're after Yeats. To kill him. You know — since he knows I'm a bounty hunter an' all. He might've figured out our plan, see, and, if so, he ain't gonna cotton to the idea of our killin' his main customer."

He glanced at Jack once more then turned back to Colter. "He might be leading us into a trap, see, is what I'm sayin'."

Colter stared across the saddle at Lou. He smiled, chuckled, and said, "Of course he does." He chuckled again and regarded Prophet skeptically. "Yeah, he probably does, Lou! I guess I sort of figured you already figured that out, so I saw no point in bringin' it up!"

Lou stared across the saddle at him, his ears burning.

Colter said, "I figured we *both* figured it was a risk worth taking, since Jack's gonna take us right up to Yeats's front doorstep an' all. I mean, how else were we gonna find the Mad Major? Hell, we're about to get a personalized introduction to the locoweed-addicted son of a buck!"

Lou's ears burned. "So, you . . . then . . . you already figured . . ."

"Yeah, of course," Colter said, grinning across the saddle. "I guess the trick is gonna be how do we do-si-do around Baja Jack and kill Yeats without getting ourselves killed in the process, since we're probably gonna have to buck both Yeats's men and Jack's men, too. Oh, and of course there's the little matter of rescuing the don's daughter from Baluarte Santiago."

Colter chuckled and wagged his head. "I don't know about you, Lou, but this trip to Mexico is turning out to be the most fun I've had in a long time. It beats running from the law up north." He winced and clutched his side. "Except for a couple of nasty bullet burns, I mean . . ."

"All right." Lou looked away in shame, tapping his fingers on his saddle. "All right, then. Never mind me . . ."

Again, Colter chuckled, turned, and walked over to his horse.

"Yeah," Lou said. "Never mind me . . ."

It was late in the afternoon after a long hot day of riding when Baja Jack reined his horse to a stop at the crest of a steep ridge.

It was one of many ridges they'd crossed that day.

Jack leaned back in his saddle, hooked one of his short, crooked legs around his saddle horn, and thumbed his sombrero back off his forehead. He lifted his chin to indicate a large, pale bastion topping the next ridge beyond, maybe a mile away as the crow flies.

"That, gents," said Jack, "is Baluarte Santiago."

Prophet stretched his gaze across the next canyon, squinting against the harsh sunlight. Baluarte Santiago was an impressive piece of Spanish masonry, at least regarding the masonry of three or four hundred years ago. The mottled pale walls appeared thick and tall from this distance and punctuated by domed defensive turrets. Inside the walls rose a heavy, blocklike building of several levels and wings and which had likely housed the bastion's garrison and commanding officers as well as stables for the garrison's horses.

Probably even a prison, the bounty hunter assumed, given the nature of men from all ages of history . . .

Prophet's party faced the old fort's west side but they were far enough forward that Lou could see the long, wide, stone-paved ramp that rose at a slant from the ground level to the edge of a moat that ringed the bulwark.

Over the moat, there'd likely been a stout drawbridge that could be raised and lowered against possible attackers by a rudimentary system of winches and pulleys. The bridge would have been pulled up to fill the large, rectangular, deeply recessed front doorway abutted by two guard turrets outfitted with loopholes for cannons.

After all these years, however — centuries, rather — even the stoutest wooden door would have long since moldered to dust and splinters. What Prophet could see stretching between the moat and the bulwark's front entrance now was likely a recently con-structed wooden bridge, but he couldn't tell for sure from this distance, squinting as he was against the sunlight reflecting off the Sea of Cortez.

Baluarte Santiago faced the deep blue, rolling waters of the Mar de Cortés, which stretched away to a far, pale horizon on Prophet's left. At this time of the day, the sea's deep, roiling waters were cobalt blue overlaid with the golden chain mail of reflected sunlight.

Baja Jack turned to smile at Lou and Colter sitting on their horses to his left. "Big old place, ain't it? Ain't nothin' purty to look at, but I reckon it did its job back in the olden days."

Jack pointed his stubby left arm toward the Sea of Cortez's sun-gilded waters stitched with the cream of rolling whitecaps. "Them stout walls protected the fort from the old buccaneer raiders from the sea — pirates, don't ya know!"

He laughed at the romance of those adventurous olden times, though Prophet would have bet that the men and maybe some women who'd resided inside the old bulwark hadn't thought the times all that romantic and adventurous.

Harrowing and dangerous maybe. But not romantic.

Jack swung his stubby arm to indicate the stark desert mountains to the right of the old fort. "The walls on that side protected the fort from the Indios that haunted all them rocks inland, including the family of my dearly departed *madre*. The Indios didn't take kindly to the Spanish invaders, especially when the Spanish forced the Indios into slave labor growing their food and building that fort and stampeding Catholicism down their throats for their trouble!"

Jack laughed again and shook his head.

He arched a brow in devilish delight at Lou and Colter, and said, "When the slaves died while building the fort, the Spanish added their bones to the mortar. You can see 'em when you get up close. In some places you can see where they added whole skulls and arm bones an' hip bones an' the like, not even botherin' to grind 'em up. Oh, them was grisly times!" Jack howled.

Prophet silently wondered how less grisly the times were at Baluarte Santiago now, with Ciaran Yeats having taken up residence . . .

He kept his gaze on the massive bulwark spread across the otherwise stark crest of the next ridge and felt a chill rise from the small of his back and spread out across his shoulder blades. He and Colter were about to meet Ciaran Yeats. They had to find a way to kill the man and rescue Alejandra de la Paz.

Back at Hacienda de la Paz, when he was under the spell of both the old don and the beguilingly lovely Señorita Marisol, the job hadn't seemed nearly as hard as it did now. Back there, it had seemed romantic and adventurous.

Now it rose before him, harrowing and dangerous.

Now he sort of wished he were lying with the dusky-skinned, chocolate-eyed señoritas of Sayulita . . .

"Come on, gents," said Baja Jack, dropping his boot back into its stirrup custom-built for a child-sized leg, and nudging his horse on down the trail. "It ain't gettin' any earlier in the day, and my throat sure ain't gettin' any wetter just sittin' here!"

He laughed.

Prophet looked at Colter, sitting to his right. The redhead was staring across the canyon and up the next ridge at Baluarte Santiago, the lair of Ciaran Yeats. He was surprised to see apprehension furling the young man's brows. He hadn't thought Colter Farrow was afraid of anything, much less his own demise. Lou had figured he was like Louisa in that way.

But, no — the kid appeared to be having second thoughts. Or if not second thoughts, at least he wasn't as much in a hurry for romance and adventure as he'd been that morning when he'd laughed in the face of all that could go wrong at the end of the trail.

Colter must have sensed Prophet's stare. He jerked his head toward the bounty hunter. He frowned, suddenly peevish. He brushed his rein ends against his coyote dun's left hip. "You heard the man, Lou," he grumbled, setting out down the ridge and into the dust kicked up by Baja Jack's mount. "Our throats ain't gettin' any wetter, sittin' here."

Prophet hoped that it wasn't a dark omen that a diamondback rattler, with a body nearly as thick as his wrist, seemed to take umbrage at Mean and Ugly and came slithering out from a patch of shade along the trail. Its diamond-shaped head was up and its eyes were flat and rife with unthinking, savage purpose. It shot as though fired out of a snake-firing cannon toward Mean's right front hock.

Old Pepe, riding on his broad-barreled donkey directly behind Prophet, saw the snake at the same time Lou did, and yelled, "Hy-yiy-yiy-yiy-*yiyy*!"

Mean swerved away from the snake, and sunfished a good four feet in the air. Prophet's heart leaped into his throat. Holding Mean's reins with one hand, he swiped his .45 from its holster, cocked it, and, seeing the snake coiled up on the right side of the trail, button tail raised, ready to strike again, Lou took quick aim.

His Peacemaker bucked six times, roaring. By the time the sixth bullet had plowed through the snake, there wasn't much meat left, the other five big rounds having hit pay dirt, as well.

What was left of the snake, which wasn't

much — it looked like a chunk of raw beef chopped up for the stewpot — lay writhing in the sand and rocks along the trail.

Prophet got Mean settled down, leaning forward and patting the horse with his left hand. Mean regarded the snake askance, withers quivering, the big heart still pumping quickly. Horses hated sidewinders as much as wildcats. Lou didn't blame them a bit.

There was a silence for a time as Prophet's gun smoke thinned and the echoes of his blasts rolled away to silence. Then the others, including Baja Jack and Colter, gathered in a ragged circle around Lou to stare down at the dead viper.

Jack and his men, including old Pepe, looked from Lou to the snake and then back at Lou, their lower jaws hanging. Lou's eyes were probably still a little glassy. Baja Jack grinned. He slapped his thigh and started laughing as though at the funniest joke he'd ever heard, and not three seconds later the others were joining in.

Their hysterical guffaws vaulted toward the heavens, echoing.

Prophet looked at them and then at Colter. The redhead looked back at him, and then he started laughing, too. Prophet didn't know what in the hell they were laughing about — hadn't they ever seen a dead snake before? — but in no time he was laughing, too.

As though at the funniest joke he'd ever heard.

CHAPTER 33

Prophet followed Baja Jack and Colter down
the ridge toward the canyon choked with
wiry brush, cactus, and boulders.

The trail switchbacked gradually. At the
bottom of the canyon, it snaked off to the
right before crossing the canyon at the only
place the debris would allow. At the other
side of the canyon, the trail meandered back
along the base of the ridge before climbing
the ridge at a steep, forty-five-degree angle.

Mean and the other horses were blowing
hard in the hot sun, their coats lathered, by
the time they trudged to the top of the ridge
upon which the impressive masonry project
of Baluarte Santiago sat like the mountain's
capstone. The regal old ruin sat facing the
sea, its back to the savage-teeming wilds of
Baja, silently sending out its challenges in
both directions.

As Lou looked at it now, head tipped back
to peer up at the grand old battlement, it

looked as abandoned as it likely had been before Ciaran Yeats had moved in. The fort shone with the cracks, dimples, gouges, and discolorations of time. Having weathered the ages not without cost, the guardian of San Luis Point was silhouetted darkly and formidably against the glowing orange sun plunging toward the far western crags.

Now Prophet saw several men with rifles standing atop the stout, high walls. They were dwarfed by the sprawling masonry structure looming behind them, inside the walls.

One of the pickets stood near the wall's right-front corner, near the snub-peaked defensive turret. The other stood to the left of the large open doorway. Both men were facing the newcomers. The one on the right stood resting a rifle on his shoulder, a *cigarro* dangling from between his lips as he stood studying the newcomers, head tipped curiously to one side.

"Holy cow — don't recollect ever seein' such a pretty sight," Colter said.

Lou turned toward the redhead, who'd swung his horse to study the ocean lapping against a white sand beach to the east. Near shore the water was more aquamarine colored than the cobalt farther out, the low waves rolling onto the shore, laced in the

417

white of a sparkling froth. Seagulls wheeled, shrieking.

Between the ocean and the bluff the fortification stood on, a village sprawled amongst the rocks and clean white sand — a humble but relatively prosperous-looking village of stone and adobe huts and mud jacales and *establos* roofed with grass or red tiles. Palm trees and organ-pipe cactus jutted among the pale structures, which appeared to stretch for at least a mile in both directions along the meandering shoreline.

Here and there stout, dark-skinned, colorfully clad women, some wearing straw sombreros, toiled in the surf, cleaning fish that had likely been hauled in from the wooden, single-masted boats that pitched at anchor out where the aquamarine water turned to cobalt. Nearly at day's end now, the boats were darkening, their masts gilded with the angling rays of the sun.

A gun barked behind Prophet and Colter.

Both men wheeled, closing their hands over their own holstered sidearms, to stare toward the bulwark. Baja Jack and Jack's men were all staring in that direction, as well, most also with their hands on their guns. Several of the horses sidestepped, jittery. One of the burros brayed, weary from the long ride and wary now, as well.

The gun barked again. Again. Again.

A man screamed.

Another laughed loudly.

Prophet turned to Baja Jack. "What the hell's that all about?"

Jack grinned edgily and lifted his shoulders in a tight shrug. "Who knows? It is Baluarte Santiago."

The laughter rose again, even more loudly than before.

It was followed by another thundering report of what sounded like a .45 revolver.

A girl screamed shrilly.

"Jesus Christ!" Prophet said, scowling at the broad, vaguely rectangular opening in the wall at the far end of the stone ramp.

Lou poked his spurs into Mean's flanks. The horse leaped onto the ramp and moved up the incline at nearly a full gallop, its shod hooves clacking on the stones.

"Lou!" Jack cried. "Wait, *pendejo*!"

The little man's admonition was nearly drowned by yet another rocketing pistol report as well as by Mean's clacking hooves. The horse thundered across the wooden bridge that spanned the wide, dry moat ringing the bastion and hurled itself and rider through the broad open gate in the thick masonry wall.

More clacking and thunder rose behind

419

Lou. He glanced briefly behind him to see Colter and Northwest hot on Mean's hocks.

"Hey, hey, hey!" yelled one of the guards on the wall above Prophet.

A rifle belched. A bullet plumed dirt in the bastion's graveled earthen yard several feet ahead of Prophet.

Lou drew back tightly on the dun's reins and stared to his left. A man lay belly down in the gravel roughly fifty yards away from him. A girl lay in the yard between the prone man and the hulking, multistoried, castle-like structure of Baluarte Santiago rising straight out away from Prophet.

Two men stood on a balcony of that great, sprawling structure. One of the men was leaning forward, crossing his arms on the balcony rail. The other — a big, red-haired, red-bearded man in jodhpurs and a red sash pulled taut over his bulging belly — was holding two big silver-chased Russian revolvers.

The fat, red-haired man was aiming one of the Russians over the balcony rail toward the girl. The gun bucked, flames lapping from its barrel. The bullet tore into the ground near the girl, who screamed and glanced back in horror over her exposed brown shoulder at the shooter.

"Get up, you disgusting *puta,*" bellowed

the Russian-wielding fat man on the balcony. "Run for your life. Go ahead — make a play for it, or I'll shoot you right where you lay! Drill ya a third eye in the back of your traitorous head!"

The dark-haired man beside him, dressed all in black, threw his head back and roared.

The girl on the ground pleaded for her life in anguished Spanish. A young girl. Prophet didn't think she was much over thirteen. She wore a short red dress with green and gold embroidering, and that was all. One of the dress's thin straps hung down her thin, brown arm.

"Hold on!" Prophet shouted then booted Mean and Ugly into a gallop once more.

"Dangit, Lou!" Colter protested behind him.

Ignoring his trail partner, Prophet and the line-back dun dashed toward the Mexican girl in the skimpy red dress.

"Hold your fire, you son of a buck!" Prophet bellowed, checking Mean down abruptly then leaping out of his saddle.

He took two running strides and then dropped to a knee beside the sobbing girl, stretching one arm around her slender shoulders while placing his right hand over his still-holstered Peacemaker's grips.

A Gatling gun rattled above and behind

him. Reacting more than thinking, Lou ripped the Peacemaker from its holster, wheeled, and saw a man crouched over a mosquito-shaped brass gun on the wall near the open gate. The man had centered the machine gun's maw on Prophet's chest, the gun's swivel squawking. He'd just started to turn the Gatling's crank when Prophet drew a bead on him and fired.

The man jerked backward, firing the Gatling gun into the dirt several feet to Prophet's left, the hiccupping reports echoing shrilly. The gunner slumped forward, cursing in Spanish, then slid forward down the brass canister and over the wall. He screamed as he stretched out in the air, spreading his arms and legs like wings before hitting the ground at the base of the wall with a loud grunt and a crunching thud.

Prophet spied movement in the corner of his right eye. He turned his head quickly to see another man run toward him, extending a rifle.

Prophet punched a bullet through the red necktie adorning the man's chest, between the flaps of a hand-tooled deerskin vest.

The man dropped to his knees in the gravel before falling and rolling. He lay on his back writhing briefly and groaning through gritted teeth before he fell silent and still in death. His bloody necktie lay slack against his chest.

Around Prophet rose the metallic rasps of rifles being cocked. Men were cursing in both English and Spanish. A cold stone dropped in Lou's belly when he realized that he was nearly surrounded by heavily armed men and they were all moving toward him fast.

"Lou!" Colter grunted out somewhere behind him.

He knew what the kid was thinking. Now he'd done it. This time, he'd really done it. *Scratch, get a fresh shovel ready . . .*

Then a man's voice shouted commandingly, "Hold your fire! Hold your fire, lads! Everyone, hold your fire and just take it easy *one bloody minute!*"

Prophet stretched his gaze toward the two men standing on the second-floor balcony. The balcony hadn't been part of the original fortification. It had been improvised with steel frames and wooden planks. The fat, red-haired, red-bearded man stared over the long barrel of his Russian revolver at Prophet. He was drawing a bead on Lou's forehead. Lou could feel that bead tickling him just above the bridge of his nose.

The sweat on his back turned cold.

The black-haired man standing beside the red-haired man also held two pistols, normal-sized. He held them down low by his legs clad in black whipcord, outside of the black fustian he wore. He stood scowling over the balcony rail at the disruptor.

Lou lowered his gaze from the massive main building of the bulwark of Santiago, to the men surrounding him. They were dirty and bearded and they were Mexicans and Yanquis and several other races. They smelled bad and they looked even worse, with angry eyes cast with a feral sort of amusement. They edged closer and closer around Lou and Colter Farrow, who had swung down from his horse and now stood holding his reins, looking around as Prophet was.

"Big man," yelled the fat redheaded gent, who was also bespectacled, Prophet now saw, the lenses of the man's small, round glasses glinting in the afternoon's softening light, "who in the bloody hell are you and just who in the bloody hell do you think you are, ridin' in here, all blood 'n' thunder, like some bloody knight in shinin' armor gallopin' in to save that there *damsel in distress*? Gallopin' in on the ugliest horse I believe I've ever laid my eyes on, I might add . . ."

Mild laughter issued from the men around Prophet in response to the slight against Mean and Ugly.

He'd spoken with an Irish accent.

That had to be Yeats himself.

Hoof thuds sounded from the direction of the bulwark's open gate.

"More comin', Major!" a man shouted from the wall. "It's Jack an' his asses!" he added with a chuckle.

Lou and everyone else swung their gazes toward where Baja Jack was leading Pepe and the burros and his dozen guards over the wooden bridge, through the main gate, and into the bulwark's yard. Jack held his *trigueño* to a slow, leisurely pace while holding both his hands in the air, palms out in supplication.

He was grinning, showing his bad teeth, that one eye crossing so severely it appeared fascinated with the tip of his beaklike nose.

"Baja Jack, you old devil!" Yeats called, looking at the most recent newcomers but keeping his Russian aimed at Prophet. "Lookee here what the cat dragged in, fellas! You got somethin' for us, Jack? We been expectin' you, you old mestizo!"

Jack chuckled, his toothy smile in place. "Just what the doctor ordered, Major! Just what the doctor ordered! As for that fella there . . ." Jack chuckled again and wagged his head, like a father with a child who'd proven an exercise in frustration. "Don't mind him. He's a loco gringo friend of mine. He's with me. Both of these fellas are!"

Jack stopped his horse just beyond the ragged circle of men bearing down on Lou and Colter with rifles and pistols. Jack's smile became a glare when he peered down at Prophet but his glowing smile was back when he turned again to Yeats, chuckling nervously.

"He's with *you*?" Yeats asked, incredulous.

"Sure enough," Jack said. "I didn't have nothin' to do with him ridin' in here all blood 'n' thunder — I'd like to make that clear!"

"What in hell does he think he's doin'?" asked the dark-haired man standing beside Yeats and who Prophet assumed was Yeats's second-in-command, Lieutenant Will-John Rhodes. Rhodes looked older than Prophet had imagined. But then, so did Yeats, which was understandable, since all the stories about them were a good twenty years old and more.

They'd been down here a long time.

Prophet glanced down at the girl cowering on her hands and knees, her forehead pressed against the ground, then shot a glare at Yeats. "What the hell were you doin' to this poor girl here, Yeats? Usin' her for target practice? I don't know where you come from, but where I come from . . ."

"Where the hell *do you* come from?" Yeats slowly lowered the Russian, scowling skeptically at the big gringo. "You tend to go easy on your vowels and roll your consonants . . . like a *Southern man.*"

He'd said those last two words with none-too-vague accusing.

CHAPTER 34

Prophet's heart gave a little hiccup.

According to what he'd heard, the Mad Major had ridden for the Union though he'd taken no part in the Civil War. At least, not back East.

He'd been in Arizona and California during the War of Northern Aggression, but he'd still worn the blue uniform of a federal soldier, all right. Prophet's having ridden for the Confederacy was likely reason enough for this old devil to kill him.

There was no denying who he was, though.

"I was a reb, born and bred in Georgia. But the war's over, Yeats. You might not have heard down here." Prophet glanced at the girl. "I was just lookin' out for this poor little ole gal here's, all. I killed those men because it was either them or me, and I reckon I tend to act before I think things through. Been accused of the same more often than I like to admit."

The girl glanced up at him in bafflement, tears streaming down her plump, coffee-colored cheeks.

"But even if I had thought it through, honey," Prophet told the girl, "I'd likely have done the same damn thing."

"The Old Southern gentleman, that it?" asked Yeats.

Prophet shrugged. "Well, I never been accused of bein' a gentleman before, but I am from the South so I reckon you're half-right, anyways."

Yeats studied him skeptically. Then he opened his mouth and threw his head back, laughing. He turned to Baja Jack. "Where in the hell did you find him, Jack? I'll be damned if I don't like him, despite his interfering in my little open-air parlor game."

"Parlor game?" Prophet said, glancing at the terrified girl again and then at the dead men lying beyond her.

"That's what I call it. A parlor game," Yeats said with challenge in his Irish brogue. "Folks who rub my fur in the wrong direction become my playthings. They all know it, but they tend to rub my fur in the wrong direction, anyway.

"That dead man over yonder is . . . er,

was . . . one of my men. He was caught smoking the magic elixir and frolicking with that whore there, little Elegra, when he was supposed to be on guard duty. That's what happens to men and whores who cross me. They get to run across the yard, and I get to use them for target practice. If they can make it to the wall, they're free. If they can't make it to the wall . . . well" — the Mad Major chuckled diabolically — "then they're dragged down to the sea and thrown to the sharks off San Luis Point."

Yeats set his right-hand pistol down on the rail before him. He plucked what appeared to be a cigarette from a tray on the rail and took a puff, drawing it deep into his lungs, his lumpy chest thickening behind his puffy-sleeved white silk tunic split low down his fleshy chest. He tipped his head back and blew the plume out over the yard and said, "Just like men, sharks gotta eat, too. And they don't mind what they eat, even human trash. And for that I thank them mighty kindly indeed, 'cause there's plenty of that to feed the seven seas!"

He grinned broadly and turned to Will-John Rhodes standing to his left and laughed exaggeratedly, with bizarre abandon. Prophet hadn't thought the man's line about the sharks had been all that funny, but maybe he just didn't have the sense of humor Ciaran Yeats did.

Or maybe the laughter came from the weed the Mad Major was smoking, wrapped into that fat quirley. Lou glanced at the other men standing around him, and it occurred to him that, judging by the haziness of their eyes and the slackness of their jaws, half of them, too, were fogged up on the stuff.

When Yeats finally stopped laughing, he took another long, pensive puff off his quirley, blew the smoke out into the yard again, and stared coolly down at Prophet. "Tell me again if you already told me, Jack — who's your friend?"

"His name's Prophet. Lou Prophet. Right capable fella. Why, he held off nearly an entire bunch of banditos his ownself. You know that big half-Pima, Gato? Bandito?"

"Ah yes, Gato, that scurvy vermin. Yes, I know of him."

"Lou an' him went head-to-head, hand-to-hand, face-to-face. Mano a mano!" Jack laughed. "Guess who won?"

Yeats frowned skeptically. "This man? The rebel?"

"You got it."

Yeats turned to Jack. "Gato is dead." He said it like a statement he was testing out to hear how it sounded.

"Sure as the summer days is long!" crowed Baja Jack, beaming at Prophet.

A collective mutter arose from the crowd.

The girl still on her knees beside Prophet looked up at him, frowning, and said softly in Spanish, "You killed Gato, señor?"

"I reckon so, señorita, though I didn't get the import at the time. I was just trying to keep my neck from bein' broke's, all."

"Well, I'll be damned," Yeats said, casting his own marveling gaze at Prophet. "I reckon I can't very well kill the man who turned Gato toe-down — now, can I? At least, not tonight."

Prophet gave a weak smile. He sort of felt like a condemned man whose death sentence had been commuted for a day.

Yeats looked at Colter. "Who's the redhead?" He chuckled. "Good lord, boy, what the hell happened to your face?"

Prophet saw an angry flush rise into the redhead's face. Colter flared his nostrils and, glaring up at Yeats, snapped, "Your mother —"

"Red!" Lou admonished him out of the side of his mouth.

Colter stopped. He drew a deep breath and said tautly, "An outlaw sheriff stamped me with the brand of his town to keep me out. I kicked him out with a cold shovel."

"Ahh." Yeats smiled. "A pair of tough gringos." He laid the quirley in its tray atop the balcony rail and slowly clapped his hands. "I like that, I like that. I get tired of all the chili-chompers around here. It's the only bad thing I've found so far about Mexico. Most of my original army died from syphilis long ago."

The few *americanos* around Prophet chuckled while the Mexicans chuffed their displeasure at their mercurial leader's slur.

"Tonight, I reckon we'd better celebrate," Yeats said. "Come on, Jack! Bring that sweet-smellin' locoweed of yours up here. Our shelves is runnin' bare! Bring it up here, every last bag. I wanna look it over and have a good sniff. Come on, little man. Bring your frankincense and myrrh . . . and your two tough gringo amigos!"

With that, Yeats collected his two long-barreled pistols, dropped them into the holsters thonged on his thighs, glanced at his second-in-command, Lieutenant Will-John Rhodes, and both men disappeared through the arched doorway flanking the balcony.

Prophet looked at Colter, who said, "So that's Yeats, eh?"

"He ain't as big as I figured."

433

"He's big enough."

"Yeah."

Prophet glanced around at Yeats's men. They were all returning to what they'd been doing before Prophet had ridden in, all fire and fury, to save the *puta*. They appeared content to leave the dead men where they lay. It was hard to tell the Americans from the Mexicans, for Yeats's original deserters had been here a long time — the few that remained on this side of the sod. Some of the gang members returned to guard duty atop the wall, climbing wooden makeshift steps, while some went back to tending cook fires crackling and smoking here and there around the grounds.

There were also several Apache-like brush jacales along the stout walls, beneath which makeshift chairs sat or hammocks hung. The whole yard of the old bastion appeared to be one big camping party, with many half-dressed Mexican girls like little Elegra here, none looking much over sixteen, serving as Yeats's men's entertainment.

Elegra looked around then turned to Prophet. Relief shone in her eyes. *"¡Por favor, señor!"* She leaned toward him and planted a soft kiss on his cheek. "If you want, I will —"

Prophet pressed two fingers to her lips.

"That there was all the thanks I need, little darlin'."

Elegra rose to her feet and scampered off, running barefoot toward the bastion's front gate, likely heading back down to the village by the sea. Her little red dress swished enticingly around her cool brown thighs.

Several little boys in white cotton tunics, cotton slacks, and rope-soled sandals had materialized out of seeming nowhere to grab the reins of Prophet's and Colter's horses and to lead them away. Other little boys, urchins who must work as swampers and hostlers around the bastion, were leading off the horses of Baja Jack and his men, as well. Pepe was freeing the locoweed-bearing canvas panniers from the *tenajas* on the burros' backs, and handing the baskets over to several of Jack's men.

Jack walked over to Lou and Colter, eyeing the urchins leading away their horses. "Don't worry," Jack assured them. "Your horses will be well cared for. Yeats pays the peon *niños* well to perform such tasks. The stables are outside the walls, to the west — a big mud jacal full of sweet hay and oats from the *campesinos*' fields. Yeats knows the value of a well-tended horse. He himself rides only the finest Morgan palominos."

He jerked his chin toward the big sprawling feat of Spanish masonry into which Ciaran Yeats and Will-John Rhodes had retreated. "Follow me. I don't know about you two, but I could use a drink."

He paused and narrowed one eye up at Prophet. "Oh, and, uh, I'd appreciate if you minded your manners, Lou. I'm a sucker for a red dress my ownself, but you damn near got us all shot."

Colter glanced at Prophet with a wry snort. "Can't take you anywhere."

"Ah hell."

"Come on, come on," Jack said, ambling toward an open doorway. "I'm purely craving a drink. Yeats has the best mezcal you'll taste anywhere. I think the peons make it down in the village."

Prophet followed Jack and Colter, respectively, through the arched doorway, which was low enough that Lou had to remove his hat. Apparently, they'd built doors for men smaller than himself back when the Spaniards threw these digs together.

As they entered a dimly lit portico, Prophet saw white fragments in the pitted walls. Remembering what Jack had told him about how the Spaniards mixed the bones of dead slaves with the mortar, his innards gave a shudder.

He followed Jack and Colter up a narrow

stairway, their boot thuds and spur chimes echoing in the cavernlike place. They passed through two large rooms that were barren of all furnishings but which stank from bird and rodent dung. Lou could hear birds flapping overhead, let in by the large open windows, and as they passed through another room with a massive crack in its floor and in one wall, letting in light from outside, he heard the screech and frenetic scuttling of what must have been a startled rat.

As he walked, boots clacking on the rough stones and avoiding the largest cracks, Lou looked around, wondering where Alejandra de la Paz was being housed. If she were still alive, that was. The idea that she might be dead hadn't occurred to him until just now. The notion had been spawned by Yeats's obvious savagery as displayed in the yard only a few minutes ago.

If Alejandra were anywhere near as headstrong as her lovely sister, Marisol, she might have done something to incur Yeats's wrath, and ended up fed to the sharks off San Luis Point.

They dropped down a short stone stairway and turned into another room from which they'd heard voices echoing as they'd approached it. Now Prophet saw that the voices belonged to Yeats and Rhodes, who sat on heavy leather sofas angled before a fireplace in which small flames popped.

Prophet felt the hair on the back of his neck prick as he entered the devil's lair.

CHAPTER 35

There were several others in the room — all young Mexican girls, it appeared. Two lay on the sofas on which Yeats and Rhodes sat, each girl curled beneath a thin quilt or a blanket, appearing to be asleep or at least dozing, oblivious as children.

Four other girls were scattered about the big, cavelike room, lounging on furniture — a fainting couch, a wing chair, and a deep brocade-upholstered chair with wooden arms scrolled in the shapes of a lion's paws. None of the furniture in this parlorlike room appeared to be arranged with any particular strategy in mind.

There were other furnishings — bookcases nearly empty of books and bearing mostly only dust and soot from the fireplace. More leather sofas were shoved back against the walls. There were small tables nearly hidden by various paraphernalia that included food scraps, clay cups and plates, playing cards, coins, and guns of all makes and calibers, as well as knives and ammunition.

One long, heavy table that belonged in a dining room, surrounded by high-backed, hand-carved chairs, was cluttered with more dirty plates and cups, pots and pans, as well as what appeared to be the remains of one large roasted chicken moldering under a swarm of flies.

The room and another beyond it, which appeared to be an extension of it, possibly a makeshift kitchen, served as an apartment, Lou saw. It appeared to be the apartment of a wealthy but extremely lazy and spoiled young royal with a penchant for weaponry and the entertainment of young *putas* whom he kept pie-eyed on marijuana, the smoke of which hung like fog in the shadowy room.

The furnishings were all heavy and expensive-looking, including several large, gilt-framed oil paintings leaning against the walls or on the fireplace's stone mantle. Sculptures were mounted on marble pedestals, some carelessly adorned with girls' frilly underwear, including a pair of pink pantalets hanging from a conquistador's raised obsidian sword. A *camisa* was draped around the conquistador's shoulders, as though against a chill.

A big shaggy cinnamon bear rug sewn against red velvet was thrown over the arm of a sofa, and one of the girls reclined against it, fidgeting as though bored, her bare legs crossed at the ankles. She was puffing a corn-husk cigarette, which was no ordinary cigarette, while staring at the ceiling.

The room was lit by delicate, colored glass lamps arranged haphazardly on the tables, in recessed wall niches, and one on the fireplace mantle. Each owned a good coating of soot and spiderwebs.

None of the furniture was native to Baluarte Santiago, of course. Whatever original furnishings the bastion had boasted would have long since turned to dust. Prophet had a keen feeling that the room's current furnishings were the booty that Yeats and Rhodes had hauled out of the haciendas they'd been raiding up and down the Baja peninsula for the past twenty years.

Prophet's eyes swept the room once more, noting that all the girls — slaves of one form or another, most likely, addicted to the locoweed by now — were Mexican. Again, he wondered where Alejandra might be . . . if not in the sea off San Luis Point.

Baja Jack ambled up to the clutter of furniture on which Yeats and Rhodes slouched, and looked around, scrubbing a thick little fist across his nose and chuckling self-effacingly. "Sure could use a little cuttin' o' the trail dust, Major. I was just tellin' *mi amigos* Prophet and Farrow that your mezcal —"

Will-John Rhodes cut the little man off with: "Ahh — there it is. I can smell it from here!" He was looking over Baja Jack's head toward Jack's men just entering the room behind Lou and Colter, the dozen or so bulging panniers from the *aparejos* hanging down their chests from ropes looped around their necks.

Jack twisted a disgruntled look up at Prophet, running his hands up and down his shirt, showing his dire need for a drink.

"Come in, come in, gentlemen!" Yeats rose from the sofa, wobbling a little from the spice likely wafting through his head similar to the way its smoke was wafting through the room. "Bring it over to the table and let me have a look at it!"

The big man with a ponderous belly barely contained by the red sash he wore stumbled toward the table, tripping over a wrinkle in the thick rug that carpeted the room and which had probably also been hauled out of a don's opulently furnished casa. He cursed and glared over his shoulder at the wrinkle. For a second, Lou thought the woolly-brained man was going to actually kick the rug.

Apparently thinking better of it, the Mad Major continued to the table to which Jack's half-dozen marijuana-laden men carried their cargo. Yeats stood glaring at the mess on the table. He hardened his jaws, and his face swelled and turned red. "I thought I told you *putas* to clear off this table! What makes you think you can disobey my orders and get away with it when I treat you like princesses? Please tell me! I demand an answer to that very simple question!"

He turned to snarl and roar, lion-like, at the six girls who scrambled to their feet and came running to the table. They were all dressed in frilly, colorful underwear that didn't cover more than a third of any of them. Two were sobbing as they approached the table. They'd obviously incurred their master's wrath before. They all appeared nearly as pie-eyed as Yeats himself, so they clumsily began gathering up some of the relics and scraps of several past meals.

One of the girls approached the table on Yeats's right side. He grabbed a handful of her hair, bellowed another curse, and slammed her forward against the table. If she hadn't managed to brace herself with her hands, her head would have slammed violently into the debris remaining there.

Colter jerked forward but Lou held his arm out in front of him, holding him back.

"What did I tell you?" Yeats fairly shrieked. His thick, curly red hair liberally spotted with gray danced madly about his head, and spittle flecked his thick mustache and the tangled mess of his red-gray beard. "Did I not tell you two days ago to get rid of this mess?"

Tears streaming down the girl's cheeks — they were all crying now — she gathered several pots and plates and ollas and straw demijohns up in her arms and scrambled toward the adjoining room, scraps tumbling from the mess in her arms to land on the carpeted floor. Not stopping, she ran into the other room, followed by the other girls sobbing over the refuse they cradled in their arms.

Yeats turned to Prophet and Colter, a vein still swollen in his high, ruddy, lightly freckled forehead above two large, glassy blue eyes that peered over the round, steel-framed spectacles sagging low on his thick nose. "How do you like that? I give these girls a home. I give them all the spice they want even though I've been running low for the past several weeks, and *I need the stuff to stay alive!* And this" — he held out his hand to indicate the litter-strewn table — "*this* is how they treat me!"

Three days' worth of leavings, eh? Prophet silently ruminated. Ciaran Yeats might have lived here like the king of his castle. But, obviously, chaos reigned. The Mad Major was indeed mad. Mad as a hatter or a tree full of owls in a lightning storm, Lou's old ma would have called him.

Savage, too.

He'd kidnapped these girls from all over Baja, got them addicted to the locoweed, enslaved them to him and his men to fulfill their wishes both in and out of their mattress sacks, and he thought *they* were indebted to *him.*

The man needed a bullet. Prophet was aching to give it to him. He just needed the right time and the right place. He also needed to find Alejandra de la Paz . . .

Where could she be?

Yeats looked down at the still-cluttered table, sighing and wagging his head. Finally, he leaned forward and ran his forearm across the table, sweeping a good third of the remaining debris onto the floor, including scrap-littered plates and ashtrays and half-filled cups.

"There now!" he intoned heartily. "They

have an even bigger mess to clean up for their sloth!" He waved impatiently at the men holding the panniers around their necks. "Come now, come now! Throw those beauties onto the table and let me see what you have for me, Jack! Is it good stuff? Of course it is. That's why I buy from you exclusively, Jack. You're the best spice farmer on the peninsula. What you lack in looks and stature you atone for by rising to the lofty heights of the locoweed-growing gods!"

Baja Jack appeared to have forgotten his thirst for the moment. Waddling up to the table, he was grinning and blushing like a virgin bride. He was breathless as usual, as though the mere act of walking six feet on his bandy legs was exhausting.

When the men had unstrapped the panniers, Jack scowled and waved at them, giving them their leave. They flushed a little, indignant, then turned and made their way back across the room but not before casting lusty glances behind them, no doubt hoping for another peek at the dusky-skinned, mostly naked señoritas, who were understandably taking their time returning to the room.

They probably figured Yeats had forgotten about them. And it appeared that he had.

His fleshy face with its rheumy, bespectacled eyes was aglow as he leaned over to slide one of the panniers toward him. He lifted the bag, hefting it, judging its weight, then opened the flap and peered inside.

He arched a brow as though in preliminary approval.

He shoved his right hand inside, raised a scoop of the green buds to the top of the bag, and fingered them, his brows hooding with concentration. He raked his thumb across the buds in the palm of his large, fleshy hand, making a soft raking, crunching sound.

"Hmm."

He opened his hand, letting the spice drop back into the bag. He lowered his thick nose to the open top of the bag, closed his eyes, and drew a slow, deep breath. He lifted his face, keeping his eyes closed and his chest swollen with the trapped inhalation.

Finally, he released the breath then repeated the action, dipping his nose into the bag again, closing his eyes, and drawing a slow, deep breath and holding it.

He didn't hold it for as long this time before releasing it and handing the bag over to Will-John Rhodes standing to his right. Rhodes went through a similar process as Yeats, who repeated his own ceremony on each of the other bags. He was in no hurry. He was taking his time, giving each pannier a thorough evaluation.

Prophet sensed Baja Jack's anxiety and saw it on the man's gnomelike features. Jack's head, still adorned by his black velvet, silver-embroidered, wagon-wheel sombrero, the thong drawn up taut beneath his chin, stared up at Yeats, his eyes wide, even the crossed one, which was angled toward the tip of his nose. He looked like a boy, albeit one with a gargoyle's face, staring up at a temperamental, arbitrary father in anticipation of long-sought praise.

Several beads of sweat cut through the dust on Jack's narrow, unshaven cheeks and rolled down over his jawline.

When Yeats had evaluated the last bag, he handed it to Will-John Rhodes. So far, the Mad Major had given no indication of the status of his evaluation aside from the occasional, intermittent, "Hmm," or just as obscure, "Uh-huh."

Rhodes, a tall, brooding man whose taciturnity seemed to go hand-in-hand with the darkness of his features and the frosty, gray-blue remoteness of his eyes, hadn't even given that much of a response. His face, which lacked definition aside from the unsettling eyes, had not betrayed even a trace of his thoughts on the matter of Baja Jack's locoweed.

Yeats kept his oblique eyes on Rhodes.

When Rhodes had finished evaluating the last pannier, he carefully strapped the flap closed, set the bag on the table, glanced at Yeats, and raised both his eyebrows maybe a quarter of an inch. That was his only response. It seemed to be enough for Yeats.

The Mad Major turned to face Baja Jack staring up at him like a tongue-tied gargoyle with the legs of a dwarf. Jack's lower jaw hung. Yeats scowled down at him, his lumpy chest rising and falling sharply behind his frilly, white cotton shirt that was unbuttoned halfway down his chest to where his pale belly began to bulge sharply.

Jack swallowed under the severity of Yeats's gaze.

Yeats planted his fists on his hips and leaned slightly forward at the waist, furling his brows as though with great disdain. "Baja Jack, you ugly little rascal — you know what I oughta do to you?"

Again, Jack swallowed. He blinked once, his crossed eye nearly straightening for a moment before rolling back to stare at the tip of his long nose. He opened his thin-lipped mouth to speak but appeared unable to find his voice. Yeats spared him a further pained attempt.

The man's face suddenly broke into a broad smile and he said, "I oughta pick you up off the damn floor and plant a big old wet kiss right on your rancid mouth, and that's exactly what I'd do if you didn't smell like a dead javelina!"

Yeats laughed.

Jack beamed.

CHAPTER 36

The Mad Major drew Baja Jack close against him in a hug of sorts. Since Jack's head didn't come up much past the bulge of Yeats's sagging paunch, it was a bizarre thing to see. They resembled a father hugging his child. At least from a distance it would have looked that way.

Unfortunately, Prophet was close enough that he could see the pair all too closely — Yeats smiling approvingly down at Baja Jack staring up at him, blushing, that one wacky eye drawn toward his long, hooked nose.

Lou thought that for his many sundry sins, he'd likely be condemned to remember the scene in vivid details on his deathbed.

He looked away quickly, blinking, trying to keep the image from burning into his brain.

Baja Jack cackled his crowlike laugh and bellowed, "Ah hell, Major. I'm just glad you like the stuff, and, uh . . . uh . . . well . . ."

He gave a nervous chuckle as he raised his thick little right hand and rubbed his thumb and index finger together. He winked.

"Oh, of course! Of course!" Yeats laughed raucously then turned to Will-John Rhodes. "Lieutenant Rhodes, will you please see to Baja Jack's compensation?"

"Of course, Major," Rhodes said, glancing at Jack still beaming like the boy who'd built the flashiest kite. "Right this way, Jack."

"Right behind you, Lieutenant!"

When Baja Jack had followed Rhodes out of the room and into the adjoining one and then beyond that one, Ciaran Yeats turned to Lou and Colter. He studied each man carefully, frowning suspiciously. Lou and the redhead didn't say anything, just cut each other skeptical, edgy glances under their quarry's careful scrutiny.

Suddenly, Yeats raised an arm, gesturing toward the mess of sofas and chairs near the fire, and said, "Please, please, gentlemen. Let's have a seat and get to know each other, shall we?"

He turned to one of the Mexican girls — the only who'd returned to clear the table and was gathering up more plates and dishes now, tentatively, fearfully.

"Chiquita," Yeats said, moderating his tone this time, "bring me an olla of the grape

pulque and one of the mezcal, *por favor.* And please apologize to the other girls for me, will you? They should be used to my temper by now, for crying in the queen's ale. Assure them that I didn't mean to hurt their feelings." Like any good bully, he appeared weary at having to sooth the nerves of those overly sensitive enough to be offended by his perhaps headstrong but otherwise benign words and deeds.

A little more of the former steel returned to his voice as he added, "Please tell them to toughen up a little, and for God's sakes get back out here and get this table cleared. Then I want you all to haul your skinny little brown bean-eating asses outside to the cookfires and rustle me up a decent meal for a change. A meal for me and the lieutenant and for Baja Jack and my new friends." He threw his arm out again, indicating Lou and Colter. "And please, please, *please* — a little efficiency for a change? Do not embarrass me this evening — *por favor,* I beg you, *chiquita!*"

He clapped his hands together and steepled them beneath his bearded chin, closing his eyes as though in prayer for calm.

With her arms full the girl hustled out of the room.

Lou and Colter shared another furtively

conferring glance. *Crazier'n a privy rat . . .*

Yeats looked around the table, found a plate that wasn't as overburdened as the others, and dumped the debris off it. He reached into one of the panniers and crumbled a handful of the locoweed onto the plate. He placed some shredded corn husks onto the plate, as well, and then led Lou and Colter over to the fireplace.

"Sit, gentlemen," Yeats said, collapsing with a sigh onto the sofa on which he'd been sitting before. "Sit and take a load off. You've had a long ride and, apparently, one that was not without trouble." He glanced meaningfully over the rims of his spectacles at Prophet.

"I reckon you could say that," Lou said, grimly fingering his swollen left eye.

"Gato, eh?"

"We weren't formally introduced."

"Thank you for scouring the trail of that vermin, Mr. Prophet. Any enemy of Baja Jack is an enemy of mine."

"Call me Lou."

"All right, then. Lou it is. And you're . . ."

The redhead shrugged. "Since we're all getting friendly, I reckon you might as well call me Colter. Or . . ." He cast an ironic glance at Lou. "Red will do, I reckon. Since most folks end up calling me that sooner or later, anyways."

Prophet hooked a wry half smile.

One of the young señoritas brought in two clay ollas and set them on the low table between Yeats and Lou and Colter, who both sat on the couch that Rhodes had been occupying when they'd entered the apartment. Another girl carried a tray holding three clay cups without handles into the room. She set the tray on the table beside the two pots and then in a voice so soft that Prophet could barely hear her, she asked Yeats if he wanted her to pour.

Yeats didn't look at her. He merely threw up his arm as though in disgust. The señoritas obviously took that as their signal to leave, which they did, nearly tripping over each other to exit the room.

"Girls that age," Yeats chuffed. "Good for one thing and they're not all that good even at that. You have to teach them every damned move. If you take them any older down here, though, they've had niños — they drop them at sixteen, seventeen years old, even younger — and their bodies have already gone to seed." He shook his head in disgust.

"Help yourselves, gentlemen." The Mad Major tapped each pot in turn. "Mezcal and the obligatory pulque, ancient drink of the

Aztecs. The Spanish conquerors turned up their noses at it, preferring wine instead. A superior race, the Spanish. Too bad so many mingled with the Aztecs, giving us the lower class of mongrel now running things — or trying to run things — in Mexico."

"I reckon I'll go with the mezcal, then," Prophet said in a wistful tone, leaning forward and lifting the wooden ladle from the mezcal pot.

He held the ladle up to Colter and arched an inquiring brow.

Colter winced, probably remembering his previous encounter with the thunder juice. Not wanting to seem impolite or worse, weak, he said, "Fill 'er up."

"Cure what ails you," Yeats said, apparently having noticed the redhead's reluctance.

Lou ladled mezcal into a cup and gave it to Colter.

"Mezcal, Major?" Prophet asked.

"Why not?"

When Lou had ladled up one cup for Yeats and one for himself, he sat back in the heavy sofa of worn, cracked bull hide and sipped the smooth liquor. The mezcal did a good job of cutting the trail dust and easing the aches and pains he still suffered from his encounter with the half-Pima, Gato. It did not, however, relieve his tension. That was all right. He needed to keep his edge here in this veritable devil's den, facing the devil himself and wondering where in hell Alejandra de la Paz might be.

Yeats was fussily grinding the weed buds between his fingers, making sure all the bits of the weed tumbled back onto the plate. He looked up frequently, curiously at Colter. "Besides your non-preference for spiritous liquids, the scar makes you distinctive. You killed the man who gave it to you?"

"Sure as tootin'."

"A sheriff?"

"Yep."

"An outlaw sheriff?"

"He killed my foster father."

"I am sorry to hear that."

Colter didn't respond to that. He just sat with his knees spread, his hat hooked on one of them, his drink resting on the other one, staring at the man's careful work with the weed, which Yeats was now rolling into a fat cigarette.

Yeats looked over his sagging spectacles at him again. "You're wanted by the law? Up north?"

"That's right."

Yeats slid his rheumy, uncertain gaze to Prophet. "How about you, Lou? Are you wanted, as well?"

Prophet reflected none too fondly on Buzzard Gulch and Roscoe Rodane. With a weary sigh, he said, "The jake had it comin' — both barrels."

Yeats laughed as he deftly rolled the big, green cylinder closed. "They all do, don't they?"

"Some more than others."

Yeats laughed even louder at that.

He sank back into his couch and glanced over at the table, which all half-dozen girls were administering to once more. It was a long table and, judging by the smell of rotten food that hung in the room beneath the grassy aroma of the weed, probably hadn't been tended for days.

Yeats barked at the *chiquitas* for a light, making them all leap with a start. One grabbed a match from a box, scratched it to life on the table, then came over, cupping the flame tenderly in the palm of her hand. Her hands shaking, she touched the flame to the end of Yeats's stogie.

When he had the big cylinder burning, filling the air with the heavy aroma of fresh-cut alfalfa, the girl returned to her work and Yeats leaned back against the sofa, turning slightly to one side and crossing one of his jodhpur-clad legs over his other knee.

He studied the ridiculously large cylinder in his large, soft hands — hands that hadn't known real work in a long time — then lifted it to his lips. He drew deeply on the quirley, making the coal glow for nearly fifteen seconds.

Prophet almost coughed, imagining the harsh smoke filling the man's lungs. Yeats was accustomed to it. His eyes glazed as he stared off across the room beyond Lou and Colter sitting across the table from him. His mouth corners rose dreamily. He held the smoke for maybe ten seconds before he lifted his chin, gathered his mouth into a near-perfect circle, then parted his lips, blowing a thin, transparent plume of the skunky-smelling smoke into the air over Lou and Colter's heads.

"You can never really tell how good the weed is until you've taken the smoke deep into your chest. You really need to bathe the old ticker in it." Yeats looked at the quirley's coal again as he held the cylinder straight up and down between his thumb and index finger. He smiled, nodded. "That ugly little mestizo is one hell of a farmer, I'll give him that."

He cast his gaze at Lou again, and then at Colter, and again curiosity shone in his eyes. "So, tell me, gentlemen — what brings you to Mexico?" He blinked once then gave a shrewd, lopsided smile as he added, "Me, perhaps?"

A snake hidden in the regal old sofa's musty cushions slithered up through a crack to lick the base of Prophet's spine. At least, that's what it felt like. A momentary chill hit him despite the fire crackling in the hearth.

He didn't look at Colter, but in the corner of his eye, he saw the redhead fidget slightly in his chair, bringing his knees a little closer together and reaching down to finger the brim of his Stetson.

"You?" Prophet said, frowning. "I don't understand."

He'd be damned if he hadn't sounded sincere. At least to his own ears.

Yeats looked at the coal of his stogie again. "As you must know, being *americanos* and all, I have quite a high bounty on my head back north in the States and territories. The last I heard, it was right up around five thousand dollars. That's a lot of dinero for most men. Believe me . . ."

He paused to take a shallow drag on the cylinder then, blowing it out, said in a pinched voice, "I've had men after me." He paused to rid his lungs of the smoke then spoke in a normal, level tone of voice, smil-

460

ing. "This was a few years ago, back when I was easier to track down. As my legend has grown down here in Baja, the wise country folks, salts of the earth, have learned not to bandy my name about overmuch. Bad things have been known to happen when they do. More than a few have lost their tongues, in fact. Those were the more fortunate ones."

Yeats smiled proudly at that.

"As for the bounty hunters who came after me," he continued, still smiling, quite pleased with himself, "their heads ended up used as kick balls for the children down in the village. Oh, what a novelty for them, as you can imagine!"

He slapped his thigh and had an overlong laugh at that.

He sobered abruptly and shuttled his penetrating gaze between Lou and Colter and said, "So . . . is it the bounty you're after? Shall I reward the village children with two more balls for their kick games?"

Prophet couldn't contain a grimace.

"Nah, nah, Major — them two ain't after you." Baja Jack had just followed Will-John Rhodes back into the room. He held a sizable buckskin pouch in his right hand and was hefting it happily. "I'll vouch for Lou and Colter my ownself. They work for me, don't ya know. After I ran into 'em along the trail, I sorta figured they might be cut out for guardin' my weed runs. It's hard to get good help these days. Hell, most gunnies would rather *prey* on me than ride guard for me. After ole Proph there pounded Gato's head so far down between his shoulders it coulda served as a lamp table, I made it official."

Jack smiled, a tad shrewdly, from Lou to Colter and back again. "Didn't I, boys?"

Lou stared back at him, suspicion buzzing around his ear like a pesky fly. What was Jack up to? Not that Lou minded, of course. Louisa had planted in his mind the well-founded suspicion that Jack, realizing that Lou and Colter were hunting Yeats, his primary patron, might have been leading the two *americanos* into a trap.

That suspicion was now replaced with another one. Why was Jack lying on Prophet and the redhead's behalf?

Lou and Colter shared another quick, conferring glance and then Prophet cleared his throat and, turning to Yeats, said, "That's right, Major. Why would we wanna do a fool thing and take down a golden goose like yourself?"

"That's right," Colter said. "If you kill the cow, no more milk!"

462

Everybody, including Lou, furled their brows at him.

Colter flushed, shrugged, and brushed his fist across his chin. "I mean . . . in a manner of speakin' . . ."

Yeats studied him closely, suspiciously. Finally, his thick lips spread inside his tangled, gray-red beard, and he chuckled. He turned to Lieutenant Rhodes standing near where Jack stood staring lustily down at the two clay ollas filled with tangleleg. Yeats said, "Why don't you roll my guests a stogie each, so they can sample Jack's wonderful ganja? Jack, too, of course."

"Oh, now — that's okay, Major," Jack said, raising his hands, palms out. "I'll stay clear. I done sampled the batch when I was concocting this potent variety just for you, and it done made me howl at the moon for hours on end." He chuckled uneasily and rubbed his hands up and down on his leather vest.

"Nonsense," Yeats insisted, glancing again at Rhodes. "A stogie for each of my guests, if you will, please, Lieutenant?"

"Comin' right up, Major." Rhodes walked over to the table where the panniers were stacked.

Prophet was about to protest. He'd tried marijuana a few times when he'd been down here in Mexico, and all it had done was turn him into an even bigger fool than he already was. But he had a feeling his protest, like Jack's, would fall on deaf ears. So he said nothing. Neither did Colter. Lou saw that the redhead wore a wary look.

Jack looked at Lou. The little man raised his arms in a shrug as though in apology. Lou wasn't sure exactly what he was apologizing for, but after he'd taken a few puffs off the stogie, he realized exactly what the apology had been about.

The marijuana was potent. Not at first. At first, it was like riding an old mare in a leisurely lope across a grassy field. It filed all the edges off a fella's tender consciousness. It made Lou feel very calm and relaxed, and it made the world around him seem uncommonly friendly and beautiful, warm and inviting, with the peace of an old church and the charms of a beautiful, sexy woman.

It made him want to keep puffing the damn stuff until too late he realized the mare he was riding was in fact an unbroke bronco broomtail cayuse, wild as a wolf and bred for hard mountain riding.

Prophet didn't realize this until several hours after he'd started smoking the stuff, chasing it with the mezcal. He and Colter and Baja Jack and the Mad Major and Will-John Rhodes all dined together on a simple but hearty meal, which was just the right padding a man needed after so many days on the trail. The Mexican-spiced goat meat and frijoles and steaming tortillas went down just fine, accompanied as it all was with more and more mezcal and then the sangria Yeats ordered one of the girls to bring up from the cellar.

The first of the evening was filled with much boisterous conversation and ribald laughter, with the señoritas serving the men at the long table and acting very flirty and teasing and sexy in their low-cut, sleeveless, brightly embroidered dresses that left their brown legs and feet bare.

Prophet talked and laughed with bunk-house abandon, and so did Colter. They both forgot all about the reason they'd come here and about Alejandra de la Paz, as well. All their tension and anxiety about the mission thinned out and disappeared like fog on a quiet morning pond. They were in a room full of new friends enjoying good food, good drink, and the flashing eyes of the young Mexican serving girls.

It was after the long meal, which must have lasted a good three hours or more, finally wound down and Will-John Rhodes rolled more marijuana cigarettes, that Prophet's mare made the unlikely transformation. It pitched and whinnied and buckkicked and took him running off across the violent waves of the evening.

The stallion had no saddle or bridle. All Lou could do was grab two fistfuls of mane and hold on.

Much of the rest of the night was a chaotic dream with only sporadic moments of fleeting lucidity. He remembered more girls coming into the Mad Major's apartment — fresh girls who were apparently hazed up here each evening from the village, like a gaggle of young geese. Lou wasn't sure who they were — if they were kidnapped girls from around Baja whom Yeats had forced into his despicable slavery, or if they were girls from the near village he'd forced into the same.

Lou didn't care. He didn't care about anything except holding on to the bronco's mane while the stallion carried him up hill and over dale of his rarefied debauch.

He had another vague, short-lived moment of clarity when he was singing along with several señoritas while he himself was strumming a mandolin, albeit crudely. (He hadn't known he could play the mandolin even crudely.) There were other such moments when his head bobbed above the waves of intoxication, as when he realized he was stumbling out through the open front gate of the bastion, each arm draped around the neck of a young señorita, each of whom was laughing and stumbling and trying feebly to keep the big man on his feet. (He had the vague sense that the bastion was always open and guarded only sparingly. Yeats must have felt confident that no one would be fool enough to try to infiltrate his ancient garrison.)

Time stopped again. Or maybe it sped up. He became aware mainly of sensations — the brush of a girl's hair against his cheek, warm lips pressed to his, more drink rolling over his tongue and down his throat. At one point he found himself stumbling through shadowy alleys that stank of privies and trash, and he had no idea how he'd gotten there or where he was going.

Dogs barked.

An old woman cajoled him loudly from the doorway of a mud jacal in rattling Spanish.

A señorita laughed madly.

Then he was in the salty ocean surf, naked as God had made him, and he thought he was making love though he wasn't sure. It felt like that for a time, but then he was alone and it was dawn and the sun was a bloodred rose rising out of the polished glass table of the Sea of Cortez.

He gathered his clothes, dressed, and stumbled back through the morning-quiet village to the bastion, dead windblown palm fronds blowing against his ankles. Seagulls shrieked in the rookery for breakfast, diving at the water behind him.

That day passed, and another evening that somehow transpired just as the previous one had. It was as though he were sucked into a whirlpool of wanton desire and a revolving intoxication, laughing, singing, having long, seemingly meaningful conversations with Ciaran Yeats or Colter or Baja Jack or some pretty girl who spoke slowly and helped him with his Spanish . . .

More food. More drink. More puffs of Baja Jack's relentlessly addictive marijuana, which, despite its eventual sledgehammer effects, also made the world make sense somehow and become what every man and every woman from the beginning of time had wanted it to be . . .

And then there was a night of sudden, strange lucidity. He wasn't sure where it came in relation to his coming to Baluarte Santiago. It could have been the third or fourth night, or the four hundredth night, for all he knew.

He opened his eyes and saw a lovely, redheaded woman in a diaphanous white gown step up to him from the rolling shadows of the seashore. Lou was on his knees in the surf, naked, his clothes bobbing around him in the lacy waves edged with sparkling foam.

He'd been laughing uncontrollably. He'd remembered a young *puta* being there with him, but she was gone now, it seemed. There was only the redheaded goddess standing over him, staring down at him. Starlight sparkled in her filmy gown, which seemed made entirely of starlight reflected off the water, as the wind buffeted about her long, bare legs.

Her red hair danced in the wind. The moon cast silver streaks into it and reflected off her dark, almond-shaped eyes.

"You have to help me," she said. "Will you help me?"

She dropped to her knees in the surf beside him, wrapped an arm around his shoulders. In Spanish-accented English she said, "You have to help me, Mr. Prophet," she begged. "Won't you please help me?"

CHAPTER 37

Prophet stared up at her, aghast. Her face was like that of a marble statue in a moonlit garden at midnight. Classical. Mysterious. Mythical in its worldly anguish.

Enthralling.

Lou reached up and gently placed his hand on it, lightly ran his thumb across the nub of her cheek, as though to prove to himself that she was really here, that she wasn't just another concoction of his inebriated imagination.

"Ale . . . Alejandra . . . ?"

"Yes." She placed her hand on his. "Yes, I'm Alejandra. Will you help me, Mr. Prophet? He can't, you see. He can't help me. I . . . I very much need your help."

"Yes." Prophet smiled. He'd found her at last! Or . . . she'd found him. "Yes, I'll help you."

She squeezed his hand. "Come."

"Wait. Now?"

"Yes, now. ¡*Vamos, por favor!* Hurry — you must!"

"All right." Lou looked around at his soaked clothes rolling in the surf.

"I'll go ahead," the girl said. "So no one suspects us.

"All . . . right . . ."

Then she was gone as abruptly as she'd materialized. He turned to stare after her, wanting to reassure himself that she was real. *Don't fall in love with her,* Marisol had warned him. Now he knew why she'd been worried. He felt that he'd already tumbled for the bewitching, red-haired goddess of the Sea of Cortez!

He could see her tall, lithe figure in the blowing gauzy dress drift away from him and the rolling wavelets. She was lifting the soaked hem of the long dress halfway up her bare legs, just above her knees. Her long legs were slender and supple and the color of alabaster.

No wonder Yeats had chosen her and secreted her away here at Baluarte Santiago, keeping her all for himself . . .

Lou gathered his clothes. He started to pull on his summer longhandles then nixed the idea. He was too drunk to go through the labor of pulling on the sopping duds. He'd walk naked back to the bastion.

Most of the village was likely asleep by now, and most of the debauchers in the bastion were likely three sheets to the wind. Aside from the guards, but they'd likely seen more than their share of debauchery and partaken in enough of it, as well, when they'd not been on guard duty. They wouldn't be overly shocked to see a naked man walking through the bastion's open gate.

Prophet walked barefoot along the trail through the village. He wasn't accustomed to walking barefoot, of course, but few rocks or thorns grieved him. Likely the nerves in his feet as elsewhere were still dead from all the liquor he'd drunk and the locoweed he'd smoked.

For a time, he could see the vague, pale figure of Alejandra walking ahead of him, but then she stretched the distance between them and disappeared into the darkness. When he mounted the stone ramp, he could feel the eyes of guards on him though he could not see them up there in the darkness capped by a sky full of stars. He heard a couple of men chuckle mockingly at him as he passed over the bridge and tramped on into the compound in which a couple of cookfires glowed softly, men slumped around them in drunken slumber.

The bastion itself loomed before him — hulking and massive, like a large pale mountain of granite.

He stopped, looked around, frowning.

Where was the girl? His blood quickened desperately, fearful he'd lost her or, worse, that she'd been spawned only by Baja Jack's locoweed.

"Pssst! Señor!"

He jerked his head in the direction from which the raspy call had come. She was a pale smudge in the darkness ahead and on his left. Leaning out from a heavy shadow, she beckoned.

Clutching his clothes before him, his shell belt, Peacemaker, and bowie knife looped over his arm, he hurried his pace. His legs and feet felt spongy from all the drink. He stumbled, nearly fell, and dropped his hat. He cursed as he stooped to pick it up and then continued walking as quickly as he could to where he'd last seen the girl though she'd disappeared again now, swallowed by the shadows of the massive masonry building.

As he approached the hulking castlelike structure, he saw a small, arched doorway near the far-left end. She reappeared in the doorway, again beckoning. "Come quickly! ¡Rápido!"

Prophet strode quickly to her. She grabbed his arm and pulled him into the entrance's deep shadows, gave a husky laugh, wrapped her arms around his neck, and kissed him.

Her lips were warm and as smooth as silk.

His heart hammered.

She gave another husky chuckle, then wheeled. "Come, come! We've no time to waste. It will be dawn soon!"

She wheeled and moved quickly into a corridor, and Prophet followed her heavily on his bare feet, not sure where they were going or what they were doing. Surely, she didn't think he could take her away from here tonight. One, he was in no condition. Two, they hadn't prepared horses . . . trail supplies . . .

These were vague concerns fluttering through his brain. More powerful was the allure of the girl herself. Even if he'd wanted to, he couldn't have done anything except follow her down a cold stone corridor then up a flight of stone stairs, stubbing his toes as he climbed. They tramped down another corridor.

He could hear the slap of the girl's bare feet ahead of him, the soft crunch of the sand clinging to the soles. He could hear her breathing. Occasionally, she chuckled — a soft, earthy, almost musical sound of barely restrained emotion.

They came to another doorway. She pushed through a heavy wooden door and into a room lit by two small arched windows through which milky moonlight angled.

"Here we are," she said, whirling toward him, wrapping her arms around his neck, and pressing her supple body against his. "Here we are, my love. Help me! *Por el amor de todos los santos en el cielo, por favor ¡sálvame de este desierto!*"

Prophet's slow-working brain translated the plea as "For the love of all the saints in heaven, please save me from this desert!"

She rose up onto her bare toes and kissed him again, hungrily, flicking her tongue between his lips. Passion hammered at him. "I will, Alejandra," he groaned. "I will . . . but . . ."

She grabbed his hand and wheeled. He dropped his clothes and his gun on the floor as she led him over to a massive bed that appeared to be one of the large room's few furnishings.

It was soon apparent that all the help she wanted at the moment was his help in her bed.

In his current stare of intoxication and raging passion, who was he to deny this young siren anything?

■ ■ ■ ■

Sunlight woke him. He could see it through his eyelids.

At first, he thought he must be lying on the seashore again, as had become his custom of late. Faintly, he could hear the surf and smell the salty tang of the air. Only the sound of the surf was too faint, the tang too light. Also, he couldn't feel the wind on his skin, only a very soft breeze.

He lifted his head, opened his eyes. He had no recognition of where he was. It must be a *puta*'s crib, only it was larger than he'd have expected — a large, cavelike, stone-floored room with a domelike ceiling and two small, arched windows hewn through a thick, masonry wall. A church? Humor touched Prophet. It was tempered by a faint disappointment.

He'd dreamed that he'd found Alejandra de la Paz on the seashore, late at night. She'd had red hair like her mother's, and she'd worn a lacy white gown, and the wind had done intoxicating things to her hair and the gown under which it had been quite obvious she'd worn nothing.

He smiled longingly as he looked around at the strange room, trying to get his bearings. Of course, it had only been a dream.

Wait.

He turned his head to his left. His eyes widened.

She lay belly up beside him, half covered by only a thin white sheet. A red-haired goddess with alabaster skin. Her head was turned to one side, her hair fanned out around the pillow like a red halo. Her face couldn't have been any more classically sculpted unless a master artist had chipped it out of ivory for the most expensive cameo pin ever made. God himself had crafted this one, smiling devilishly as he'd done so, knowing full well that it was a face to ravage the hearts of mortal men.

Prophet's heart hiccupped. No, it hadn't been a dream. She was real. He had only a vague recollection of what they'd done here in this bed last night, but what he remembered stirred him once again. He felt a dull ache in his right shoulder, and he turned to see a bite mark.

He smiled at that. They'd had a good time, all right.

He ran his gaze down her body. The sheet covered only her legs. He couldn't help lifting it for a peek beneath.

"My God," he heard himself whisper.

She groaned, stirred, opened her eyes. She

stared up at him and smiled. Her enchanting brown eyes flashed in the sunlight angling through one of the room's two arched windows.

Lou let the sheet drop back down, covering her legs. "Beg your pardon."

"It's all right. I like being appreciated." Her smile widened. "Most of all, I like being satisfied." She sat up, brushed her lips across his. She frowned at the tooth marks on his shoulder then kissed them softly, lowering her gaze demurely, a soft flush rising in her creamy cheeks. "Sorry."

"The mark of satisfaction."

"I don't remember doing that."

"I don't remember feeling it."

"We had a good time. *Gracias, amigo.*" Alejandra kissed his cheek then lay back down against her pillow, not bothering to draw the sheet up any farther than it already was. She crooked her arms behind her head. "You better go now. You don't want to be found in here."

"I reckon not."

Prophet climbed off the bed, wincing against the ravages of a violent hangover, bells clanging in his ears. It took him a while to dress for he was still a little drunk and wobbly on his feet. His clothes were damp but they'd dry out quickly in the desert sun.

He crouched to pluck his boots off the floor then sat on the edge of the bed to pull them on. There were few other furnishings besides the bed. There was a large armoire, a marble-topped washstand with a bowl and a pitcher, and a single chair. A fine one, upholstered in brocade and with wide, finely scrolled arms, but the only one. It was buried under the mess of a woman's fine wardrobe likely taken hastily from her bedroom at Hacienda de la Paz.

There was no glass in the windows. Beyond them, birds flew across the bastion's yard, and Lou could hear the regular wash of the sea rolling its waves onto the shore. Gulls cried.

He finished pulling on a boot with a grunt and turned to where Alejandra lay on the bed, watching him with a dreamy smile showing the ends of her fine, white teeth. "I'll be back."

Again, her smile broadened. "Tonight?"

"When I can get you out of here."

She frowned a little with her eyes, leaving the smile on her lips. "What do you mean?"

"I'll come back. Later. I have to work out a plan first with the kid. We gotta get you a horse and . . ."

Lou let his voice trail off. He didn't like the way she was looking at him now, all

479

traces of her smile gone. Her lovely brows formed a severe ridge.

"I figured you must've realized," he said, sitting there on the edge of the bed, only one boot on, twisting around to regard her on the bed behind him. "Your father sent me. He hired me to kill Yeats and get you out of this perdition."

Slowly, staring at him in shock, Alejandra pulled her hands out from behind her head. "My father sent you?"

"Yeah. I thought you knew. Since you knew my name."

"I overheard the major talking to you. I saw you out in the courtyard, facing his men. I saw what you did . . . and . . . well, it stirred me. You're a big, strapping man, Señor Prophet. Ciaran . . ." She shook her head slowly. "He can't . . . he can't . . . you know . . . *hacer el amor.* He wants to. He tries. But always he leaves howling and sobbing in frustration, leaving me here in this big room he gave me, sobbing and howling in frustration. I need a man to please me, señor. That man was you. I don't want to be rescued from this perdition, as you call it. The perdition, Mr. Prophet, is Hacienda de la Paz!"

Lou stared at her in hang-jawed shock.

Fury flared in the girl's eyes. "My father

sent you to kill Yeats? What a cowardly old devil. If he wanted me back so badly, the least he could have done was come for me himself. Him and his men. But he and they are all useless. They are old women. I like my life here. I didn't want to come at first, but the major has given me the life of a queen, complete with all the spice I could ever want."

"Ah, Jesus," Prophet said, rubbing his jaw in astonishment. "You're all woolly-headed on the stuff. You're addicted. You want to stay here and . . ."

"Life is good here. It is paradise!" Alejandra turned her fine chin toward one of the windows and screamed in Spanish, "Rape! Someone help me, this *americano* is trying to have his way with me. *¡Violación!*"

CHAPTER 38

"Violación, my ass!" Prophet bounced up from the bed and stared toward the windows looking out on the bastion's broad yard. He threw out an arm to Alejandra. "Pipe down, you crazy wench. I'm here to save your loco hide. You don't wanna stay here and lounge around like some hop-headed queen of Sheba!"

"¡Violación! ¡Violación! ¡Violación!" the girl screamed at the top of her lungs.

On the other hand, it appeared she did.

Prophet's heart turned painful somersaults in his chest. His head throbbed miserably, nearly blurring his vision. He stood in shock, staring toward the windows, as the señorita de la Paz continued to scream in Spanish for someone to help her, the *americano bastardo* was raping her!

How in the hell do I get myself into these situations?

Lou ran to one of the windows and peered

into the yard. Men were shrugging out of their drunken slumbers from various encampments by the near wall, where fire pits were mounded with cold, gray ashes and where small flames leaped in others as a few men, awake now that it must have been nearly midmorning, were preparing coffee.

Several had already grabbed guns and, staring puzzledly toward the señorita's windows, were striding clumsily this way. Others, also staring toward the señorita's room, pulled on boots and strapped cartridge belts around their waists.

"Ah hell!"

Lou lifted his gaze toward the wall facing the Sea of Cortez. The Gatling gun swung toward him, a guard hunkered on one knee behind it, aiming down the barrel. Another guard standing on the wall nearly straight out from Prophet was aiming a rifle toward Lou, the guard's head tipped sideways against the rear stock.

The rifle blossomed smoke and flames. The bullet slammed into the masonry wall to the right of the window, only six or seven inches from Prophet's head. Lou pulled back behind the casement, gritting his teeth. The hammering concussion of the bullet pummeled his ears and brainpan. He thought for a second he was going to pass out.

He cussed loudly and turned to the girl sitting up and smiling smugly on the bed at him. "That tears it!"

"Whatever that means, you stupid gringo, it sure does tear it!" She laughed.

Half to himself, he said, "Goddess, my ass."

"What?"

"More like a viper hiding inside the thousand-dollar body of a spoiled *puta*."

Alejandra's eyes drew sharply up at the corners as she glared at him. "How dare you call me that! You better run, run, *run* the hell out of here, *pendejo.* Run if you can, but there's nowhere the major and Lieutenant Rhodes won't find you. Not after what you've done to me." She smiled again, mockingly. "What a brute you are to force me to do such horrible things!"

Prophet ran back to the bed, picked up his right boot, and pulled it on. "Throw something on that purty body of yours, Alejandra!"

"What?"

"Get dressed. You're comin' with me."

"Go to hell!"

Prophet shucked his pistol from its holster, aimed it straight out from his right shoulder at the girl, and clicked the hammer back. "Throw something on and do it now, or I'll drill a hole through your pretty head."

"You wouldn't!"

Prophet manufactured a devilish grin. It wasn't hard to do. Outside, men were shouting and he could hear them running toward Alejandra's chamber, cocking rifles. He drew his index finger taut against the Peacemaker's trigger. "By the count of three . . ."

He couldn't kill her. He knew that. But she didn't.

"One . . . two . . ."

Giving a frightened cry, she scrambled off the bed and picked up the gown she'd been wearing last night. She shook it out quickly, eyeing Prophet fearfully, glancing at the big .45 bearing down on her. She pulled the gown up over her head and let it tumble bewitchingly down that long, slender, high-busted, creamy body until the still-damp hem settled around her ankles.

"Let's go!" Prophet grabbed her arm and half dragged, half led her to the door.

"Ow — that hurts, you brute!"

"Not as much as a bullet between the eyes!"

He opened the door and peered into a stone-floored hallway. It looked as derelict as most of the rest of the bastion though

485

someone had informed him over the past several days of his debauch that parts of it had once been used by the *federalistas* as a prison, so parts had been somewhat modernized. The hallway was deserted but he could hear the clacks of running boots down the cavernlike hall to his right.

"Come on!"

"Help me!" Alejandra screamed in Spanish, in the direction of the oncoming men. "Help me — the brute is trying to kidnap me!"

Prophet ran down the hall, weaving around gouges in the ancient stone floor as well as masonry fallen out of the walls or the ceiling.

The footsteps grew louder behind him — several men coming fast. The clattering echoed loudly. *"¡Ahí!"* There!

A gun barked.

Alejandra screamed.

"Damn fools!" Prophet stopped suddenly, wheeled, extended his Peacemaker, and fired three quick rounds. Two of the running men — it was too dark in the hall for him to see exactly how many there were — fell and rolled, howling. The others stopped and dropped to their knees, extending pistols or rifles.

One shouted, "Don't shoot, you fools! If

we hit the girl, Yeats will string us up by our *cojones*!"

Prophet grabbed Alejandra's arm and kept running, the girl groaning and trying to pull away, her bare feet slapping on the rough stone floor. Prophet slowed when he approached a T in the hall. Boots clattered down the wing to his right.

"More are coming!" the girl reveled. "You'll never get away, you big, stupid — !"

Prophet wheeled on her, glaring and snugging his revolver's barrel up taut against her left temple. "You scream out one more time, I'm gonna kill you, señorita. You got that?"

He pressed the gun barrel even harder against her head, driving the point home.

Wide-eyed, she nodded once but rasped out wickedly, "Brute!"

Prophet continued forward, pulling her along behind him with his left hand. He stepped to the wall on the hall's right side and raked his shoulder against it as he continued to the T. The clatter of running men grew louder.

Prophet swung his gun hand around the corner and aimed down the hall on his right, saw a handful of men run up into the light offered by a large, ragged-edged hole in the ceiling. The men running ahead of the others widened their eyes in shock and began to open their mouths to shout, but neither got a word out before Prophet shot them both and one more.

Screams vaulted around the hallway, on the heels of Lou's loudly echoing gun reports.

Prophet pulled his gun back into the hall he stood at the corner of. He shoved the girl down to her knees. She gave a clipped, indignant scream. *"¡Bastardo!"*

"I told you to shut up." Lou also fell to a knee, flicked open the smoking revolver's loading gate, and rotated the cylinder, quickly shaking out the spent cartridges.

"Yeats will catch you and if he doesn't kill you he will draw and quarter you and gut you like a pig!"

Hurriedly thumbing fresh rounds into the Colt's empty chambers, Prophet glanced down at the girl, who stared up at him from below his left shoulder. Her brown eyes were slitted. They blazed like two nuggets of high-grade gold. Her copper-red hair was a lovely, tangled mess all about her head and slender shoulders. He chuckled, flicked the loading gate closed, and said, "Goddess, my ass . . ."

She snarled at him, flaring her nostrils again defiantly. "You enjoyed me, though — didn't you? Admit it!"

"Oh, I had a grand old time," Prophet said. "What I can remember of it. Don't forget" — he patted the shoulder she'd sunk her teeth into — "you did, too, sweetheart."

He laughed.

A flush rose up Alejandra's fine neck and into her cheeks, and she dropped her eyes in chagrin. Prophet peered down the hall he'd fired into and where one man was sobbing shrilly and asking Saint Peter to forgive him for his earthly sins. "It was Yeats's fault, San Pedro!" he bellowed. "I was a good man before I fell into bad company!"

"Likely story." Lou hurled two more rounds down the hall where he could see several faces peering toward him from the dense shadows. The faces jerked back or dropped toward the floor as the two reports reverberated like cannon fire in the close confines.

Before the echoes had fallen silent, Prophet leaped to his feet, jerked the girl up, as well, and bounded down the hall opening on his left. "Sure wish I had my barn-blaster," he complained as he ran, pulling the girl along behind him. "Nothin' better'n two wads of twelve-gauge buck in close quarters. Hell, I could take out two, three of these bean-eaters at a time."

"What are you saying, you gringo

pendejo?" the girl asked, breathless.

"Don't mind me — I just yak it up when I'm nervous." Prophet leaped another large, jagged crack in the stone floor. "Watch your step, princess!"

Prophet laughed.

"*¡Cabrón!*"

They dropped down a crumbling staircase, climbed another.

Prophet heard men running down an open corridor to his left, so he swung right, climbed another staircase, ran down another open corridor, then hung a right at an intersecting corridor that appeared to be an ancient cellblock, with banded iron doors on either side.

Men turned a corner ahead of him and ran toward them. They were all wielding pistols.

They saw him a second after he saw them. Lou was already aiming his Peacemaker.

The big, burly, mustached Mexican running out front of the others stopped suddenly and threw his arms out to his sides, trying to forestall the others behind him. His large, drink-bleary brown eyes found Prophet, and he yelled, *"Noooo!"*

There were seven of them, including the big man out front. Prophet emptied his Colt into them, taking out all seven because one of the six madly fired his own pistol into the neck of one of the others as he twisted around, dying and spewing blood and howling like a lobo.

"Damn, you're good with that thing!" Alejandra stared up at him, aghast.

Prophet flicked open the Colt's loading gate. "If I remember correct, that's what you said last night."

He couldn't help laughing at his joke as he spun out another batch of spent cartridges. She gave an angry wail and lunged at him, punching him with her tightly clenched fists. Prophet crouched beneath her onslaught as he thumbed a fresh round of six cartridges into the Peacemaker's cylinder.

"Ouch, damnit — that one hurt!" he complained as she kneed him very close to where she'd intended to. He flung out his elbow to hold her off. He must have flung it out harder than he'd meant to, because she gave a scream and flew backward, hitting the back of her head with a clang against an iron-banded door.

Her eyes rolled back in her head, and she sagged to her butt, legs sticking nearly straight out before her. Her head flopped to one side, chin resting against her shoulder.

Prophet stared down at her, frowning.

"Princess?"

She didn't move.

"Princess?" Prophet's heart lurched. *Oh, for Pete's sake — did you kill her, ya big galoot?* he silently berated himself.

He crouched over her. He could hear her breathing, saw her ample bosom rising and falling slowly behind the gown's low-cut bodice. He gave a sigh of relief, then, hearing footsteps growing louder behind him, he said, "Quieter this way," and grabbed her hand and pulled her up over his left shoulder like a hundred-pound sack of potatoes. "Much more pleasant . . ."

He took off running, wincing under the weight. Not that she was all that heavy, but he was still slightly drunk and hungover and cracked bells were tolling in his ears and badly assaulting the exposed nerve of his brain. When he came to a corner, he swung left. He wanted to get away from the main yard and the damn Gatling gun over there.

It wasn't going to happen. On his left men were running toward him down another open corridor. Lieutenant Will-John Rhodes was in the lead, holding a pistol in each hand.

"There!" he shouted, raising both guns toward Prophet.

Lou raised his own Peacemaker to the

girl's side and cocked the hammer back. "I'll kill her, Lieutenant! I'll drill a hole right through both kidneys! Stay back or you'll have to explain the death of this purty little devil here to the Mad Major!"

"Hold up!" Rhodes shouted to the men running behind him. He stopped and raised both his Colts barrel-up.

Prophet heard more footsteps behind him, coming from the direction of the yard. Ahead rose a cracked stone wall. Behind him, more running feet clattered as another pack of Yeats's wolves was charging hard in his direction.

His heart pounded. Sweat streaked his face.

They had him cornered.

Quickly, he thought through his options.

Options? Hell, what options? He almost laughed at the thought. He was a dead man.

If he had any hope at all, it was the main gate. If he could get through the main gate — which was one mighty big *if* — he *might* have a chance. A slim one, but what the hell else was he going to do except run in circles until he exhausted himself or one of Yeats's rannies finally called his bluff on his threat to kill the princess and kicked him out with a cold shovel?

He swung around to face the men running toward him from the yard. They'd just climbed the top of the stone steps, and now the first men had seen him and were widening their eyes beneath their sombrero brims and raising their guns.

"Back!" Lou shouted, trying to put as much crazy-wild rebel in his voice as possible, which wasn't too hard, given where he hailed from and his current predicament. "Back, you chili-chompin' curs, or I'll drill the princess here a pill she won't digest!"

CHAPTER 39

Prophet wasn't sure if the Mexicans now gathered at the top of the stone steps had understood what he'd said. If not, they'd apparently gotten the overall drift. They looked from the gun Lou was pressing against Alejandra's side to Prophet's eyes. They must have seen bloody murder there. Or thought they did.

A couple of men at the head of the pack gestured for the others to lower their weapons while the pack leaders lowered their own.

Prophet whipped around toward where Will-John Rhodes was walking slowly toward him, his own small gang close on his heels. "Back, Rhodes!" Lou gritted his teeth and tightened his grip on the Colt's handle.

Rhodes stopped and held his guns out flat to each side, and raised and lowered them slowly, indicating the others to stand down, as well.

Prophet whipped back around toward the gang of eight men gathered at the top of the stone steps. "Back, back!" He moved toward them, keeping the Colt pressed against the señorita's side. "Back!" he repeated.

"*¡Espalda! ¡Espalda!*" yelled one of the leaders, gesturing at the others behind him.

"Yeah, *¡espalda, espalda!*" Lou repeated.

The group lowered their weapons and began backing or sidestepping down the stone staircase beside which an ancient Spanish cannon rusted, a bird's nest sprouting from its maw. The cannon reminded Lou of the damn Gatling gun on the wall near the bastion's main gate. He was going to have to face the blasted thing whether he wanted to or not. He just hoped the fella manning it didn't have an itchy trigger finger or had been smoking Baja Jack's locoweed . . .

"*Mierda,*" he said, the word in Spanish coming nearly as easily to his lips at it did in his own tongue.

He moved forward, gritting his teeth, making his eyes blaze, hoping that all the men backing down the steps away from him swallowed his ruse. If just one realized that he had no intention of shooting the pretty girl on his shoulder, his goose was cooked. Yeats would kill him slow.

The Mexicans edged away from him down the steps and along a short corridor between two crumbling walls then out into the main yard. Prophet stepped out into the yard, as well, the group forming a ragged semicircle around him, backing away from him as though he were a wounded grizzly.

"Out of the way!" he yelled at two men impeding his way toward the main gate.

They separated quickly, sidestepping, one tripping over his own feet and almost falling. Lou strode through the opening they'd left, tramping out into the middle of the yard, angling toward the gate ahead and on his left.

He looked up at the wall to the right of the open gate. That damn Gatling gun was manned, as usual, and the man manning it canted the brass canister down toward Prophet. Lou could hear the soft chirp of the swivel as the man behind the gun swung it slowly, tracking his target. He opened and closed his gloved hand on the crank's wooden handle, squinting one eye as he aimed down the barrel.

The skin pricked under the collar of Lou's buckskin tunic, which was still damp from last night though he wasn't aware of anything at the moment besides the Gatling gun and the men standing around him, regarding him warily but also shrewdly, wanting desperately to make a play.

"Alejandra!"

The bellowing cry had risen from Prophet's left. A burly, red-bearded man in a red sash, frilly cotton shirt, and jodhpurs stumbled forward from a group standing atop a portico. Yeats ambled down the steps and into the yard, holding his two silver-chased Russians straight out in both hands.

"Put her down, you dog!" Yeats wailed, lances of raw fury caroming from his glassy blue eyes set deep in his fleshy, sunburned face, behind his sagging spectacles.

Behind Prophet, Will-John Rhodes said, "He says he'll kill her, Major! If we don't give him safe passage, he'll kill her!"

"You son of the devil!" Yeats barked at Prophet. He stopped at the bottom of the portico's steps, keeping his Russians aimed at Lou's head. He cocked them both at the same time. The ratcheting clicks of the hammers sounded inordinately loud in the funereal silence of the yard.

"Put the hoglegs down, Major!" Lou swung around to face Yeats, keeping his cocked Colt pressed against Alejandra's side. "I'll kill her! I walk out of here, or she and I both die! I'll take her with me to the smoking gates, Major. I swear I will!" It wasn't too hard to make his voice sound brittle with desperation.

Yeats squinted one eye as he aimed down the barrel of one of the aimed Buntlines. "How do I know she isn't already dead?"

"You'll just have to take my word for it."

"Suppose I choose not to?"

Lou thought he saw quick movement to his hard right. He looked that way but saw a dozen men flanking him on that side, standing still but watching him with wide-eyed expectation, some holding guns, others fingering weapons that remained in their holsters. One man was caressing a knife handle as though he were considering a quick throw at the big bounty hunter's back.

Lou fired a quick look over his right shoulder. That damn Gatling gun was still aimed at the back of his head.

Christ, what a mess!

If on the off chance Lou made it out of this little entanglement intact, he was spending next winter north of the border. Give him a raging prairie blizzard over this bailiwick any day of the week!

"As you can see," Yeats said in a maddeningly reasonable tone, "there is no chance of your getting out of here, Prophet! Now, why don't you put down the señorita? You and I can go inside. We will have a drink

499

together. You can enjoy a last meal with a drink and a smoke. Baja Jack's wonderful weed will make death less painful for you. I promise to kill you quick. I won't make you suffer. All right? Do we have a deal, compadre?"

Prophet continued backing toward the gate. "Put down the Russians, damnit, Yeats!"

Yeats smiled broadly. "I don't think you can kill her."

Lou's heart thudded. "What?"

"I'm calling your bluff, Lou. I don't think you're holding a winning hand. I think you're holding the same hand that Wild Bill Hickok was holding when he suffered his untimely demise — the dead man's hand."

"I'll kill her!"

"No, you won't." Yeats shook his head slowly, knowingly. "I don't think you can do it. If so, go ahead. She is a rare beauty, for sure, but there are more rare beauties in the world. True, it takes some looking, but I have plenty of time!"

Ah hell . . .

"What the devil's goin' on?"

The familiar voice made Lou stop in his tracks and lurch with a start. He glanced over his shoulder.

Colter stood in the middle of the open

gate, looking blearily toward where Prophet stood holding the girl on his shoulder. The redhead appeared to have just woken somewhere — probably in some *puta*'s crib. His shirttails were untucked. His hair hung in tangles to his shoulders. He looked pale, his eyes rheumy from the long debauch.

The kid looked beyond Prophet to Yeats, and he said with grim understanding, "Ah hell."

"Kid," Prophet said with a weary sigh, "you got the worst timing of anyone in the world."

Yeats laughed. Lou swung his head back forward. Yeats was drawing a bead on his forehead and, closing his lips together, started taking up the slack in his trigger finger.

Lou heard a soft snicking sound from behind and above him. A man gasped, groaned.

Yeats took his eye off Prophet's forehead to peer up and behind Lou, who turned his head just in time to see the Gatling gunner drop down onto one knee beside the Gatling gun, grimacing, his sombrero tumbling off his shoulder to hang down his back by its neck thong. *"¡Dios mio!"* He pitched slowly forward, dropped over the edge of the wall, and turned a single somersault before hitting the ground at the base of the wall with a heavy thud.

The wooden handle of a small *cuchillo* poked up from his back.

What in tarnation?

A figure rose from behind the Gatling gun. "Now, then, what do you say we get this dance started right an' proper!" came the crackling, raspy, crowlike caw. Prophet blinked in disbelief when he saw Baja Jack tip up the Gatling gun's canister with a loud chirp of the swivel and wrap one small, gloved hand around the crank handle. Just then Prophet realized the furtive movement he'd spied a minute ago on his right had been Jack scuttling along the wall to the ladder giving access to the Gatling gun. No one else had seen him, or paid him any interest, because all eyes had been on Lou and the girl.

Baja Jack's buzzardlike face beneath the broad brim of his black velvet sombrero blossomed into a wide-eyed grin of pure jubilation as he began turning the crank with his crooked little arm while cackling like a dozen witches freed from hell. *The rat-tat-tat*s of the revolving rifle quickly drowned out Jack's crowing though not the screams of the men his first bullets found.

Prophet cursed in exasperation as he

pulled Alejandra down off his shoulder, set her on the ground, and then threw himself on top of her, shielding her body with his. He looked up to see Ciaran Yeats running up the portico steps and then diving through the doorway as Jack hurled bullets in his direction, several plowing into the men around him and hammering the masonry walls to either side of the door.

Most of the men who hadn't yet been shot spun and ran for cover, a couple triggering bullets toward Jack as they did. Will-John Rhodes dropped to a knee and raised both his pistols but he got off only one shot before he jerked suddenly as one of the Gatling gun's bullets plowed into his belly, just above the buckle of his cartridge belt.

A second bullet walloped his chest over his heart before a third and a fourth drilled his upper chest and then his right cheek respectively, throwing him backward onto the ground already reddened with the blood the bullets had blown out of his back. The lieutenant lay spread-eagle, quivering as he died.

More men twisted and fell, screaming, as the Gatling gun continued plundering the flesh around where Prophet lay stretched out over the girl, who was regaining con-sciousness now. He could feel her squirming around beneath him.

Suddenly, the Gatling gun stopped its cackling. As its echoes faded, rocketing off the wall and the big bastion, Prophet heard the yips and howls and raucous wails of Baja Jack. The Gatling's swivel squawked.

Prophet looked at the wall to see Jack rising from behind the smoking maw of the Gatling gun, giving one more raucous roar before turning and yelling over the far side of the wall, *"¡Pepe, trae los burros y los caballos, viejo réprobo!"*

Prophet stared at him, frowning. "What the . . . ?"

Baja Jack stepped to the edge of the wall and looked around, his Colt .44 in his right hand. He looked at Prophet and said, "Cover me, Lou!"

Prophet looked around again at the dead men strewn around the yard. There must have been at least twenty of them. A few were alive but wounded and writhing or trying to crawl away, clutching bloody wounds. Lou didn't see any more guards on the front wall. All but the one manning the Gatling gun must have climbed down to investigate Alejandra's pleas for help. Now they either lay amongst the dead in the yard or were cowering behind cover with the other survivors of Baja Jack's lead storm.

Jack ran toward the gate. A ladder leaned against the wall over there. He dropped onto the ladder and descended quickly, his thick little body making the ladder buck and creak. He was breathing hard from excitement.

Prophet, sitting up and looking around the yard, saw one of the fallen men aim a gun at Jack. Lou dispatched the man with a bullet through his brisket. He could see a few men peering out through the fortification's arched doorways. One extended a rifle but Prophet discouraged him with a bullet that sent the man cursing back into the shadows.

Colter was on one knee in front of the open gate, looking around with his Remington extended, also hurling lead here and there where men poked their heads out from behind cover.

Baja Jack leaped down from the ladder and ran toward the gate, grinning at Prophet, beckoning with his left arm. "Come on, Lou. Come on, old son. We're burnin' daylight!" His eyes widened suddenly. He wheeled toward Prophet, raising his .44, and fired.

Lou ducked. A man behind him grunted. Lou turned to see a man fall near the portico in which Yeats had retreated.

Jack laughed and twirled the Colt on his finger. "Just like shootin' rats off a trash heap!" He scowled at Prophet. "Come on, Lou! We ain't got all day. I killed a good many o' them rascals but there's a small army still kickin' for sure!"

Prophet looked down at Alejandra. She lay belly down, looking around at the dead men in shock, her red hair blowing around her head in a rising wind off the sea.

Prophet grabbed her arm. "Come on, sweetheart."

She climbed to her feet and turned a withering glare to him. "Go to hell!" She slapped Lou hard across his right cheek.

Angrily, he crouched, threw her over his shoulder, and hurried after Baja Jack, who'd crossed the bridge fording the moat and was heading down the stone ramp. Colter stood facing Lou, his cocked Remington in his hand. He was frowning, shaking his head. "Would you mind tellin' me what in the hell's goin' on, Lou?"

Prophet shrugged a shoulder. "Your guess is as good as mine, Red, but I reckon we done wore out our welcome at Baluarte Santiago." He brushed past Colter and crossed the wooden bridge. "Come on. There's still some snakes wrigglin' around in the lair back there, includin' Yeats." He had a feeling they were all cowed by the shock of Baja Jack's sudden attack, but they'd recover soon and organize themselves into a catch party.

Very soon. And they'd be more than a little hot under the collar.

Prophet had just stepped onto the stone ramp when he stopped suddenly. He stared at where the old burro wrangler, Pepe, came galloping toward the bastion from the adobe stables. Sitting astride his mule, he led a string of pack burros and horses, Baja Jack's *trigueño,* Colter's Northwest, and Lou's very own Mean and Ugly.

Lou poked his hat back off his forehead. "I'll be damned."

Colter stepped up beside him and did likewise. "I'll be double damned."

The horses were saddled. The pack burros were outfitted with their *aparejos.* The panniers hung from the pack frames, bulging.

Prophet and Colter hurried down off the ramp toward where Pepe stopped the string of mounts and where Baja Jack was leaping up off the edge of the ramp to shove his boot into a short stirrup hanging from the side of the *trigueño.*

Slumped over Lou's shoulder, the girl cursed and kicked and pounded his back with her fists. *"¡Bastardo! ¡Gran bastardo americano feo!"*

Baja Jack triggered a round toward the bastion. "Best hurry, amigos. They're trying to get back up on the walls. We really prodded the snake, I think!"

Prophet was glad to see his Richards hanging by its lanyard from his saddle horn, his Winchester in its sheath. Old Pepe had done well. Prophet unhooked the shotgun from the horn and slung it over his shoulder. "Did you hit Yeats?"

"I think so. Not where I was aimin', but I think I hit him, all right!" Jack slapped his thigh and squealed a laugh. "Did you see how I shredded that mean an' nasty Will-John Rhodes?"

"Yeah, I seen."

"Hah — served him right, the cold-eyed son of a buck!"

"Where're your guards, Jack?"

"Probably still curled up with the *putas* somewhere in the village. Don't worry about them. I'll explain later. *Vamos,* Lou!"

Lou tossed the girl up onto his saddle, grabbed his reins off the tail of the burro in front of him, and then swung up behind Alejandra, who was still cursing a blue streak in Spanish. "Say, Jack — what's in the panniers?"

"It's a surprise, amigo!" Jack laughed.

"Oh, it's a surprise, all right! A fine one, you will agree. Just now, however, I reckon we'd best haul our freight. When Yeats and his men recover from the shellacking I just gave them, compliments of their own Gatling gun, they will be angrier than a pack of rabid lobos!"

Pepe had already galloped off on his mule, pulling the jackasses, who were complaining mightily. Jack galloped after the old wrangler. Prophet and Colter did, as well, Colter sidling up to Prophet, looking befuddled. "I don't get it. How'd he know to have our mounts saddled?"

"I don't know, kid," Prophet said, hunkering low as he prodded Mean into an even faster lope, because guns were now crackling from the bastion walls behind them. "But you know the old saying . . ."

"Yeah, I know," Colter yelled above the clatter of their horses' galloping hooves. "Never look a gift hoss in the mouth!"

CHAPTER 40

Prophet reined Mean to a halt on the far side of the canyon north of the promontory atop which Baluarte Santiago sprawled. He curveted the horse so that he could see back out over the canyon toward the bastion.

Colter came up behind him and stopped Northwest, looking back toward the old fort, as well. "Any sign of 'em?"

Jack and Pepe had stopped their own mounts and the burros a little farther up the trail and higher on the mountain shoulder the party was climbing.

Lou shielded the bright morning sunlight, glinting painfully off the breeze-rippled sea, with his hand. "Not yet."

"Maybe I hit Yeats worse than I thought I did," Jack said, also staring back toward the bastion bathed in the smoky haze of lemony morning light. "Without Yeats —"

"Forget it." Lou saw several riders galloping out from the far side of the bastion, from the direction of the stables. It was hard to tell for sure from this distance, but the big man riding point, with a red sash tied around his waist, appeared to be Yeats himself. "If you hit him at all, you must've only winged the son of Satan."

"*¡Mierda!*" Jack said.

"Yeah," Lou agreed.

Colter whistled as he stared, counting. "You were right about one thing, Jack. There's still a small army of 'em!"

Sitting his mule beside Jack, old Pepe crossed himself.

"That's all right," Jack said. "We'll lose 'em in my canyon!"

He cackled out his crowlike laugh, reined his *trigueño* around, and booted it on up the trail. Pepe spurred his mule along behind the little man, tugging the lead line of the five burros tied tail to tail and sporting the *aparejos* and bulging panniers.

"I wonder what he's got in them packs," Colter wondered aloud as he and Prophet booted their own mounts into the dust kicked up by the lead riders and the burros.

"Took the thought right out of my head," Lou muttered. As Mean loped up the rising trail toward a high, craggy ridge crest, Prophet looked down at Alejandra riding before him. She sat stiff-backed in the saddle, her hands wrapped around the horn. "You're mighty quiet," he observed.

She turned her pretty face to him, but her eyes were slitted into a devil's smug grin. She spread her compressed lips in a frigid smile. "It's enough for me to know he's coming. If he's coming, he'll run you down. There is nowhere for you to run, nowhere to hide, *cabrón.* You have taken his most prized possession from him. *Me!*"

She smiled with demonic delight, nearly closing her eyes as she gazed up and back at Prophet.

"You're as modest as you are charming, princess."

She winkled her nose at him, hardened her jaws. "Stop calling me that. You're only mocking me."

"Sorry . . . princess."

She spit against his cheek. Prophet didn't bother wiping it away. He'd swapped more than that with her the night before, and he'd enjoyed the taste. Besides, the dust-filled wind blowing against him as Mean continued to climb would dry it in a minute.

He gave a wry chuckle. "Like I said, as modest as you are charming . . ."

They rode hard for another hour.

Then two hours . . . then three.

512

Occasionally, Prophet peered along their back trail but it was impossible to tell if Yeats were gaining on them. The country they were traversing was a dinosaur's mouth of steep rocky ridges, dry arroyos, and violently carved barrancas choked with desert scrub and bristling with cirios and elephant trees.

He hadn't had a clear view of more than a quarter mile behind him since they'd left the canyon ridge overlooking the bastion. A couple of times he thought he saw dust rising, but in the bright glare of desert sunshine, it was impossible to see anything clearly.

He knew Yeats was behind him, of course. For the very reason the señorita had pointed out. And for revenge, a dish better served cold in Mexico.

And then there was the matter of what Baja Jack had in his panniers.

They rode hard for another two hours, pausing only long enough to water their horses and burros at a rare spring. Mounting up again quickly, wanting to put as much ground between them and Yeats as possible, for this was no country to make a stand in — at least, not against a small army that had you badly outnumbered — they rode for another hour and a half before Jack reined his *trigueño* to a stop and swung back to face old Pepe, Lou, and Colter.

"This here's where we leave the main trail for my secret canyon." Jack pointed his hawk's beak down into a stone-choked barranca to his left.

Lou poked his hat back off his forehead. "You mean we came up out of there on the way to the bastion?"

"We sure did."

"Funny, I don't recognize it."

"That's the way of this crazy country. It's a maze. That's where we came from, all right. The canyon's another hour's ride down through that old river gorge. Only I know the way." Jack grinned proudly.

Colter said, "Jack, are you sure Yeats don't know about *your* canyon?" He glanced at Prophet. "I sure would hate to get trapped in there, with only two ways in or out."

"No one knows about that canyon but me!" Jack was exasperated, rising up in his short stirrups. "Ole Pepe knows, of course, but he ain't long for this world. Hell, he's damn near as old as that canyon. Hah!"

If the old burro wrangler had understood, he didn't let on. He sat his mule, casually smoking a loosely rolled corn-husk cigarette and regarding Jack with a bland smile. The smile widened as Jack laughed but still

514

Prophet didn't think the old man had understood. He was only reacting to Jack's amusement.

Jack continued with: "Now you two know about it, of course, but hell, you'll never remember how to find it. Hell, you didn't even remember this is where we turn off the main trail to get to it! We'll lose Yeats right here, I tell you. The word of John Brian Rynn-Douglas may not be good on a lot of things, but it's bond on that!"

"All right, all right, we'll take your word for it," Prophet said. "Let's mosey, old son. Mean's getting tired of carryin' double. Um . . . no offense, princess."

She turned one of her frigid smiles on him and said sharply but softly. "Go to hell." She turned her head forward again, silently fuming.

Jack reined his horse to one side and waved the others ahead. "You all go on. I'm gonna stay back and cover our trail."

"Jack, tell us real quick what you got in them pouches," Prophet asked. "I been dyin' to know all day."

Jack grinned his rotten-toothed grin. "In good time, *mi amigo.* In good time. Now get on with ya so I can cover the trail before Yeats shows!"

"All right, all right," Prophet grumbled,

booting Mean off the main trail and into the rocks. He glanced at Colter riding beside him. "He just loves keepin' us in suspense, that little buzzard does."

Colter glanced behind as he and Prophet followed old Pepe and the burros down the slope toward the knife-slash barranca. "Lou?"

"Yeah, Red?"

"What about Yeats?"

"What about him?"

Colter glanced at Alejandra sitting astride Lou's saddle then narrowed one eye at Prophet. "You know . . . the agreement we made with the don . . . ?"

"To kill him, you mean?" Prophet wasn't afraid of offending the princess. "I don't know, Red." He glanced behind at the stark, jagged, rocky, sun-hammered country they'd just traversed. "I have a nasty feelin' we ain't seen the last of Ciaran Yeats. We might get another shot at him, though we might not survive it."

Alejandra threw her head back and gave an ominous laugh.

"You should act more like a lady," Prophet told her. "Since you look like one an' all."

"Go to hell."

"I figured that's what you were gonna tell me to do. You got your sister's pepper, all right. But I don't think she would've made the poor choice you made, throwin' in with Yeats."

Alejandra glanced back at him in surprise. "Oh? You met my sister, eh? Hmm." She turned her head forward.

"Hmm, what?"

"Are you in love with her?"

Prophet laughed.

Again, she glanced at him. "What's funny?"

"She warned me not to fall in love with you. Now I reckon I know why."

Alejandra slid a lock of windblown hair back from her right eye, tucking it behind her ear. It was a distinctive gesture in the particular way she did it. Prophet remembered Marisol making the same one. "Answer my question," she ordered in her imperious tone.

"I don't know the señorita well enough. I gotta admit, though, I wouldn't mind getting to know her a whole lot better."

"Every man falls in love with Marisol the moment they lay eyes on her. My father loves her, too. Far more than he loves me."

Prophet scowled down at her skeptically. After his conversation with the don, Prophet was left with the impression that the old man loved Alejandra very much indeed.

Maybe even more than he loved Marisol.

"*Sí,* it is true. You see, we had an older brother who died when he fell from his horse and snakes bit him."

"Salvador."

"She told you the story?"

"Yeah, but I got a feeling you have a different version."

"After Salvador died, my father turned his attention to Marisol. You see, I was the youngest and nothing but a distraction. With Marisol, he could ride about the hacienda. She became a substitute Salvador for him, I think. I felt left out, alone."

Prophet let out a breath.

"Why do you sigh?"

"You wouldn't understand," Lou said, marveling at the complexities of families. How could people of the same blood and who lived practically on top of each other for years misunderstand each other so completely?

"Yeats gave me a way out," Alejandra said. "He gave me the spice. It made me forget my problems."

"Locoweed ain't a way out," Prophet told her. "It's just a way to numb yourself, a way to feel just fine doing nothin'. Baluarte Santiago was no place for you, livin' like that old man's *puta* in a crumbling ruin of

518

a place. Livin' with outlaws. Murderers. Rapists. Gettin' all hop-headed on the locoweed. You got a family that loves you, Alejandra. You might not see it, but I do, and they ain't gonna be around forever, so you'd better learn to appreciate 'em while you still can."

Alejandra looked up at him again, this time less accusingly, more speculatively. "You sound as though you speak from experience, Mr. Prophet."

"I lost a lot of my folks in the war. That's why I been runnin' off my leash out West for the past twenty years, tryin' to find somethin' I realized a while back might not even exist. Not only that but I know a pretty young lady your age who lost her entire family to cutthroats. There ain't a night that goes by she don't suffer the most terrible nightmares from missin' 'em so." Prophet shook his head. "You got folks who love you, señorita. And I'm takin' you home to 'em. Maybe someday you'll thank me for it."

She didn't say anything more. She just sat staring straight ahead though Prophet thought she wasn't holding herself quite as rigid as before.

Thinking about Louisa now, Lou glanced around. They were nearly to the bottom of the barranca. As he kept scanning the rugged mounds of rock and ancient volcanic lava piled around him, spiked with cirios and cactus, Colter frowned at him. "You see somethin' out there?"

"What? No. I was just lookin' for somebody. Turns out I got me a guardian angel I didn't know I had till we were in that crazy canyon we're headed back to. I was just wonderin' where she was now. We could sure use another gun hand, and she's one of the best but I'll thank you not to tell her I said so."

"Who're you talkin' about, Lou? You don't mean . . ."

"The Vengeance Queen."

Colter glanced around as if half expecting Louisa to raise her pretty blond head up from behind a near rock. "She's out here? Nah!"

"Sure enough."

Colter chuckled at him. "You're imagining things!"

"Hell, no, I'm not." Lou reached back to stuff his hand into the back pocket in which he'd tucked the pink handkerchief Louisa had given him.

He frowned.

"What is it?" Colter asked.

Lou probed the pocket deeper with his fingers. "I'll be damned." It wasn't there.

"See?" Colter said.

"No, it was here. I know it was." Prophet frowned, staring straight ahead and saying softly, half to himself, "I musta . . . I musta lost it on that long bender we took at Baluarte Santiago."

"Yeah, that must be it," Colter said with a sarcastic snort.

"Yeah, that must be it," Lou said, though he was beginning to wonder now himself.

The pound of hooves sounded behind them.

CHAPTER 41

Lou turned to see Baja Jack riding toward him atop his brown Arab with tricolor shading.

"Got the trail covered," Jack said, grinning, his wild eye rolling toward his nose. "We're safe now, amigos. Yeats will drive himself madder'n he already is scouring these rocks but he'll never find us. We'll wait in my canyon until tomorrow night and then flee under cover of darkness."

"He'll hunt you down, Jack," Colter said. "He'll follow you back to the farm where you grow your locoweed. I don't know what the 'purty ones' are carryin', but you pissburned him positive with that Gatling gun." They were riding along single file now, Jack riding drag behind Prophet and Alejandra. Pepe and the burros led the way into the deep, forbidding gorge carved by an ancient river. The rocks on each side of the knifelike slash of the canyon were limned brightly with ancient paintings — haunting, harrowing scenes of savage pageantry from long ago.

"*Sí, sí,*" Jack said. "You got that right, Red. He *would* follow me, all right. But I'm not goin' back there."

They all looked over their shoulders at him, including Alejandra.

"Where the hell you goin' if you're not goin' back to your farm?" Prophet asked.

Jack rode along leisurely, casually rolling a quirley, one thick leg bent around his silver-capped saddle horn. "Me? I'm gonna head east to New York, Philadelphia, Washington City, which I hear they call Washington, D.C., now. Look around a bit. My dear old pa told me about some things I should see before I snuggle with the diamondbacks and angleworms. I'm gonna go to the museums, the Smithsonian an' such. Hell, I'm gonna see the elephant!" He laughed. "And then I'm gonna hop a steamer and head on over to Pa's home — Rynn-Douglas Manor in Newcastle. I'm gonna meet my long-lost relatives, don't ya know. Hell, won't they break the teapot when they get a load of me?"

He slapped his thigh and threw his head back in silent laughter. He snapped a lucifer to life on his thumbnail and lit the quirley, inhaling deeply, his wild eye rolling queerly back in its socket.

Prophet narrowed an eye at the odd little man, curiously. "What's in the panniers, Jack?"

Smiling merrily, Jack blew smoke out his mouth and nose and said, "Soon, Proph. Very soon now, indeed."

"Whatever it is, it must be worth a sizable fortune."

"Soon, Proph," Jack repeated. "Very soon indeed."

Lou gave a caustic snort. Jack was enjoying tormenting him and Colter with his secret. Lou couldn't help chuckling. Baja Jack had a special way about him, Jack did. Lou had met some characters in his life, but none more colorful than Baja Jack.

Lou drew back on Mean's reins. "Let's stop here."

"Why?" Jack said, checking the *trigueño* down behind Prophet.

"I wanna check our back trail." Lou shoved his left boot into his stirrup then swung his right leg over Mean's rump before dropping to the ground.

"What for?"

"I wanna make sure Yeats ain't behind us. If we get trapped in your canyon, Jack, our goose is done scalded, plucked, and greased for the pan. The only English family you're gonna meet are them that's done been planted six feet down."

Jack rolled his head and grimaced. "What a negative nancy you are, Lou!"

Lou gazed up at Alejandra. "Do I need to tie you to the saddle?"

She turned to him, blinking once, slowly. "In case you hadn't noticed, I'm not exactly dressed for a run across the desert."

Prophet looked at her sheer dress, her bare feet, and smiled. "I noticed."

Lou tied Mean's reins to a twisted bush growing from a crack in the stony embankment. He grabbed his field glasses out of his saddlebags and glanced at Colter. "Come on, Red. Four eyes are better than two."

Colter swung his right foot over his saddle horn and dropped smoothly to the ground.

"That old *borrachón* ain't behind us, I tell ya," said Baja Jack, his voice indignant as well as adamant. "I covered the trail, what little sign we left in the rocks, an' I know for a fact I'm the only one who knows about that canyon."

"Keep movin', Jack," Lou said as he started climbing the steep escarpment rising on the barranca's right side. "We're gonna take a gander and then we'll be along."

Jack pulled his horse around Mean and Ugly and Northwest, and gestured for Pepe to continue on down the barranca. "Wastin' your time, boys!" he called smugly over his shoulder, his quirley dangling from one corner of his mouth. "Just 'cause I'm short an' ugly don't mean I'm stupid!"

Lou traced a winding course up the incline, so steep that he occasionally dropped to his hands and knees. When he gained the crest of the one-hundred-foot-high formation, he lay at the base of a fingerlike protrusion jutting straight up toward the sky, rising still another hundred feet.

He was sweating and breathing hard.

"What's the matter, Lou?" Colter said, crawling up behind him. "Don't tell me you're gettin' too old for a leisurely climb."

Lou spat to one side and raised the field glasses. "It ain't the years, Red, it's the trail of sins I've left behind me."

Prophet aimed the binoculars back along the path they'd taken down from a ridge two ridges to the west. There was no path, exactly, so he was mainly looking for movement behind him.

All he could see were rock and cirios, the occasional candelabra cactus, and thin clumps of saltbush. A lone hawk hunted high above the ridge down which they'd ridden into the barranca. For a time, the raptor appeared to be holding absolutely still but then a sudden dip of either wing told of its riding a thermal, looking for an early supper along the shoulder of the ridge below it.

"Anything back there?" Colter asked.

"I don't see nothin'." Prophet handed the glasses over to the redhead. "You give it a try. Your eyes are probably better than these sinful old peepers of mine."

Colter poked up his hat brim, held the glasses to his face, and adjusted the focus. He slid the binoculars left, back to the right, then slowly left again.

"Nothin' but that hawk up yonder. Oh, wait!"

Prophet's heart quickened. "What?"

Colter lowered the glasses, grinning. "Coyote."

Prophet released a held breath, scowling at the younker. "You ought not torment your elders so."

"Sorry, Lou. I think Jack has it right. If Yeats knew about the canyon, we'd see him by now. He wasn't that far behind us, and he's gotta be madder'n an old wet hen."

Prophet looked off, pensive.

527

"What is it?" Colter asked him.

"What was that coyote doin'?"

"Huh?"

"Was it just moseyin' along or was it runnin'?"

Colter hiked a shoulder. "It was sort of joggin'."

"Joggin' an' lookin' behind it, or was it chasin' a rabbit or a mouse or some such, looking *forward*?"

"It was lookin' behind," Colter answered, studying Prophet curiously though apprehension was building slowly in his eyes.

"Give me them glasses."

Prophet rose to his knees, held the binoculars to his face, and scanned the rocky terrain flanking them once again. The coyote must have drifted off through the rocks, for there was no sign of it. No sign of trouble, either. There was nothing along their back trail but more rocks and cactus climbing one ridge after another until all the ridges merged into one big blue blur beyond which lay the Pacific Ocean.

"Hmmm," Lou said. "That brush wolf must've been watchin' his shadow. Or maybe we spooked him."

Colter smiled at him. "Satisfied?"

"No, I ain't satisfied. I'm gonna keep an eyeball skinned and so should you, but I

528

reckon I'm ready to head to Jack's canyon. I could use a good, quiet night's sleep for a change, though that ain't the ideal place for it."

He and Colter made their careful way back to their horses. Alejandra was where Lou had left her, sitting atop Mean. She sat slumped forward, head hanging, her thick red hair obscuring her face. Prophet pulled his reins free of the shrub and frowned at her.

"You all right, señorita?"

She turned to him and brushed her hair out of her eyes, throwing it straight back over her head. She looked weary and drawn, probably foggy from all the weed she'd smoked for the past several weeks she'd been housed in Yeats's lair. Maybe now that reality was settling over her, she was realizing the mistake she'd made, forsaking her family for Ciaran Yeats and his locoweed.

She said nothing but merely returned her gaze to the pommel of Lou's saddle.

Prophet mounted up and, Colter following close behind him, continued along the barranca's twisting course between high red ridge walls painted by the ancients and flecked with the bones of dinosaurs and likely with a few of the ancient folks' bones, as well. Prophet didn't relish the prospect of spending another night in the canyon amidst all the ghosts that lingered in the ancient village. Despite the strange haunts of the place, though, it was likely the best sanctuary around.

If Baja Jack was right, that was, and Yeats didn't know about the canyon — didn't know that the mysterious cliff dwellings were where Jack would be heading with whatever he was carrying on his burros.

Prophet's uneasiness ratcheted up when a croaking cry rose from ahead along the barranca. A strangled wail followed, echoing. A mule brayed.

Lou glanced back at Colter, whose eyes popped wide as the strange sounds that could only be from a man in distress continued to vault off the canyon's close walls. Prophet whipped his head back forward and ground his spurs into Mean's flanks, the dun giving an indignant whinny and lunging off its rear hooves.

Prophet galloped around a bend in the barranca and then, spying movement ahead of him, shucked his Peacemaker from its holster, holding the gun barrel-up in his right hand. When Mean had taken three more long, galloping strides, Lou jerked back on the horse's reins and stared ahead

in shock toward where the canyon's back
door was a black hole before him.

Pepe and the burros were clumped near
Jack's *trigueño* in front of the portal. The
trigueño's saddle was empty, its reins hanging. The Arabian's neck and tail were arched
and it was looking up and dancing around
nervously. Pepe, mounted on his mule, was
also looking up and shaking his head and
yelling in shrill Spanish, gesturing with one
gloved hand.

What the old man and the *trigueño* were
gaping at was none other than Baja Jack
himself, who dangled six feet off the ground
before the canyon's narrow entrance. He
was suspended in the air, sort of dancing
and twisting and snarling like a leg-trapped
bobcat. A rope encircled his chest, drawn
up taut beneath his arms. He clawed at the
hemp with his fat little hands.

Lower jaw hanging in befuddlement,
wondering if the cavern's strange magic
wasn't already in play, Lou followed the
rope straight up from Baja Jack's sombrero-
clad head. Lou's jaw hung even lower and
his eyes grew even wider when he saw . . .
or *thought* he saw . . . Louisa Bonaventure
kneeling on a ledge over the cavern's portal.
Her pinto horse flanked her.

The rope suspending Baja Jack over the

531

portal angled over Louisa's right shoulder and curved up and over her saddle horn. She held the end of the taut rope in both her gloved hands down close to the ground, keeping a firm grip on the hemp.

The Vengeance Queen's jaws were taut. Her face was red from strain. She glared down at the thick little man dancing the midair two-step beneath her. She appeared to be saying something to Jack, but Prophet couldn't hear her above Jack's crowlike rasps and wails and his shrill curses as well as the hoarse protests of old Pepe and the braying of the old man's mule.

Prophet blinked and shook his head as though to clear his vision.

Surely he was seeing an image spawned by his weed-fogged brain or the canyon's dark magic. But when he opened his eyes again, Louisa was still there on the ledge above the canyon's mouth, dangling Baja Jack over the portal like a worm on a fishing hook hanging into a lake.

When Lou finally found his voice, he bellowed, "Louisa, for the love o' Uncle Mike, stop playin' cat's cradle with Baja Jack, you crazy catamount!"

CHAPTER 42

Louisa turned her head from where Baja Jack dangled below her, kicking and twisting at the end of the rope. She held Lou's gaze, frowning at him curiously from beneath the brim of her tan Stetson.

Lou gestured wildly with his right hand still holding his Peacemaker. "Turn him loose! Turn the old buzzard loose, fer chrissakes!"

Louisa shrugged. She released the rope, and Baja Jack plummeted the six feet to the ground. He landed with a sharp grunt followed by an indignant wail. Dust wafted around where the little man lay writhing.

"Heaven help you if you killed that little bastard!" Prophet swung down from Mean's back and ran up through the nervous burros and Jack's horse and Pepe's loudly braying mule.

He dropped to a knee beside Jack, who snarled and shook his head and madly tried to free himself of the noose that hung slack around his lumpy torso.

"Ease up, Jack," Lou said. "Lemme help you!"

When Jack relaxed a little, sitting up, Lou lifted the rope up over his head and tossed it away.

He set a hand on the little man's shoulder. "You all right, John Brian? She didn't hurt ya none, did she?"

Jack was flushed, his buzzard face swollen and red behind his natural dirty-brown. He was breathing hard and reaching forward to caress his left ankle curled before him. "Oh, Lordy — I think my ankle is broke!"

"You think so?"

"Oh, mercy, what an indignity I've suffered!" His face creased with misery, Jack looked at Lou and Colter, who was also kneeling beside him now, regarding the little man with concern. "I was just ridin' along, mindin' my own damn business, headin' into the canyon when lo an' behold out of nowhere someone drops a ketch rope over my head from above!"

Jack jerked his head slightly to his left, and his eyes nearly popped out of their sockets. He jutted his left arm out in wild fury. "There she is! That's her now! She's the one who lifted me right up out of my

534

saddle and hung me there to dry!"

Lou turned to see Louisa descending the ridge a hundred feet to the right of the canyon mouth, her pinto stepping carefully down what appeared to be a steep game path. At the canyon bottom, the blond Vengeance Queen swung the pinto over to where Lou and Colter were on their knees beside the indignant Baja Jack.

Louisa rode easily in her saddle, her face expressionless, hazel eyes as unruffled as ever.

"There she is right there! That's the one!" Jack exclaimed.

Stopping the pinto, Louisa poked her Stetson back off her forehead and leaned casually forward against her saddle horn. "Don't get your drawers in a twist, little man," she said. "It played out differently than I figured."

"Jesus, Louisa," Lou said, staring up at her in exasperation. "Why in the hell did you throw a long loop over Baja Jack?"

"When I saw just him and his burros heading toward the cavern, I figured he must have thrown you to that lion, Ciaran Yeats. I wanted to get the story from the horse's mouth, and I thought maybe hanging him up for a bit would loosen his tongue."

"He didn't throw me to no lion," Prophet told her. "He saved my hide, as a matter of fact. Both me and the kid's."

Colter rose to his feet, doffed his hat, and held it over his heart. He smiled shyly up at the pretty blonde Vengeance Queen sitting atop the big pinto. "I'm Colter Farrow."

Prophet glanced at the love-struck redhead and snorted a laugh. "Don't swallow your tongue over her, Red. She ain't worth it. She eats men for breakfast, lunch, an' supper."

"Only when there's a paucity of anything more appetizing," Louisa said. "Like scorpions or rattlesnakes."

Lou straightened to stand beside Colter gazing up at Louisa. While love at first sight glittered in the redhead's eyes, Prophet's gaze was dubious, deep lines cut across his forehead beneath the brim of his battered, funnel-brimmed Stetson.

"What're you staring at?" Louisa asked her sometime partner, sometime lover.

"It really was you the other night."

Louisa hiked a shoulder. She was ignoring Colter gazing dreamily up at her. "Someone has to watch your back."

"What're you doing here?"

"Waiting for you. And Yeats."

Lou scowled, incredulous. "Huh?"

"I had a feeling you were going to skin out of Baluarte Santiago with Ciaran Yeats tight on your back trail. You have a habit of skinning out of places with men tight on your back trail. When you showed up here, which I knew you would, thinking you could escape him this way . . ."

Louisa gave a self-satisfied smile as she reached out to caress the stock of the Winchester repeating rifle jutting up from its saddle scabbard on her right.

"You'd blow Yeats out of his saddle?" Lou said, skeptically.

"Right between the eyes."

"So I was *bait*?"

Louisa shrugged.

Prophet laughed without mirth. "The joke might've been on you, you know, you crazy blond polecat. If Yeats was behind us, there'd be a few more than just the Mad Major himself, you have to figure!"

"They'd die bloody. Or I would . . . after a bloody battle. But at least Yeats would be dancing with the devil. I've wanted him for years, for all the girls he's taken from their families, mostly poor peon families. I just never found a way to get him." Again, Louisa smiled that irritating, unflappable smile of hers. "Until I saw that you were stupid enough to go after him without a plan of any kind . . ." She glanced snidely at Alejandra sitting on Lou's saddle atop Mean and Ugly. "Only knowing there was a beautiful girl at the end of the trail . . . just trailing along behind this . . . this . . ."

Louisa indicated Baja Jack with her hand, leaving the question open, her lips shaping a grimace.

Caressing his ankle, Jack glared back at the Vengeance Queen. "Who does this crazy gringa think she is, Lou? Don't she know it ain't polite to come down here to Mexico and long-loop unsuspecting hombres out of their saddles?"

"Which question you want me to answer first, Jack?"

Baja Jack shook an exasperated finger at Louisa still sitting her saddle like a queen upon her throne. "You, young lady . . . you need to be taken in hand. If you were my woman, you'd walk behind me, never ahead, and when I told you to jump, you'd ask how high!" He'd intoned this tirade with his good eye flashing bayonets of glinting fury, his wild eye dancing around in its socket like a demented mouse in its hole.

Louisa furled her brows at him bemusedly. "Do you have a woman, little man?"

Jack compressed his lips at her, looking indignant and vaguely sheepish. "At the moment, I'm between women."

"I'm between women, too, Miss Bonaventure," Colter said, still holding his hat in his hands, like a boy who'd come calling on the preacher's daughter with whom he wanted to share the porch swing for an hour or two.

"That there's the *Vengeance Queen?*" Baja Jack asked, skeptically.

"That's her," Colter said through a fawning smile.

Baja Jack croaked out his crowlike laugh. "She don't look like so much to me! What she does look like to me is a girl in need of a man taking her over his knee!"

"If you think you're that man . . ." Louisa closed a hand over one of her fancy, pearl-gripped, silver-chased Colts. "Come and get it."

"Ah, fer chrissakes — stand down, Louisa!" Prophet dropped to a knee again beside Jack. "Don't let her get to ya, John Brian. How you feelin' now? Think you can stand?"

"No, I don't think I can stand," Jack whined. "I think she busted my ankle for me, the crazy polecat!"

"How does this feel?" Lou waggled the little man's child-sized foot clad in the child-sized black, hand-tooled boot.

Jack gasped and stiffened. "That hurts like hell!"

Lou smiled. "If it was broke you'd scream a lot louder than that, Jack."

"I can't scream any louder than that, Lou. I'm in too much pain!"

After further albeit brief examination, it was determined that Baja Jack's ankle was only sprained, and Lou and Colter pulled the little man to his feet. Jack yipped and howled and sucked sharp breaths through gritted teeth as he settled his weight on the ankle in question, but finally they got Jack and themselves and all the horses, burros, and old Pepe into the canyon, where they could set up camp for the night. They gathered around where Louisa had built a small cookfire over which a coffeepot — or a teapot in Louisa's case, since she drank only tea and abstained from all form of tangleleg — steamed on an iron spider.

While Jack limped around, trying to keep his ankle from stiffening up, Prophet pulled Alejandra down from Mean's back. Louisa led her pinto up near Prophet, glanced at Alejandra in her filmy gown, and gave a snort. "You sure know how to pick them — don't you, Lou?"

Alejandra gave Louisa the woolly eyeball then turned to Prophet. "Who is she, Lou?"

Louisa arched a brow. "It's 'Lou' already, eh?"

Prophet's ears warmed a little as he said to Alejandra, "That there is . . ."

"I know who she is," Alejandra said crisply, giving Louisa the slow, critical up-and-down. "I mean — who is she to *you*?"

Prophet's ears got even warmer. Louisa saved him from a response by giving a response of her own: "Don't worry, honey, our relationship is purely adversarial."

Alejandra looked at Lou and said with a skeptical, vaguely jealous air, "Is that right?"

Jesus, Lou thought. *I was safer back at Baluarte Santiago!*

Colter, who was pouring water into his hat for his horse, chuckled and shook his head.

"Shut up, Red," Prophet said.

"I didn't say nothin'."

"Shut up, anyway."

"All right."

Prophet decided to leave the ladies to their stare-down. He turned to where Jack was still trying to walk off his injury while old Pepe, like Colter, watered his mount from his hat. "What I want to know once an' for all," said the bounty hunter, moving to one of the burros and opening a pannier strapped to the *aparejo,* "is what in the holy hell you have . . ."

He let his voice trail off. His eyes grew wide. He looked at Jack, who stood with the bulk of his weight on one foot, and said, "Is that what I think it is?"

Jack smiled, both eyes glistening, even the one staring at the tip of his nose.

"What is it?" Colter asked, loosening Northwest's latigo straps so the horse could drink freely.

Lou was numb with shock. He turned his gaze back to the pannier and slowly dipped his hand inside. Colter hurried over to another burro and opened a pannier on its back. The redhead dipped a gloved hand into the pouch and withdrew a handful of . . .

"Pearls?" he said, turning his incredulous gaze to Lou.

Prophet held a handful of the pale, luminous little objects, some as small as the tip of his index finger and some as large as jawbreakers. Most were perfectly round and as smooth as polished marble. Some were nearly eggshell-white while others seemed to radiate the soft blue of a late-summer sky.

Prophet dipped his other paw into the pannier and pulled up another handful, letting the little baubles trickle from between his fingers, making soft clacking sounds. Smooth, supple, and perfect, they were as kind to the touch as a young woman's breast.

"Pearls," Lou said, turning to Jack, his eyes still wide with exasperation. "Where in the hell did you get these, you old reprobate?"

Jack stood grinning deviously. "Yeats always pays me in pearls. It was our special arrangement."

"He paid you for your locoweed with all these pearls?" Colter asked, opening yet another flap and dipping his hand inside.

Baja Jack shook his head. "No, no, no. He paid me a single pouchful. The others, you see . . ." He paused as he made his way over to a low stone shelf at the base of the towering cliff dwellings. He sat down on the shelf with a soft sigh of pain and crossed his stubby arms on his thick chest, smiling like a banker. "The rest, you see, we stole. Will-John Rhodes and myself."

He cackled softly, his shoulders jerking, thoroughly enjoying the rapt attention of his listeners.

CHAPTER 43

"You an' Rhodes?" Prophet said, closing the pannier flap and putting his back to the burro, staring skeptically down at Baja Jack. "I don't follow."

All eyes were on Jack now. Jack loved the attention.

Old Pepe stood leaning back against the hindquarters of the burro named Escorpión, filling his corncob pipe from a hide sack of chopped tobacco. He chuckled softly to himself. Lou didn't think the old man understood English, but he obviously caught the gist of Jack's story. He was a character in it, after all.

Jack said, "On my last weed run to Baluarte Santiago, Rhodes and I threw in together to separate the Mad Major from his pearls. Rhodes was tired of Yeats's mad ways and of runnin' wild down here in Baja. He wanted to go home to America, but he needed a stake. So he set his sights on the pearls that he and the Mad Major had been plundering from *hacendados* up and down the coast of the Sea of Cortez for years. Pearls, you see, are the preferred currency for most business transactions around here. Pearls have been in the families of the landed muckety-mucks for generations, starting way back when the first Spaniard set foot on the peninsula. Hell, some of the Indios even traded in pearls!

"Anyway, to make a long story short, me an' Rhodes threw in together, because Yeats wouldn't give the lieutenant a cut of the pearls and let him leave a wealthy man. No, sir — the Mad Major was hoarding them pearls, and the other men backed his play on account of how they loved his weed so much . . . and the young girls, of course. No, Rhodes was gettin' mighty sore against Yeats, an' mighty desperate.

"So, for the past four nights, while Yeats and you and most everybody else at Balu-arte Santiago was stompin' with your tails up, three sheets to the wind, thanks to my specially formulated locoweed, me an' Rhodes smuggled the pearls out of the strongbox in the bastion's dungeon. We took only a few fist-sized pouches at a time, so we wouldn't get caught and shot by firin' squad, or made to make a mad dash to the wall with Yeats usin' us as target practice for them Russians of his. We carried the bags out — staggerin' like we was drunk like the rest of you, only at night, late at night when Yeats was in his cups. Little by little, we filled Pepe's panniers."

The old ass-wrangler chuckled delightedly around the stem of his corncob pipe.

"We was gonna pull out tonight," Baja Jack continued, turning his gaze to Lou. "But when I heard the señorita kickin' up a fuss and then guns blazin' like it was a Mexican's birthday" — Baja Jack cackled a delighted laugh at his quip — "I just had me a feelin' it was you, Lou. Of course, I knew you was here to kill Yeats. Why the hell else would a gringo bounty hunter be here if not for the bounty on the Mad Major's head?"

Louisa fired a haughty look at Prophet. "I told you he knew!"

Ignoring her, Prophet kept his eyes on Jack. "You didn't need me to kill him for you. You or Rhodes could've done it when he was . . ."

"Sure, sure," Jack said. "We could've killed him when he was pie-eyed, just before we lit out. Which was our plan. But I figured if you did it, you'd kick up just the diversion I needed to make a run for it with the pearls and the burros, and if by some slim chance you managed to kill Yeats, all the better!"

"So why didn't you and Rhodes just light out with the pearls when Yeats's men were chasing Lou around the bastion?" Colter wanted to know.

"That's what I was gonna do. As soon as I heard the fuss, I sent Pepe out to saddle up the purty ones and the horses, yours included. I figured I owed you a chance, anyways, for your trouble." Jack grinned. "When I seen that damn Gatlin' gun, I couldn't resist." He slid his smiling gaze between Lou and Colter. "I don't have that many friends, ya see, an' I reckon I count you two among 'em, even though we ain't known each other that long. Besides, Yeats purely was . . . er, is . . . needin' a bullet."

The little man rubbed his hands together, deviously grinning. "Besides, I saw a chance to kill both Yeats an' Rhodes in one fell swoop . . ."

"And then all the pearls would be yours," Lou said, smiling knowingly. "What about your guards, though, Jack? Why'd you leave them behind?"

Jack made a face. "With this many pearls, I didn't think I coulda trusted 'em any more than I coulda trusted Will-John Rhodes not to slit my throat some night as I slept. Now, you fellas . . ." He smiled again at Lou and Colter. "I figured I could trust you two to help me get the loot to a bank in San Diego. For a price, o' course. I aim to pay you both very well if you see me all the way to California!"

He slid his gaze to Pepe. "Me an' Pepe, that is." Jack heaved himself to his feet and limped over to stand beside the older Mexican, who wasn't much taller than Baja Jack himself. Smiling up at Pepe, he said, "My old amigo's gonna join me on my tour of the world, don't ya know? I've named him my private secretary!"

He laughed then translated for the benefit of Pepe, who chuckled around the stem of his pipe, showing teeth in no better condition than Jack's own.

Mean and Ugly lifted his head suddenly, turning toward the canyon's mouth — the one they'd entered by — and giving a shrill warning whinny. A gun cracked. Pepe lurched forward, eyes snapping wide as his pipe dropped from his teeth.

"Pepe!" Jack cried as he reached up to catch his old friend. Pepe was too much of a load for the little man, however. As Pepe fell, blood welling from the fist-sized hole where the bullet had exited his forehead, he toppled Jack over onto his back.

Jack screamed and flopped his arms and legs.

Prophet swung his surprised gaze toward the canyon entrance through which they'd come. A snake flopped in his belly as he saw several horsemen galloping toward him, guns flashing, bullets screeching in the air around his head.

Prophet cursed as he ran over to Mean and Ugly and shucked his Winchester from its scabbard. Alejandra screamed as more guns cracked, triggered by more riders thundering into the canyon.

"Yeats don't know about *your* canyon — eh, Jack?" he shouted, racking a cartridge into the Winchester's breech.

Lou dropped to a knee and fired the rifle into the group of riders bearing down on him, blowing two men out of their saddles and wounding another before a bullet carved a burn along his left side. He cursed, racked another cartridge into the rifle's action, aimed hastily at another rider galloping toward him, and fired.

Louisa and Colter took knees to either side of him, hurling lead toward the horseback riders silhouetted against the rear opening roughly fifty yards away. The echoing cacophony of the rifles was punctuated by the metallic rasp of the cocking levers and the pinging of the empty cartridges falling to the canyon's stone floor and dancing around the boots of the three defenders.

Lou watched in satisfaction as several more of Yeats's men were thrown from their saddles, hitting the canyon floor and rolling, wailing, some being kicked by their horses as the mounts wheeled and ran back in the direction from which they'd come.

Chaos had exploded like dynamite in the canyon as the rifles cracked and horses bucked and whinnied and the burros pitched wildly, hee-hawing and kicking. Yeats's men shouted and cursed. A bullet hammered into one of the burros, which went down screaming.

"No!" Lou heard Jack wailing beneath the din of gunfire, hoof thuds, and the screams of the horses and the braying of Pepe's mule. *My pearls! My pearls! My pearls!*

Prophet emptied his Winchester into Yeats's men, unseating two more and causing the others to draw back on their mounts' reins, leap from their saddles, and dive for cover. "Let's mount up and hightail it!" Lou shouted to Colter and Louisa.

"Don't have to tell me twice!" the redhead said, running toward where his coyote dun was dancing with its tail arched.

"Where's Yeats?" Louisa yelled, staring

toward where guns flashed near the far entrance.

"Forget him," Lou yelled at her. "Mount your horse!"

"You may have gotten what . . . or *who* . . . you came for, but I'm here for Yeats!" Louisa shot back at him.

Prophet lunged for Mean's reins. The horse was wheeling this way and that as the bullets flew around him, some hammering the floor near his prancing hooves. Again, Prophet grabbed at the reins, catching them this time and leaping into his saddle.

As he rode over to where Alejandra lay near a dead burro and the dead Pepe, covering her head with her arms, Prophet saw Baja Jack standing as though in shock, gazing wide-eyed and hang-jawed at the pearls now littering the canyon floor.

Apparently, the burros, several of which were now dead or wounded, had in their frenzy caused the precious pearls to bleed from the panniers. There were so many pearls on the canyon floor that it appeared as if a hailstorm had recently passed.

"My pearls!" wailed Baja Jack, sandwiching his crowlike face in his small, thick hands. *"My pearls! My pearls! My precious pearls!"*

"Forget the pearls, Jack!" Prophet shouted. "Mount up!"

"¡Vamos, señorita!" he yelled at Alejandra, who lowered her arms and gazed up at him, eyes dull with shock. Lou extended his hand to her. She took it, and he swung her up behind him even as he neck-reined Mean and Ugly hard toward the canyon's other mouth, opposite the end from where Yeats's men were firing on them.

The horse took two lunging strides before Lou jerked back on the reins, yelling, *"Whoa!"*

Just then galloping riders had burst through the front door, triggering pistols and rifles.

Colter checked down his own horse, staring straight ahead in horror. He whipped a wide-eyed look back at Lou. "We're trapped!"

While Colter and Louisa, who'd apparently given up on Yeats, threw lead at the riders heading toward them from the *front* door, Lou swung his head around to stare toward the men moving toward him from the *back* door, most of them now on foot and running, crouching and firing from rock rubble strewn at the bases of the two high ridges of stacked cliff dwellings.

Lou snapped up his Colt and hurled three .45 rounds, trying to hold the attackers from that direction at bay.

Meanwhile, Baja Jack was on his hands and knees, gathering up his pearls and jamming them into the pockets of his deerskin charro leggings. He screamed when a bullet sliced across his left cheek and another tore through the nap of his vest but he continued gathering pearls. His *trigueño* was prancing and whinnying angrily on the far side of the canyon, panicked by the gunfire.

Lou slung three more rounds toward the back door, glad when one of the shooters cursed and dropped, shooting his own pistol into the canyon floor. But it wasn't enough. Yeats's men were working their way toward Lou's party from both ends of the canyon. They'd caught them in a whipsaw and there was only one way out.

The thought had brushed like a shadow over Lou's consciousness.

The underground river.

It was their only escape. Probably an escape to a watery death, but it was their only chance.

Horrified and repelled by the thought of leaping into the black water, not knowing where it came from or its exact course on the way to the Sea. Lou swung his head around. "Colter! Louisa! We have to get to the river!" He turned to Baja Jack. "Jack, get your horse. We have to get to the river!"

Baja Jack paid no attention to him; he continued gathering his consarned pearls.

"Jack!" Lou bellowed at the top of his lungs.

Jack lifted his head, gazing at him glassily, his wild eye wobbling around untethered in its socket. "The river, Jack!"

Jack blinked, looked at the pearls rolling around him. He looked at Lou again, his brows ridged dubiously. "Help me gather my pearls, Lou!" He heaved himself to his feet and threw his arms out in pleading. "Help me gather my pearls, Lou! Please! I can't leave them. They're all I've got, Lou!"

His head jerked sharply forward and to one side. Blood and brain matter lapped from his left temple.

"Ah shit!" Lou cried. "Damnit, Jack!"

A bullet curled the air off Prophet's left ear. Another one carved a hot line along the outside of his right thigh. That braced him, jerked his mind from Baja Jack, who now crumpled and lay dead upon his blood-washed pearls, to the river.

Lou turned back to where Louisa was hurling lead in both directions now from atop her wheeling pinto, shooting each one of her pretty Colts in turn while Colter crouched in his own saddle, quickly thumbing fresh cartridges into his Henry's loading tube.

"We have to get to the river!" Prophet shouted.

He booted Mean and Ugly over to the far side of the canyon. The dun was sporting several bloody bullet grazes himself now, his eyes wide, glassy, and white-ringed. Lou took his Richards sawed-off in both hands and sent a wad of double-ought buck hurling toward the shooters at both ends of the canyon, evoking a couple of shrill, satisfying cries of agony.

When he reached the steps that, if he remembered correctly, rose to the cavern that led to the river, he swung down from Mean's back and lifted Alejandra down, as well. Colter and Louisa galloped up behind him, crouching in their saddles, both streaked with the blood of wounds or grazes. They were both firing toward the shooters at both ends of the canyon, so far holding the onslaught at bay.

Prophet shoved Alejandra down beside him and dropped to a knee, trying to shield her body with his own. As he reloaded his shotgun, he looked at Colter and Louisa, who both swung down from their own saddles. "We have to get our horses up these steps, into that cavern. Leastways, I think that's the one."

Colter fired a round toward their attackers then glanced incredulously at Prophet. He shook his head. "I don't like that idea. I don't like it at all, Lou!"

"What river?" Louisa asked, looking at Prophet as though he were addlepated.

Lou thrust his reins into Colter's hands. "Show her, Red! Take my horse and take Alejandra! The river's our only way out of here!"

"It's a hell of a way out of here!"

A bullet blew Colter's hat off his head. The redhead flinched and looked sharply toward where the bullet had come from.

"You got a better plan?" Prophet asked him.

Without replying, Colter picked up his hat, stuffed it onto his head, and then began coaxing both his horse and Mean and Ugly up the steep stone steps.

Louisa, holding the reins of her own horse, stepped up to Lou. Her eyes were bright with incredulity. "What river?"

"You'll see." Prophet had reloaded his shotgun and slid it back behind his shoulder. Now, casting desperate looks toward both ends of the canyon, where Yeats's men were moving on them more quickly, he punched fresh cartridges through his Winchester's loading gate.

He glanced at Louisa, laughed mirthlessly, and shook his head. "I just hope you can swim, darlin'!"

CHAPTER 44

The horses balked at being led up the cliff
wall.

At least, they balked until Lou triggered
one of his wads of twelve-gauge buck toward
the attackers scurrying into the canyon from
the rear door, and another wad toward those
running and firing from the front door. The
twin blasts, one on top of the other, made
all three horses whinny shrilly and leap on
up the steps, in a hurry to escape the din as
well as the bullets hammering the cliff
around them.

Mean and Ugly knocked Alejandra to her
knees. Colter grabbed her, pulled her to her
feet, and then continued leading Mean and
his own horse, the redheaded beauty scrambling along behind him barefoot. Louisa led
her pinto behind them both, occasionally
stopping to use one of her Colts to sling
lead into the canyon.

When they and the horses were safely into

the cavern, Lou ran up the cliff steps, crouching, wincing against the lead screeching through the air around him and spanging off the slope to each side. One bullet pinged off his right spur, sending the rowel spinning off and away.

"That's no way to treat a spur, you filthy swine!"

Gaining the cavern entrance, he stopped, swung around, and flung himself belly down to the cavern floor. He poked his head and rifle back out through the door. Yeats's men were running toward the steps. There must have been thirty of them. Lou pumped a cartridge into the Winchester's action, ready to buy Louisa and Colter some time to get the horses into the river.

He centered his sights on one of the onrushing attackers but held fire. Movement from the other side of the canyon had distracted him. A chunk of that ridge, above the cliff dwellings, had suddenly broken away from the ridge proper. It leaned precariously forward, seemed to hang suspended there for a couple of seconds, and then plunged straight down the ridge.

It slammed into the slope and broke into several pieces, all of which continued rolling and causing more of the ridge to break away and to roll after it. Those pieces hammered into the cliff dwellings lower down, and chunks of the mud houses, too, began to break away from the slope and tumble down the ridge.

Lou stared over his Winchester's barrel in wide-eyed shock as more and more of that ridge broke away from itself and plunged toward the canyon, the pieces slamming into one another and rolling and thundering and kicking up dust and causing the cavern floor beneath Lou to reverberate like the rumbling of a giant's sore belly.

The attackers stopped, one by one and two by two, to look around in befuddlement. Seeing the ridge wall plunging toward them in chunks the size of wagons and privies, even some as large as cabins, they cursed shrilly in Spanish and began running back toward the canyon's two openings. An enormous chunk of rock slammed into the canyon floor to Lou's left, obliterating a good half-dozen fleeing attackers, turning them into a great, brown, billowing cloud of ground rock and dust.

Screams were drowned by the cacophony.

The thunder grew louder. The cavern floor beneath Lou pitched wildly, nearly nudging him onto a shoulder. He looked up to see chunks of his own ridge breaking away and rolling toward the canyon floor.

Lou held his breath and stared in shock. "Holy . . ."

The gunfire must have triggered an earthquake. The old ridge walls were coming alive as though enraged by all the human drama playing out below them.

A grinding noise rose from nearby. Prophet turned his head forward and left, and his eyes grew even more shocked. A zigzagging crack opened up in the cavern's front wall. It grew wider . . . and wider . . .

Lou cursed as he crabbed straight back on his belly. He leaped to his feet but the vibrating floor tripped him and he fell to a knee. He heaved himself up and forward into the velvet black darkness of the inside of the ridge, crouching and wincing and holding his rifle out in front of him in both hands, shielding himself from a possible painful run-in with an unforgiving rock wall.

From far away in front of him, he could hear the stony echoes of shrieking horses amidst a man's and a woman's anxious shouting. Louisa and Colter were trying to force the horses into the river, and the horses weren't buying into the plan. Lou didn't blame them. He didn't buy into it, either. The problem was there wasn't another one for sale.

Ahead, a murky light grew. He quickened

his pace, stumbling from side to side like a drunk as the cavern floor bucked and pitched around him.

Small chunks of stone dropped from the ceiling; he couldn't see them but he could feel them plunging past his shoulders. He saw the horses silhouetted against the light radiating from the lonely chasm through which the blacksnake of the river wound, roaring.

Both mounts had their heads and tails down. The rumble of the river now covered the thunder of the crumbling ridges.

"They don't wanna go swimmin', Lou!" Colter yelled above the near-deafening pounding of the river when he saw Prophet stagger onto the stone embankment. Colter was tugging on Mean's and Northwest's reins while Louisa was tugging on the bridle straps of her pinto. Alejandra was pushing against the pinto's rear, leaning forward, one strap of her gown hanging off her shoulder.

Prophet hurried forward. He tied his shotgun's lanyard over his saddle horn. He slipped his Winchester into its scabbard.

"Get out of the way!" he bellowed.

He stepped back, raised his Colt, and triggered three thundering reports into the stone, mineral-encrusted ceiling five feet above his head.

All three horses jerked forward off the bank then down four feet into the roiling black water that glinted like the surface of a star-shrouded lake harassed by the gale of all gales.

Colter, Louisa, and Alejandra looked down as the water swept the wide-eyed mounts off to the right, the horrified beasts twisting and turning and then disappearing on down the mysterious, stony bed toward the Sea.

"Our turn!" Prophet said.

Louisa glanced at him with uncustomary wariness. "Where does it go?"

"You're about to find out."

Louisa's mouth and eyes popped wide as Lou stepped toward her, smiling. "No, wai—"

Her protest was swallowed by the river's roar as Lou nudged her off the bank and into the water. He looked at Colter eyeing him skeptically, edgily.

"There's no goin' back, Red!" he yelled. "The canyon's gone, and this place ain't gonna be here much longer, neither." He knew it was true. Already dust was wafting from the corridor through which they'd gained the river. The entrance cavern was likely already buried beneath several million tons of ridge.

The corridor itself would be next . . . then the river gorge.

"All right, then." Colter stepped up to the edge of the bank. He sniffed an armpit. "I been needin' a bath for months, anyway!"

He stepped forward, raising his arms out slightly, and dropped lithely into the dark, churning cauldron. Like the horses and Louisa, he was swept eerily away, suddenly gone.

Alejandra moved up to Prophet, placed her hands on his broad chest. "Lou, I'm frightened!"

"Take my hand!"

She placed her hand in his. She jerked her head suddenly to the right with a gasp. She screamed and slapped a hand to her mouth.

As Lou wheeled, he inadvertently nudged Alejandra off the bank and into the river. Ciaran Yeats lunged toward him like a specter from the corridor's darkness. The big man's spectacles hung low on his nose, and his eyes flashed with animallike savagery. He raised a razor-edged, obsidian-handled, pearl-encrusted *cuchillo* in his right hand and, gritting his teeth, thrust the blade down in an arc toward Prophet's left eye.

Lou reached up and grabbed the Mad Major's wrist just before the slender blade of the savage pig-sticker would have impaled his eyeball. He raked his spurs until the bank was no longer beneath him. He angled backward and down toward the roiling black water, still holding Yeats's wrist as he and the big major plunged into the water like two lovers deciding to take a dip hand in hand.

As Lou sank backward into the maelstrom, Yeats's wrist was wrenched from his grasp. Lou had the vague sense of Yeats himself being whipped away from him, the competing currents sweeping him back over Prophet's right shoulder as Lou was spun and then hurled on down the near-black chasm.

Lou fought the cold hands of the whirlpool, trying to keep his head above water. The waves beat him about the head and shoulders, sneaky currents reaching up to grab his ankles and pull him down, down, turning him sideways, determined to drown him. He fought those watery devils with his hands and feet, flailing for the surface, forcing his head above the churning waves once more and sucking a desperate breath into his lungs but choking because he'd sucked water in, as well.

A foot . . . or what felt like a foot . . . kicked him in the right kidney. He glanced to his right and thought he saw Yeats's foot draw back in the froth-fringed, darkly billowing torrent. Or maybe it had been a rock. A rock now slammed against his left shoulder and sent him spinning, wincing against the sudden pain in his ribs.

As the waves continued to batter him, he peered above them and down the sarcophagus-like chasm, seeing only more foaming water following the stone corridor's bending course. More rocks hammered against him from either side, spinning him, one sending him against another on the chasm's opposite side.

Gradually light grew around and over Prophet.

Hope lifted him.

He was hurled another harrowing twenty, thirty, fifty feet, following the river's bends, when suddenly the stone chasm shot back behind him and the sky opened over him. The vast bowl was blue and brassy and the sunlight lanced out of it painfully, reflecting harshly off the foaming water.

He'd never seen a more beautiful sight. He'd been afraid he'd been condemned to spend the rest of his life, however short it may be, fighting the enraged river deep in the prisonlike darkness at the earth's bowels. The current seemed to slow a little, offering even more hope.

As the river turned him so that he was facing slightly upstream and toward the bank on his left, a man's wet head and broad shoulders lunged toward him. Yeats grimaced insanely as sunlight glinted off the blade of the obsidian-handled stiletto still clenched in his right fist. He lurched up and over toward Lou, swinging the stiletto in another downward arc.

Again, Lou grabbed the man's wrist and stared up for a second at the small, sharp tip of the blade smiling menacingly down at him, sunlit water beading along the razor edge like liquid gold.

Lou tried to punch Yeats's grimacing face with his right fist but he fell back as the current grabbed his legs. The current spun him and his assailant, once more ripping the man's wrist out of Lou's grasp. He went hurling down the stream again, away from Yeats, but now not only worried about the water itself and rocks, but about Yeats and that damned jewel-limned pig-sticker lurking somewhere in the water, stalking him even while they were both hurled headlong toward the Sea of Cortez.

The current spun him again, again.

Prophet's heart leaped when Yeats appeared out of the maelstrom, the man grimacing again and once more lunging toward Prophet. Lou grabbed the man's wrist with his left hand, swung it down and away from him. As he did, he hammered his right fist hard against Yeats's left cheek. He punched him again and again, and still the Mad Major managed to hold on to the stiletto.

They spun together like dancers in the current, both trying to punch each other while Lou maintained his grip on the major's right wrist. Yeats swam in close to Prophet, stretched his lips from his teeth, and then rammed his forehead hard against Lou's.

Lou fell back, releasing his grip again on Yeats's knife hand.

Lou's ears rang. The major's attack addled him. He fought to bring his head up out of the water again as he turned a slow circle, and when the water washed down over his eyes and the world around him swam back into focus, Yeats was before him once more, grinning savagely, cocking that damned stiletto again for yet another attempt at carving out Lou's left eye.

Prophet was falling back, unable to lift his hand. He was able to kick up with his right boot, however. He landed the blow exactly where he'd hoped. The soft flesh between the major's stout thighs, just beneath his sagging belly, yielded.

The Mad Major cried out, his face crumpling with agony.

He recovered quickly and lunged at Lou again. This time Lou was rising with the current. He hurled all of his two-hundred-plus pounds at Yeats's left arm. He grabbed the man's forearm with both his hands and drove himself downward, holding the arm fast against his chest, driving Yeats down toward the river's bottom.

Prophet opened his eyes. In the blue-green water striped with the lemon yellow of the sun, Yeats glared back at him wide-eyed, bubbles rising from his flared nostrils and his compressed lips. His long, curly, red-gray hair swirled around his head, obscuring his face. Lou pulled Yeats by his arm to the gravelly bottom.

A large, gray rock churned into view, embedded in the bottom of the river. Prophet drove the man's hand against the rock. He heard Yeats give a watery yell beneath the sound of bubbles crackling in his ears. Still the major held on to the knife. Prophet slid his right hand up to Yeats's face, dug his thumb and forefinger into the man's eyes.

Again, Yeats yelled.

Grinding his fingers deeper into the Mad

569

Major's eye sockets, Lou smashed the man's hand against the rock again. This time the hand opened, the knife slithered out and tumbled slowly toward the river's bottom. At the same time, Yeats gave another, louder wail and drove his knee into Lou's crotch.

As the burning lance of misery bored through his belly and deep into his bowels, Prophet released his grip on Yeats's face. He tumbled away as they continued to roll downstream, Prophet glimpsing the major's bulk pitching away from him on his right.

Lou pushed his feet off the stream's floor, surprised to find the surface much nearer than he'd expected. He lifted his head above the water, his chest coming free of the river also and so suddenly that he pitched forward by the force of his own momentum and forward into the river again.

As the water flung him back up, Yeats bulled into him, punching his belly and ribs with both fists.

Pushing off the bottom with his right boot, Prophet rolled Yeats onto his back. He head-butted him. Yeats's eyes rolled up in their sockets. Prophet moved in quickly, punching the man's face with his right fist.

Yeats cried out, grabbed the collar of Lou's buckskin shirt with both his fists, stretching his lips back from his teeth. He tried to knee Lou in the oysters again, but, anticipating the attack, Lou stepped sideways, and the man's knee glanced off his hip.

Prophet hardened his jaws in fury as he slammed his clenched right fist again into Yeats's right cheek. He punched him in the mouth, across the nose, in the mouth again, against the ridge of his left brow, and then on the lower-left jaw — vicious, pummeling blows that made the Mad Major's broad, fleshy, bearded face resemble a bloody mop.

Prophet held the man by his shirt collar and punched him again, again, and again . . . until he realized Yeats was no longer resisting. Now it was like punching a fifty-pound bag of cracked corn. Yeats slumped below him, head down, arms sagging, legs curled slack before him.

Prophet pulled his fist back and did not bring it forward again.

He released the major's collar and was surprised to find that when the man's head and shoulders slumped downward, it was not into water. The river had disappeared. Now Yeats lay stretched out on wet sand and gravel over and around which the last of the river's water slithered like transparent snakes. Small bubbles popped in the sand.

Lou looked down at himself. He was

standing slumped on the riverbed, over the slack body of Ciaran Yeats. Water dripped from his soaked clothes. He looked downstream, astonished to see the river slithering away from him, like a silver rug pulled out from beneath him, leaving behind it only dark, wet sand and gravel and small pools that collected in bowls between large rocks and boulders. Farther and farther away the water retreated, glinting in the sunlight, resembling nothing so much as a desert mirage.

Then the last of the river turned a bend and disappeared, leaving Prophet standing in wide-eyed shock and awe.

He swung around to stare upstream. The riverbed resembled a desert arroyo in the aftermath of a mountain downpour, after the water had washed off to the sea or been sucked into the earth. Lou lifted his gaze beyond and above the sucking wet bed toward the crags of Baja Jack's canyon.

Only, like poor ole Baja Jack himself, the canyon was gone. Or if not entirely gone, at least obscured by a giant mushroom cloud of gently billowing dust. The gorge in which he and the others had entered the river had collapsed. The river was sealed off. Or, if not sealed, at least looking around desperately for another way out of the millions of tons of collapsed rock. It would find one soon, and another river would be born.

Prophet blinked, dazed, the intoxication of the savage struggle starting to abate so that he was beginning to feel his sundry aches and pains and the burns of the bullets Yeats's men had hurled at him.

"Lou!"

Prophet followed the sound of the familiar voice to the river's southern bank. Colter stood on a rock several feet out from the embankment, waving one arm. Louisa stood on the grassy shore behind the redhead. Alejandra stood near Louisa. They were all as wet as river rats, but relatively intact, Lou was happy to see. The horses stood beyond them in the tall grass amongst the palms, grazing, their saddles hanging askew.

Behind Prophet sounded a gurgling groan.

He turned to stare down at Yeats. The Mad Major rolled onto his back, staring up at Prophet from the bloody mask of his bearded face. He threw up one hand in pleading. It didn't rise very far, however, before it plopped back down to the wet sand.

"Finish me," Yeats begged. "Just finish me. It's all over, anyway. You took it all." He gritted his teeth as he glared up at Prophet. "You an' Baja Jack!"

Lou shook his head. "Forget it, Major. I'm taking you back north. Hell, you're worth a small fortune. You might have lost your black empire, but I'm finally flush!" He figured that cashing in the Mad Major for the big bounty on his head was worth tangling with the authorities again over the little misunderstanding involving the untimely demise of one Roscoe Rodane.

"The rabies'll kill me," Yeats said.

"I hope not before they hang you," Prophet told him.

He scrubbed a sleeve across his wet, bloody cheek. "I'm gonna take your bounty money and spend next winter up in Dakota. After all this down here — hell, them chill winds and three-day blizzards sound right refreshing to this old rebel son of the Confederate South!"

He laughed, used his other sleeve to swab more blood and sand from his face. "Sit tight, Major. I'll be back with the shackles soon."

He turned and strode wearily over to the grassy bank. His boots squawked loudly with every step. Colter grinned from his rock, chuckling and shaking his head. "Next time I think about following you to Mexico, I'm gonna think again."

Lou smiled, nodded. "That'd be wise,

Red. The cost is way too high."

He climbed onto the bank with a weary grunt. Louisa stepped up before him. Alejandra stood several yards behind her, looking downright ravishing in that wet gown in the sunlight.

Prophet slid his eyes back to his partner and grinned. "Enjoy your swim, darlin'?"

He laughed.

Louisa was holding one of her pretty Colts in her right hand. She swung it up and forward with a wicked-sounding grunt.

Lou didn't even feel the blow of the silver-chased barrel laid across his temple before everything went black.

ABOUT THE AUTHOR

Western novelist **Peter Brandvold** was born and raised in North Dakota. He has penned over one hundred fast-action westerns under his own name and his pen name, Frank Leslie. Head honcho at Mean Pete Publishing, publisher of lightning-fast western ebooks, he has lived all over the American West but currently lives in western Minnesota. Follow his life and works at www.peterbrandvold.blogspot.com.